Microsoft®

Agent

Software
Development Kit

Microsoft Pre

PUBLISHED BY
Microsoft Press
A Division of Microsoft Corporation
One Microsoft Way
Redmond, Washington 98052-6399

Library of Congress Cataloging-in-Publication Data
Microsoft Agent Software Development Kit / Microsoft Corporation.
     p.   cm.
   Includes index.
   ISBN 0-7356-0567-X
    1. Intelligent agents (Computer software)   2. Computer software-
-Development. 3. Microsoft Windows (Computer file) I. Microsoft
Corporation.
QA76.76.I58M53   1999
005.1--dc21   98-52127
                                         CIP

Printed and bound in the United States of America.

1 2 3 4 5 6 7 8 9 MLML 4 3 2 1 0 9

Distributed to the book trade in Canada by ITP Nelson, a division of Thomson Canada Limited.

A CIP catalogue record for this book is available from the British Library.

Microsoft Press books are available through booksellers and distributors worldwide. For further information about international editions, contact your local Microsoft Corporation office or contact Microsoft Press International directly at fax (425) 936-7329. Visit our web site at mspress.microsoft.com.

Intel is a registered trademark of Intel Corporation. ActiveX, JScript, Microsoft, Microsoft Press, MS-DOS, Visual Basic, Visual C++, Win32, Windows, and Windows NT are either registered trademarks or trademarks of Microsoft Corporation in the United States and/or other countries. Other product and company names mentioned herein may be the trademarks of their respective owners.

The example companies, organizations, products, people, and events depicted herein are fictitious. No association with any real company, organization, product, person, or event is intended or should be inferred.

Acquisitions Editor: Ben Ryan
Project Editor: Rebecca McKay

Contents

Introduction to Microsoft Agent

Microsoft Agent is a set of programmable software services that supports the presentation of interactive animated characters within the Microsoft Windows interface. Developers can use characters as interactive assistants to introduce, guide, entertain, or otherwise enhance their Web pages or applications in addition to the conventional use of windows, menus, and controls.

Microsoft Agent enables software developers and Web authors to incorporate a new form of user interaction, known as *conversational interfaces*, which leverages natural aspects of human social communication. In addition to mouse and keyboard input, Microsoft Agent includes optional support for speech recognition so applications can respond to voice commands. Characters can respond using synthesized speech, recorded audio, or text in a cartoon word balloon.

The conversational interface approach facilitated by the Microsoft Agent services does not replace conventional graphical user interface (GUI) design. Instead, character interaction can be easily blended with the conventional interface components such as windows, menus, and controls to extend and enhance your application's interface.

Microsoft Agent's programming interfaces make it easy to animate a character to respond to user input. Animated characters appear in their own window, providing maximum flexibility for where they can be displayed on the screen. Microsoft Agent includes an ActiveX control that makes its services accessible to programming languages that support ActiveX, including Web scripting languages such as Visual Basic Scripting Edition (VBScript). This means that character interaction can be programmed even from HTML pages using the <OBJECT> tag.

System Requirements

To use the Microsoft Agent SDK on CD-ROM, your system needs:

- Intel Pentium 120 or compatible microprocessor
- 64 MB of memory (RAM)
- VGA or higher-resolution video adapter
- At least 50 MB of hard disk space for a complete installation
- Microsoft Windows 95, Windows 98, Windows NT 4.0, or Windows 2000
- Microsoft Internet Explorer 4 or later

To work with the optional speech components, your system must also include:

- Windows-compatible sound card
- Microphone
- Headphones or speakers

Support

Every effort has been made to ensure the accuracy of this book and the contents of the companion disc. Microsoft Press provides corrections for books through the World Wide Web at *http://mspress.microsoft.com/support/*.

If you have comments, questions, or ideas regarding this book or the companion disc, please send them to Microsoft Press using either of the following methods:

Postal Mail:

> Microsoft Press
> Attn: Microsoft Agent Software Development Kit Editor
> One Microsoft Way
> Redmond, WA 98052-6399

E-mail:

> MSPINPUT@MICROSOFT.COM

Please note that support for the Microsoft Agent product is not offered through the above mail addresses. You can receive support for Microsoft Agent by calling 1-800-936-5800 in the United States. Outside the United States, please contact your local Microsoft subsidiary for your local support number. You can also submit questions electronically through *http://support.microsoft.com/support/*. Both of these options will charge on a pay-per-incident basis unless you are a member of MSDN or already have a support contract with Microsoft. You can also try the Microsoft Agent newsgroup, *http://microsoft.public.msagent,* for free (connect charges may apply) peer-to-peer support. The newsgroup provides for exchange of information with other developers.

C H A P T E R   1

The Microsoft Agent User Interface

Microsoft Agent enables Web sites and conventional applications to include an enhanced form of user interaction. It provides several user interface components that enable users to access and interact with the character, know the character's status, and change global settings that affect all characters. This chapter describes these basic elements of the Microsoft Agent user interface.

The Character Window

Microsoft Agent displays animated characters in their own windows that always appear at the top of the window z-order (that is, always on top). A user can move a character's window by dragging the character with the left mouse button. The character image moves with the pointer. In addition, an application can move a character using the **MoveTo** method.

When the user right-clicks a character, a pop-up menu appears that displays the following commands:

Open | Close Voice Commands Window
Hide

Command
…

OtherHostingApplicationCaption
…

Note Commands listed are based on the input-active client. Entries listed are all other applications currently hosting the character. For more information on defining commands that appear in the pop-up menu, as well as more information on defining this particular entry, see Chapter 3, "The Microsoft Agent Programming Interface Overview."

The Open | Close Voice Commands Window command controls the display of the Commands Window of the current active character. If speech recognition services are disabled, this command is disabled. If speech recognition services are not installed, this command does not appear.

The Hide command hides the character. The animation assigned to the character's **Hiding** state plays and hides the character. The letter "H" in hide is the command's access key (mnemonic).

The commands for the application(s) currently hosting the character follow the Hide command, preceded by a separator. Then the names of other applications using the character appear, also preceded by a separator.

The Character Taskbar Icon

If a character has been authored to include an icon, the icon appears in the notification area of the taskbar when Microsoft Agent runs. This icon provides access to the character's pop-up menu, which provides access to Agent's global commands such as those that hide and show the character.

FIGURE 1-1. The Character Taskbar Icon

Moving the pointer over the taskbar icon displays a tip window that reflects the name of the character (in the current language of the system). Single-clicking the character's taskbar icon displays the character. The action associated with double-clicking the icon depends on the current application controlling that character.

Right-clicking the icon displays a pop-up menu. When the character is visible, the pop-up menu displays the same commands as those displayed when right-clicking the character. If the character is hidden, only the Open (or Close) Voice Commands Window and Show commands appear.

The Voice Commands Window

If a compatible speech engine is installed, Microsoft Agent supplies a special window called the Voice Commands Window that displays the commands that have been voice-enabled for speech recognition. The Voice Commands Window serves as a visual prompt for what can be spoken as input (commands cannot be selected with the mouse).

The window appears when a user selects the Open Voice Commands Window command, either by speaking the command or right-clicking the character and choosing the command from the character's pop-up menu. However, if the user disables speech input, the Voice Commands Window is not accessible.

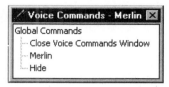

FIGURE 1-2. The Voice Commands Window

The Voice Commands Window displays voice-enabled commands as a tree. If the current hosting application supplies voice commands, they appear expanded and at the top of the window. Entries also appear for other applications using the character. The window also includes the global voice commands supplied by Microsoft Agent. If the current hosting application has no voice commands, the global voice commands appear expanded and at the top of the window.

The user can size and move the Voice Commands Window. Microsoft Agent remembers the last location of the window and redisplays it at that location if the user closes and re-opens the window. If the entries in the window exceed the current display size of the window, scroll bars appear.

The Word Balloon

In addition to spoken audio output, the Microsoft Agent interface supports textual captioning in the form of text output in cartoon-style word balloons. Words appear in the balloon as they are spoken. The balloon hides when spoken output is completed. The Advanced Character Options window provides options to disable the balloon's display as well as control attributes related to its appearance.

FIGURE 1-3. The Word Balloon

The Listening Tip Window

If speech is enabled, a special tooltip window appears when the user presses the push-to-talk key to begin voice input. The Listening Tip displays contextual information related to the current input state of Microsoft Agent. If compatible speech recognition has not been installed or has been disabled, the Listening Tip does not appear.

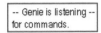

FIGURE 1-4. The Listening Tip

The Advanced Character Options Window

Microsoft Agent maintains certain global settings that enable a user to control interaction with all characters. The Advanced Character Options window displays these options and their current settings, and can be shown by any hosting application using the Microsoft Agent programming interface. Microsoft Agent remembers the last page viewed and displays that page when the property sheet appears.

The Output Page

This page includes properties that control character output. For example, the user can determine whether to display output in the word balloon, determine how balloon output should appear, play spoken output as audio, play character sound effects, display the restart prompt, and adjust the speaking speed.

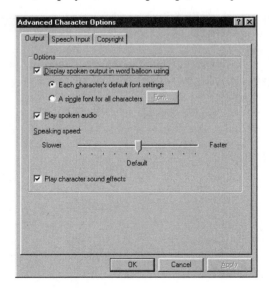

FIGURE 1-5. Output Property Page

The Speech Input Page

A user can adjust speech input options on this property page. The user can disable speech input, set the listening input key, choose whether to display the Listening Tip window, and choose to play a MIDI tone to indicate when speech input is available.

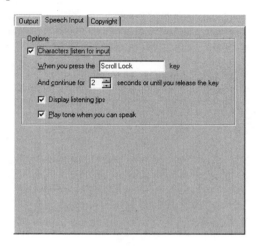

FIGURE 1-6. Speech Input Property Page

The Copyright Page

This page displays the copyright and version information for Microsoft Agent.

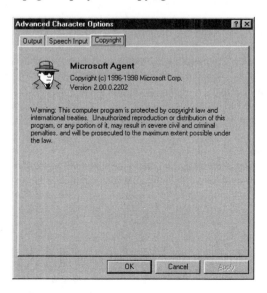

FIGURE 1-7. Copyright Page

The Default Character Properties Window

In addition to enabling applications to load a specific character, applications can load a character that is a shared resource for the user, known as the *default character*. The default character is accessible from any application, but the character is only selectable by the user. To facilitate selection of this character, Agent provides a window that provides access to selecting this character, called the default character properties window. Access to this window is supported from the Agent API.

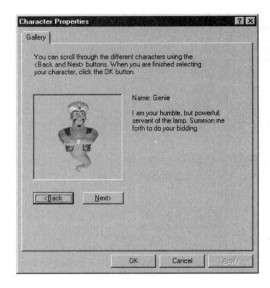

FIGURE 1-8. Default Character Properties Window

The default ch aracter properties window cannot be used to provide character selection other than for the default character.

C H A P T E R   2

Guidelines for Designing Character Interaction

This chapter outlines guidelines for designing user interfaces that incorporate interactive characters created with Microsoft Agent. For specific information on designing character animation, see Chapter 7, "Designing Characters for Microsoft Agent."

General Character Interaction Guidelines

Principles of good user interface design also apply to designing an interface using Microsoft Agent. You should understand your users and their goals as well as follow a good user interface design process. *The Windows Interface Guidelines for Software Design* (Microsoft Press, 1995) provides an excellent overview of general design principles and methodology.

Be Non-Exclusive

Interactive characters can be employed in the user interface as assistants, guides, entertainers, storytellers, sales agents, or in a variety of other roles. A character that automatically performs or assists should not be designed contrary to the design principle of keeping the user in control. When adding a character to the interface of a Web site or conventional application, use the character as an enhancement—rather than a replacement—of the primary interface. Avoid implementing any feature or operation that exclusively requires a character.

Similarly, let users choose when they want to interact with your character. A user should be able to dismiss the character and have it return only with the user's permission. Forcing character interaction on users can have a serious negative effect. To support user control of character interaction, Microsoft Agent automatically includes Hide and Show commands. The Microsoft Agent API also supports these methods, so you can include support for these functions in your own interface. In addition, Microsoft Agent's user interface includes global properties that enable the user to override certain character output options. To ensure that the user's preferences are maintained, these properties cannot be overridden through the API.

Provide Appropriate Feedback

Quality, appropriateness, and timing are important factors to consider when providing feedback in any interface design. When you incorporate interactive characters, the opportunities for natural forms of feedback increase, as does the user's expectation that the feedback conform to appropriate social interaction. A character can be designed to provide verbal and non-verbal conversational cues in addition to spoken audio output. Use gestures or facial expressions to convey information about its mood or intent. The face is especially important in communication, so always consider the character's facial expression. Keep in mind that the absence of facial expression is itself a facial expression.

We humans have an orienting reflex that causes us to attend to changes in our environment, especially changes in motion, volume, or contrast. Therefore, character animation and sound effects should be kept at a minimum to avoid distracting users when they aren't directly interacting with the character. This doesn't mean the character must freeze, but natural idling behavior such as breathing or looking around is preferable to greater movement. Idling behavior maintains the illusion of social context and availability of the character without distracting the user. You may also want to consider removing the character if the user hasn't interacted with it for a set time period, but make sure the user understands why the character is going away.

Conversely, large body motion, unusual body motion, or highly active animation is very effective if you want to capture the user's attention, particularly if the animation occurs outside the user's current focus. Note also that motion toward the user can effectively gain the user's attention.

Placement and movement of the character should be appropriate to its participation in the user's current task. If the current task involves the character, the character can be placed at the point of focus. When the user is not interacting with the character, move it to a consistent "standby" location or where it will not interfere with tasks or distract the user. Always provide a rationale for how the character gets from one location to another. Similarly, users feel most comfortable when the character appears in the same screen location from which it departed.

Use Natural Variation

While consistency of presentation in your application's conventional interface, such as menus and dialog boxes, makes the interface more predictable, do vary the animation and spoken output in the character's interface. Appropriately varying the character's responses provides a more natural interface. If a character always addresses the user exactly the same way; for example, always saying the same words, the user is likely to consider the character boring, disinterested, or even rude. Human communication rarely involves precise repetition. Even when repeating something in a similar situation, we may change wording, gestures, or facial expression.

Microsoft Agent enables you to build in some variation for a character. When defining a character's animations, you can use branching probabilities on any animation frame to change an animation when it plays. You can also assign multiple animations to each state. Microsoft Agent randomly chooses one of the assigned animations each time it initiates a state. For speech output, you can also include vertical bar characters in your output text to automatically vary the text spoken. For example, Microsoft Agent will randomly select one of the following statements when processing this text as part of the **Speak** method:

"I can say this. | I can say that. | I can say something else."

Social Interaction

Human communication is fundamentally social. From the time we are born, we begin reacting to the social cues in our environment and learning the appropriate rules for effective interaction, which include verbal behaviors such as intonation or word ordering, and also non-verbal behaviors such as posture, gestures, and facial expressions. These behaviors convey attitudes, identities, and emotions that color our communication. We often create substitute conventions for communication channels that don't naturally provide bandwidth for non-verbal cues, such as e-mail or online chat sessions.

Unfortunately, the majority of software interface design has focused primarily on the cognitive aspects of communication, overlooking most social aspects. However, recent research has demonstrated that human beings naturally react to social stimuli presented in an interactive context. Further, the reactions often follow the same conventions that people use with each other. Even the smallest cues, such as colors presented or word choice in messages, can trigger this automatic response. The presentation of an animated character with eyes and a mouth heightens the social expectations of and strength of responses to the character. Never assume that users expect a character's behavior to be less socially appropriate because they know it is artificial. Knowing this, it is important to consider the social aspects of interaction when designing character interaction. *The Media Equation: How People Treat Computers, Televisions, and New Media as Real People and Places* by Byron Reeves and Clifford Nass (New York: Cambridge University Press, 1996) is an excellent reference on current research in this area.

Create Personality

We quickly classify the personality of people we meet based on the simplest of social cues, such as posture, gesture, appearance, word choice, and style. So the first impression a character makes is very important. Creating personality doesn't require artificial intelligence or realistic rendering. Great animators have known this for years and have used the simplest social cues to create rich personalities for inanimate objects. Consider, for example, the flying carpet in Disney's

Aladdin, and Lassiter's *Luxo Jr.*, a humorous animated video of a pair of desk lamps. Beginning animators at Disney were often given the challenge of drawing flour sacks that expressed emotion.

A character's name, how it introduces itself, how it speaks, how it moves, and how it responds to user input can all contribute to establishing its basic personality. For example, an authoritative or dominant style of personality can be established by a character making assertions, demonstrating confidence, and issuing commands, whereas a submissive personality may be characterized by phrasing things as questions or making suggestions. Similarly, personality can be conveyed in the sequence of interaction. Dominant personalities always go first. It is important to provide a distinct, well-defined personality type, regardless of which personality type you are creating. Everyone generally dislikes weakly defined or ambiguous personalities.

The kind of personality you choose for a character depends on your objective. If the character's purpose is to direct users toward specific goals, use a dominant, assertive personality. If the character's purpose is to respond to users' requests, use a more submissive personality.

Another approach is to adapt a character's personality to the user's. Studies have shown that users prefer interaction with personalities most like themselves. You might offer the user a choice of characters with different personalities or observe the user's style of interaction with the character and modify the character's interactive style. Research shows that when attempting to match a user's personality you don't always have to be 100 percent correct. Humans tend to show flexibility in their relationships and, because of the nature of social relationships, are also likely to modify their own behavior somewhat to working with a character.

Observe Appropriate Etiquette

All people learn rules of social etiquette. Moreover, we judge others based on how well they conform to these rules. The presence of a character in your interface makes rules of etiquette directly applicable to your design.

We expect reciprocity in our interaction and when it doesn't happen we tend to view the behavior as incompetent or offensive. In new or formal situations, politeness is usually expected. Only after a relationship is established does familiarity allow for less formal interaction. So when in doubt, be polite.

For example, consider the appropriate protocol for starting and ending a social interaction. When engaging in a new social context, we generally greet each other and indicate our intent to leave before we depart. You can apply this model directly to character interaction; avoid the character appearing or disappearing without an appropriate indication.

A part of politeness is how we respond. We expect responses that are appropriate. For example, if you ask, "What day is it?" you don't expect the response to be "10 apples." However, accuracy and relevance are not enough; you may also need to determine the context. An accurate response could be "Monday" or "August 25th." Similarly, the wording of a response can be accurate but still be offensive, depending on intonation, facial expression, or other non-verbal behaviors.

In addition, we address each other while talking: we face the person, turning only to direct attention to something. Turning one's back, without some purpose, implies disinterest and is generally considered to be impolite.

Politeness also affects the way we respond to or perceive others. For example, social research indicates that we are more likely to be honest about our evaluation of others when asked by another person than when the people ask about themselves. Similarly, we accept positive evaluations of others more readily than positive self-evaluations. Immodest behavior is generally considered impolite. Therefore, unless intentionally trying to promote an impolite personality style, avoid having the character compliment its own performance.

Also consider the cultural impact on social etiquette. This may apply to the character's attire, gestures, or word choice. While polite behaviors may vary by culture, the concept of politeness is cross-cultural.

Use Praise

People respond better to praise than criticism, even when the praise may be unwarranted. Although most software interfaces strive to avoid evaluative feedback, praise is demonstrably more effective than providing no evaluation at all. Further, many interfaces designed as neutral are often perceived as critical by users, because they rarely get positive feedback when things are operating normally, and error messages when things go wrong. Similarly, wording that tells the user that there is a better way to perform a task implicitly criticizes the user.

Because characters create a social context, careful use of praise and criticism is even more important than in a traditional user interface. While few people enjoy sycophantic behavior, the limits of the liberal use of praise have yet to be demonstrated. Praise is especially effective in situations where users are less confident about their performance of a task. On the other hand, criticism should be used sparingly. Even when you think criticism is appropriate, be aware that people have a tendency to dismiss it or redirect it back to its source.

However, avoid self-praise unless it is a humorous part of the personality the character projects. We tend to judge self-conceit with skepticism. If you want to direct approbation to a character, have it directed from another source, such as another character or descriptive explanation.

Create a Team Player

When a team is created, group dynamics have a powerful effect on the members in the group. First, people in a group or team context have a tendency to identify more with the other people on the team than they typically would in a non-team setting. As a result, they can also identify more with their teammates than those outside the team. But equally important, members of a team are more willing to cooperate and modify their attitudes and behavior. Because the social dynamics of a team affect its members' interaction, it can be useful to consider when designing interaction with characters.

Creating a sense of team involves two factors: identity and interdependence. You can create identity by creating a team name, color, symbol, or other identifier that the user and character share. For example, you could provide a sticker the user could affix to his or her computer or enable the user to pick a team name or icon that would appear with the character. Team identity may also be established by what the character says. For example, you could have the character refer to itself as a partner or to the user and itself as a team.

Interdependence may be harder to implement or take longer to establish, though it is important to consider because interdependence seems to have a stronger social impact than team identity. This is illustrated by the product brand loyalty that marketing organizations endeavor to establish. Creating a sense of interdependence involves demonstrating continuing usefulness and reliability for the user. Important questions to answer are "Does the character provide value?" and "Does the character operate predictability and reliably?" An important factor here is how the character's relationship is established with the user. To engender a sense of team interdependence, the character needs to be presented as a peer to the user. Although it may be useful in some scenarios to present the character as an expert or a servant, to leverage the collaborative benefits of team dynamics, there must be a sense of equality where the user can be dependent on the character without a sense of inferiority. This may be as simple as having the character refer to itself as a teammate or companion rather than as a wizard. It can also be influenced by how the character requests information from the user. For example, a character might say, "Let's work together to answer this question…"

Consider Gender Effects

Social responses can be affected by gender. For example, Nass and Reeves' work indicates that in the U.S., male personalities are stereotypically considered to understand more about technical subjects, while females are attributed to be better experts in interpersonal subjects like love and relationships. This doesn't suggest that you should perpetuate gender stereotypes, only that you be aware that they may exist and understand how they might affect interaction with your character.

Remember that a character's perceived gender isn't solely established by its name or appearance. Even a gender-neutral character may convey gender based on its voice characteristics, speech patterns, and movement.

Speech Recognition

Speech recognition provides a very natural and familiar interface for interacting with characters. However, speech input also presents many challenges. Speech engines currently operate without substantial parts of the human speech communication repertoire, such as gestures, intonation, and facial expressions. Further, natural speech is typically unbounded. It is easy for the speaker to exceed the current vocabulary, or *grammar*, of the engine. Similarly, wording or word order can vary for any given request or response. In addition, speech recognition engines must often deal with large variations in the speaker's environment. For example, background noise, microphone quality, and location can affect input quality. Similarly, different speaker pronunciations or even same-speaker variations, such as when the speaker has a cold, make it a challenge to convert the acoustic data into representational understanding. Finally, speech engines must also deal with similar sounding words or phrases in a language, such as "new," "knew," and "gnu," or "wreck a nice beach" and "recognize speech."

Speech isn't always the best form of input for a task. Because of the turn-taking nature of speech, it can often be slower than other forms of input. Like the keyboard, speech input is a poor interface for pointing unless some type of mnemonic representation is provided. Therefore, always consider whether speech is the most appropriate input for a task. It is best to avoid using speech as the exclusive interface to any task. Provide other ways to access any basic functionality using methods such as the mouse or keyboard. In addition, take advantage of the multi-modal nature of using speech in the visual interface by combining speech input with visual information that helps specify the context and options.

Finally, the successful use of speech input is due only in part to the quality of the technology. Even human recognition, which exceeds any current recognition technology, sometimes fails. However, in human communication we use strategies that improve the probability of success and that provide error recovery when something goes wrong. Therefore, the effectiveness of speech input also depends on the quality of the user interface that presents it.

Studying human models of speech interaction can be useful when designing more natural speech interfaces. Recording actual human speech dialogues for particular scenarios may help you better understand the constructs and patterns used as well as effective forms of feedback and error recovery. It can help determine the appropriate vocabulary to use (for input and output). It is better to design a speech interface based on how people actually speak than to simply derive it from the graphical interface in which it operates.

Note that Microsoft Agent uses the Microsoft Speech API (SAPI) to support speech recognition. This enables Microsoft Agent to be used with a variety of compatible engines. Although Microsoft Agent specifies certain basic interfaces, the performance requirements and quality of an engine may vary.

Speech is not the only means of supporting conversational interfaces. You can also use natural-language processing of keyboard input in place of or in addition to speech. In those situations, you can still generally apply guidelines for speech input.

Listen, Don't Just Recognize

Successful communication involves more than recognition of words. The process of dialogue implies exchanging cues to signal turn-taking and understanding. Characters can improve conversational interfaces by providing cues like head tilts, nods, or shakes to indicate when the speech engine is in the listening state and when something is recognized. For example, Microsoft Agent plays animations assigned to the **Listening** state when a user presses the push-to-talk listening key and animations assigned to the **Hearing** state when an utterance is detected. When defining your own character, make sure you create and assign appropriate animations to these states. For more information on designing characters, see Chapter 7, "Designing Characters for Microsoft Agent."

In addition to non-verbal cues, a conversation involves a common context between the conversing parties. Similarly, speech input scenarios with characters are more likely to succeed when the context is well established. Establishing the context enables you to better interpret similar-sounding phrases like "check's in the mail" and "check my mail." You may also want to enable the user to query the context by providing a command, such as "Help" or "Where am I," to which you respond by restating the current context, such as the last action your application performed.

Microsoft Agent provides interfaces that enable you to access the best match and the two next best alternatives returned by the speech recognition engine. In addition, you can access confidence scores for all matches. You can use this information to better determine what was spoken. For example, if the confidence scores of the best match and first alternative are close, it may indicate that the speech engine had difficulty discerning the difference between them. In such a case, you may want to ask the user to repeat or rephrase the request in an effort to improve performance. However, if the best match and first or second alternatives return the same command, it strengthens the indication of the correct recognition.

The nature of a conversation or dialogue implies that there should be a response to spoken input. Therefore, a user's input should always be responded to with verbal or visual feedback that indicates an action was performed or a problem was encountered, or provides an appropriate reply.

Clarify and Limit Choices

Speech recognition becomes more successful when the user learns the range of appropriate grammar. It also works better when the range of choices is limited. The less open-ended the input, the better the speech engine can analyze the acoustic information input.

Microsoft Agent includes several built-in provisions that increase the success of speech input. The first is the Commands Window displayed when the user says, "Open Commands Window," or "What can I say?" (or when the user chooses Open Commands Window from the character's pop-up menu). The Command Window serves as a visual guide to the active grammar of the speech engine. It also reduces recognition errors by activating only the speech grammar of the input-active application and Microsoft Agent's global commands. Therefore, the active grammar of the speech engine applies to the immediate context. For more information on the Commands Window, see Chapter 3, "Microsoft Agent Programming Interface Overview."

When you create Microsoft Agent voice-enabled commands, you can author the caption text that appears in Commands Window as well as its voice text (grammar), the words that the engine should use for matching this command. Always try to make your commands as distinctive as possible. The greater the difference between the wording of commands, especially for the voice text, the more likely the speech engine will be able to discriminate between spoken commands and provide an accurate match. Also avoid single-word or very short commands. Generally, more acoustic information in a spoken utterance gives the engine a better chance to make an accurate match.

When defining the voice text for a command, provide a reasonable variety of wording. Requests that mean the same thing can be phrased very differently, as illustrated in the following example:

User: Add some pepperoni.
Character: I'd like some pepperoni.
User: Could you add some pepperoni?
Character: Pepperoni, please.

Microsoft Agent enables you to easily specify alternatives or optional words for the voice grammar for your application. You enclose alternative words or phrases between parentheses, separated by a vertical bar character. You can define optional words by enclosing them between square bracket characters. You can also nest alternatives or optional words. In addition, you can also use an ellipsis (...) in voice text as a placeholder for any word. However, using ellipses too frequently may make it more difficult for the engine to distinguish between different voice commands. In any case, always make sure that your voice text includes at least one distinctive word for each command that is not optional. Typically, this should match a word or words in the caption text you define that appears in the Commands Window.

Although you can include symbols, punctuation, or abbreviations in your caption text, avoid them in your voice text. Many speech recognition engines cannot handle symbols and abbreviations or may use them to set special input parameters. In addition, spell out numbers. This also ensures more reliable recognition support.

You can also use directive prompts to avoid open-ended input. Directive prompts implicitly reference the choices or explicitly state them, as shown in the following examples:

What do you want?	Too general, an open-ended request
Choose a pizza style or ingredient.	Good, if choices are visible, but still general
Say "Hawaiian," "Chicago," or "The Works."	Better, an explicit directive with specific options

This guides the user toward issuing a valid command. By suggesting the words or phrase, you are more likely to elicit expected wording in return. To avoid unnatural repetitiveness, change the wording or shorten the original for subsequent presentation as the user becomes more experienced with the input style. Directive prompts can also be used in situations where the user fails to issue a command within a prescribed time or fails to provide an expected command. Directive prompts can be provided using speech output, your application interfaces, or both. The key is helping the user know the appropriate choices.

Wording influences the success of a prompt. For example, the prompt, "Would you like to order your pizza?" could generate either a "Yes" or "No" response, but it might also generate an order request. Define prompts to be non-ambiguous or be prepared to accept a larger variety of possible responses. In addition, note the tendency for people to mimic words and constructs they hear. This can often be used to help evoke an appropriate response as in the following example:

User: Show me all messages from Paul.
Character: Do you mean Paul Allen or Paul Maritz?

This is more likely to elicit the full name of one of the parties with the possible prefix of "I mean" or "I meant."

Because Microsoft Agent characters operate within the visual interface of Windows, you can use visual elements to provide directive prompts for speech input. For example, you can have the character gesture at a list of choices and request that the user select one, or display choices in a dialog box or message window. This has two benefits: it explicitly suggests the words you want the user to speak and it provides an alternate way for the user to reply.

You can also use other modes of interaction to subtly suggest to users the appropriate speech grammar, as shown in the following example:

User: (Clicks Hawaiian-style pizza option with the mouse)
Character: Hawaiian-style pizza.
User: (Clicks Extra Cheese option with the mouse)
Character: Add "Extra Cheese."

Another important factor in successful speech input is cueing the user when the engine is ready for input, because many speech engines allow only a single utterance at a time. Microsoft Agent provides support for this in two ways. First, if the sound card supports MIDI, Microsoft Agent generates a brief tone to signal when the speech-input channel is available. Second, the Listening Tip window displays an appropriate text prompt when the character (speech engine) is listening for input. In addition, this tip displays what the engine heard.

Provide Good Error Recovery

As with any well-designed interface, the interactive process should minimize the circumstances that lead to errors. However, it is rarely possible to eliminate all errors, so supporting good error recovery is essential to maintain the confidence and interest of the user. In general, error recovery involves detecting an error, determining the cause, and defining a way to resolve the error. Users respond better to interfaces that are cooperative, that work with the user to accomplish a task.

The first step in speech error recovery is detecting the failure condition. Speech recognition can fail due to a variety of errors. Error conditions can usually be detected as the result of invalid input, explicit user correction or cancellation, or user repetition.

A *rejection error* occurs when the recognition engine has no match for what the user has said. Background noise or early starts are also common causes of recognition failure, so asking the user to repeat a command is often a good initial solution. However, if the phrase is outside of the current active grammar, asking the user to rephrase the request may solve the problem. The difference in wording may result in a match with something in the current grammar. Listing or suggesting appropriate expected input options is another alternative.

A good strategy for rejection error recovery is to combine these techniques to get the user back on track, offering increasingly more assistance if the failure persists. For example, you can begin by responding to the initial failure with an interrogative like "Huh?" or "What?" or a hand-to-the-ear gesture. A short response increases the likelihood that the user's repeated statement will not fail because the user spoke too soon. Upon a repeated failure, the subsequent request to rephrase improves the chance of matching something within the given grammar. From here, providing explicit prompts of accepted commands further increases the chance of a match. This technique is illustrated in the following example:

User: I'd like a Chicago-style pizza with anchovies.

Character: (Hand to ear) Huh?

User: I want a Chicago pizza with anchovies.

Character: (Head shake) Please rephrase your request.

User: I said Chicago pizza, with anchovies.

Character: (Shrug) I'm sorry. Tell me the style of pizza you want.

User: Chicago, with anchovies.

Character: Still no luck. Here's what you can say: "Chicago," "Hawaiian," or "Combo."

To make the error handling feel more natural, make sure you provide a degree of random variation when responding to errors. In addition, a natural user reaction to any request to repeat a response is to exaggerate or increase the volume when repeating the statement. It may be useful to occasionally remind the user to speak normally and clearly, as the exaggeration or increased volume may make it harder for the speech engine to recognize the words.

Progressive assistance should do more than bring the error to the user's attention; it should guide the user toward speaking in the current grammar by successively providing more informative messages. Interfaces that appear to be trying to understand encourage a high degree of satisfaction and tolerance from the user.

Substitution errors, where the speech engine recognizes the input but matches the wrong command, are harder to resolve because the speech engine detects a matching utterance. A mismatch can also occur when the speech engine interprets extraneous sounds as valid input (also known as an *insertion error*). In these situations, the user's assistance is needed to identify the error condition. To do this, you can repeat what the speech engine returned and ask the user to confirm it before proceeding:

User: I'd like a Chicago-style pizza.

Character: Did you say you'd like a "Chicago-style pizza"?

User: Yes.

Character: What additional ingredients would you like on it?

User: Anchovies.

Character: Did you say "anchovies"?

User: Yes.

However, using this technique for every utterance becomes inefficient and tiresome. To handle this, restrict confirmation to situations that have significant negative consequences or increase the complexity of the immediate task. If it is easy for the user to make or reverse changes, you may be able to avoid requesting confirmation of his or her choices. Similarly, if you make choices visible you may not need to provide explicit correction. For example, choosing an item from a list may not require verification because the user can see the results and easily change them. You can also use confidence and alternative scores to provide a threshold for confirmation. You might adjust the threshold by keeping a history of the user's actions in a given situation and eliminating verification based on consistent user confirmation. Finally, consider the multi-modal nature of the interface. Confirmation from the mouse or keyboard may also be appropriate.

Carefully choose the wording of confirmations. For example, "Did you say...?" or "I think you said..." are better than "Do you really want to...?" because the former phrases imply that the accuracy of the character's listening (recognition) is being queried, not that the user may have misspoke.

Also consider the grammar for a response. For example, a negative response is likely to generate a rejection error, requiring an additional prompt as shown in the following example:

User: I'd like some pepperoni.
Character: Did you say "no ham"?
User: No, I said pepperoni.
Character: Huh?
User: Pepperoni.

Modifying your grammar to include prefixes to handle natural response variations increases the efficiency of the recovery process, especially when the user doesn't confirm the verification prompt. In this example, the confirmation could have been handled in a single step by modifying the grammar for the "pepperoni" by also including "no I said pepperoni", "I said pepperoni", and "no pepperoni".

You can also handle substitution errors using the alternative matches returned by the speech engine as the corrective confirmation:

User: I'd like some pepperoni.
Character: (Hears "no ham" as best match, "pepperoni" as first alternative) Did you say "no ham"?
User: No, pepperoni.
Character: (Still hears "no ham" as best match, but now offers first alternative) "Pepperoni"?

Similarly, you can keep a history of common substitution errors and if a particular error is frequent, offer the alternative the first time.

In any recognition error situation, avoid blaming the user. If the character suggests or even implies that the user is to blame, or the character seems indifferent to the error, the user may become offended. Here also, carefully choose wording that explicitly accepts responsibility, is appropriate to the situation, and uses variety to create a more natural response. When expressing an apology, avoid ambiguous words like "oops" or "uh-oh" that could be interpreted as blaming the user. Instead, use phrases like "I'm sorry" or "My mistake." Repeated or more serious errors might use a more elaborate apology like "I am really sorry about that." Also consider the personality of the character when determining the type of response. Another option is to blame an external situation. Comments such as, "Boy, it's noisy out there," take the blame away from the user *and* the character. Reminding the user of the cooperative nature of the interaction may be helpful as well: consider phrases such as, "Let's see what we can do to make this work."

Microsoft Agent also supports some automatic feedback for recognition. When an utterance is detected, the Listening Tip displays the voice text of the best match heard. You can set your own text to display based on the confidence setting for a command you define.

Because of error potential, always require confirmation for any choices that have serious negative consequences and are irreversible. Naturally, you'll want to require confirmation when the results of an action could be destructive. However, consider also requiring confirmation for situations that abort any lengthy process or operation.

Speech Output

Like speech input, speech output is a familiar and natural form of communication, so it is also an appropriate complement in a character-based interface. However, speech output also has its liabilities. In some environments, speech output may not be preferred or audible. In addition, by itself, speech is invisible and has no persistent output, relying heavily on short-term memory. These factors limit its capacity and speed for processing large amounts of information. Similarly, speech output can also disrupt user input, particularly when speech is the input method. Speech engines generally have little support that enables the user to interrupt when speech or other audio has the output channel.

As a result, avoid using speech as the exclusive form of output. However, because Microsoft Agent presents characters as a part of the Windows interface, it provides several advantages over speech-only environments. Characters can be combined with other forms of input and output to make options and actions visible, enabling a more effective interface than one that is exclusively visual or speech-based.

In addition, to make speech output more visible, Microsoft Agent includes the option of authoring a character with a cartoon-style word balloon. Other settings enable you to determine how text appears in the balloon and when the balloon is removed. You can also determine what font to use. Although you can set a character's word balloon attributes, be aware that the user can override these settings.

Be Efficient and Natural

When accomplishing tasks, effective human conversations are typically exchanges of brief information. Often, elements in the discussion are established between the parties and then referred to indirectly using abbreviated responses. These forms of abbreviation are beneficial because they are efficient, and they also imply that the speaker and listener have a common context; that is, that they are communicating. Using appropriate forms of abbreviation also makes a dialogue more natural.

One form of conversational abbreviation is the use of contractions. When they are not used, they make a speaker seem more formal and rigid, and sometimes less human. Most conversations demonstrate more freedom in the linguistic rules than written text.

Another common form of abbreviation in conversations is *anaphora*, the use of pronouns. For example, when someone asks, "Have you seen Bill today?" responses that substitute "him" for "Bill" are more natural than repeating the name again. The substitution is a cue that the parties in the dialogue share a common context of *who* "him" is. Keep in mind that the word "I" refers to the character when he or she says it.

Shared context is also communicated by the use of linguistic *ellipsis*, the truncation of many of the words in the original query. For example, the listener could respond, "Yes, I saw him," demonstrating the shared context of *when* or even respond with a simple "Yes" that demonstrates the shared context of *who* and *when*.

Implicit understanding can also be conveyed through other forms of abbreviated conversational style, where content is inferred without repetition, as shown in the following example:

User: I'd like a Chicago-style pizza.
Character: With "Extra Cheese"?

Similarly, if someone says, "It is hot in here," the phrase is understandable and requires no further detail if you know where the speaker is. However, if the context is not well established or is ambiguous, eliminating all contextual references may leave the user confused.

When using abbreviated communication, always consider the user's context and the type of content. It is appropriate to use longer descriptions for new and unfamiliar information. However, even with long descriptive information, try to break it up into smaller chunks. This gives you the ability to change the animation as the character speaks. It also provides greater opportunity for the user to interrupt the character, especially when using speech input.

Consistency is important in speech output. Strange speech patterns or prosody may be interpreted as downgrading the intelligence of the character. Similarly, switching between TTS and recorded speech may cause users to interpret the character as strange or possessing more than one personality. Lip-synced mouth movements can improve intelligibility of speech. Microsoft Agent automatically supports lip-syncing for TTS engines that comply with its required SAPI interfaces. However, lip-syncing is also supported for recorded speech. Sound files can also be enhanced with the Microsoft Linguistic Sound Editing Tool.

Use the Active Voice

When using speech output to provide directive information or to elicit a user response, use the active voice and clearly specify the user's expected action. The following example illustrates the differences:

Let me repeat your number.	No user action
The number will be repeated.	Passive voice, no user action
Listen while the number is repeated.	Passive voice
Listen to the repetition.	Best choice

In addition, construct your output to unfold the key information at the end of the phrase as shown in the following examples:

Instead of: "Is three the next digit?"   **Use:** "Is the next digit three?"

Instead of: "Click OK to begin."   **Use:** "To begin, click OK."

Instead of: "Say 'Done' to complete your order."   **Use:** "To complete your order, say 'Done.'"

Use Appropriate Timing and Emphasis

Like all feedback, the effectiveness of speech output depends on timing and emphasis. A good deal of information can be communicated in the pace, volume, and pitch used when something is spoken. If you use a text-to-speech engine as your character's voice, most engines let you set the speed, pauses, pitch, and emphasis of words or phrases. You can use these attributes to indicate interest and understanding of the character as well as direct the user's attention or indicate your character's intent. For further information on how to set speech attributes, see Chapter 6, "Speech Output Tags." If you are using sound files as your character's output, consider these factors as well in your recorded audio.

C H A P T E R   3

Microsoft Agent Programming Interface Overview

The Microsoft Agent API provides services that support the display and animation of animated characters. Implemented as an OLE Automation/Component Object Model (COM) server, Microsoft Agent enables multiple applications, called *clients* or *client applications*, to host and access its animation, input, and output services at the same time. A client can be any application that connects to the Microsoft Agent's COM interfaces.

As a COM server, Microsoft Agent automatically starts up only when a client application uses the COM interfaces and requests to connect to it. It remains running until all clients close their connections. When no connected clients remain, Microsoft Agent automatically exits.

Although you can call Microsoft Agent's COM interfaces directly, Microsoft Agent also includes an ActiveX control. This control makes it easy to access Microsoft Agent's services from programming languages that support the ActiveX control interface. For more information on the specific API supported from the Agent server and control interfaces, see Chapter 4, "Programming the Microsoft Agent Control," and Chapter 5, "Programming the Microsoft Agent Server Interface."

In addition to supporting stand-alone programs written for Windows, Agent can be scripted to support Web pages, provided that the browser supports the ActiveX interface. Microsoft Internet Explorer includes support for ActiveX as well as scripting languages that you can use to program Agent. If you are not using Internet Explorer, consult with your vendor or supplier about the browser's support for ActiveX.

Microsoft Agent is an extension of Microsoft Windows. As a result, it currently supports only Windows 95 or later versions. Microsoft Agent also requires certain system libraries (dlls). The best way to ensure that you have these libraries (and their correct versions) is to install Internet Explorer 4.0 or later. You can download the browser from the Microsoft Internet Explorer Web site.

Licensing and Distribution

The Microsoft Agent self-extracting executable installs a number of system files and registry entries. Web developers can include the CLSID in the <OBJECT> tag of their HTML page, subject to the provisions of the license agreement displayed when the control is downloaded and installed.

Application developers who want to distribute Microsoft Agent services and any of its components (including Microsoft Agent character files) as part of their application or from their own server must complete a distribution license for Microsoft Agent. For more information on licensing requirements for Microsoft Agent, see the Licensing document at the Microsoft Agent Web site at *http:// www.microsoft.com/msagent/licensing.asp*.

Animation Services

Microsoft Agent's animation services manage the animation and movement of a character's image in its own window on the screen. An animation is defined as a sequence of timed and optionally branched frames, composed of one or more images.

Loading a Character

To animate a character, you must first load the character. Use the **Load** method to load the character's data. Microsoft Agent supports two formats for character and animation data: a single structured file and separate files. Typically, you use the single file format (.ACS) when the data is stored locally. The multiple file format (.ACF, .ACA) works best when you want to download animations individually, such as when accessing animations from an HTTP server.

A client application can load only a single instance of the same character. Any attempt to load the same character more than once will fail. However, an application can have multiple instances of the same character loaded by providing separate connections to Microsoft Agent. For example, an application could load the same character from two copies of the Microsoft Agent control.

Microsoft Agent provides a set of characters you can download and use, subject to the provisions of the license agreement. The Microsoft Agent Characters can be downloaded from the Microsoft Agent Web site at *http://www.microsoft.com/ msagent/characterdata.asp*. They are also included in this book's CD.

You can also define your own characters for use with Microsoft Agent. You may use any rendering tool you prefer to create the images, provided that you end up with Windows bitmap format files. To assemble and compile a character's images into animations for use with Microsoft Agent, use the Microsoft Agent Character Editor. This tool enables you to define a character's default properties as well as define animations for the character. The Microsoft Agent Character Editor also enables you to select the appropriate file format when you create a character. You can download the Microsoft Agent Character Editor from the Microsoft Agent Web site at *http://www.microsoft.com/msagent/agentdevdl.asp*. The editor is also included on this book's CD.

Loading the Default Character

Instead of loading only a specific character directly by specifying its filename, you can load the *default character*. The default character is a service intended to provide a shared, central Windows assistant that the user chooses. Microsoft Agent includes a property sheet as part of the default character service, known as the Character Properties window, which enables the user to change their selection of the default character.

Selection of the default character is limited to a character that supports the standard animation set, ensuring a basic level of consistency across characters. This does not exclude a character from having additional animations.

However, because the default character is intended for general-purpose use and can be shared by other applications at the same time, avoid loading the default character when you want a character exclusively for your application.

To load the default character, call the **Load** method without specifying a filename or path. Microsoft Agent automatically loads the current character set as the default character. If the user has not yet selected a default character, Agent will select the first character that supports the standard animation set. If none is available, the method will fail and report back the cause.

Although a client application can inquire as to the identity of the character, only a user can change its settings. You can use the **ShowDefaultCharacter-Properties** to display the Character Properties window.

The server will notify clients that have loaded the default character when a user changes a character selection, and pass the GUID of the new character. The server automatically unloads the former character and reloads the new character. The queues of any clients that have loaded the default character are halted and flushed. However, the queues of clients that have loaded the character explicitly using the character's filename are not affected. If necessary, the server also handles automatically resetting the text-to-speech (TTS) engine for the new character.

Animating a Character

Once a character is loaded, you can use several of Microsoft Agent's methods for animating the character. The first one you use is typically the **Show** method. **Show** makes the character's frame visible and plays the animation assigned to the character's **Showing** state.

Once the character's frame is visible, you can use the **Play** method, specifying the name of an animation, to play that animation. Animation names are specific to a character definition. As an animation plays, the shape of its window changes to match the image in the frame. This results in a movable graphic image, or *sprite*, displayed on top of the desktop and all windows, or *z-order*.

If the character's file is stored locally, you can simply call the **Play** method. In other cases, such as when you have loaded an .ACF character from an HTTP server, you must use the **Get** (or **Prepare**) method to first retrieve the animation data. This will cause Agent to request the animation file from the server and store it in the browser's buffer on the local machine.

The **Speak** method enables you to program the character to speak, automatically lip-syncing the output. Further details are covered in the Output section of this document.

You can use the **MoveTo** method to position the character at a new location. When you call the **MoveTo** method, Microsoft Agent automatically plays the appropriate animation based on the character's current location, then moves the character's frame. Similarly, when you call **GestureAt**, Microsoft Agent plays the appropriate gesturing animation based on the character's location and the location specified in the call.

To hide the character, call the **Hide** method. This automatically plays the character associated with the character's **Hiding** state, then hides the character's frame. However, you can also hide or show a character by setting the character's **Visible** property.

Microsoft Agent processes all animation calls, or *requests*, asynchronously. This enables your application's code to continue handling other events while the request is being processed. For example, calls to the **Play** method place the animation in a queue for the character so that the animations can be played sequentially. However, this means you cannot assume that a call to other functions will necessarily execute after an animation it follows in your code. For example, typically, a statement following a call to **Play** or **MoveTo** will execute before the animation finishes.

You can synchronize your code with animations in a character's queue by creating an object reference to the animation request, and, when the animation starts or completes, monitoring the **Request** events that the server uses to notify clients of the character. For example, if you want a message box to appear when the character finishes an animation, you can put the message box call in your **Request-Complete** event handling subroutine, checking for the particular request ID.

When a character is hidden, the server does not play animations; however, it still queues and processes the animation request (plays the animation) and passes a request status back to the client. In the hidden state, the character cannot become input-active. However, if the user speaks the name of the character (when speech input is enabled), the server automatically shows the character.

When your client application loads multiple characters at the same time, Microsoft Agent's animation services enable you to animate characters independently or use the **Wait**, **Interrupt**, or **Stop** methods to synchronize their animation with each other.

Microsoft Agent also plays other animations automatically for you. For example, if the character's state has not changed for several seconds, Agent begins playing animations assigned to the character's **Idling** animations. Similarly, when speech input is enabled, Agent plays the character's **Listening** animations and then **Hearing** animations when an utterance is detected. These server-managed animations are called *states*, and are defined when a character is created. For more information, see Chapter 9, "Using The Microsoft Agent Character Editor."

Input Services

A client application provides the primary user interface for interaction with a character. You can program a character to respond to any form of input, from button-clicks to typed-in text. In addition, Microsoft Agent provides events so you can program what happens when the user clicks, double-clicks, or drags the character. The server passes the coordinates of the pointer and any modifier key state for these events.

Input-Active Client

Because multiple client applications can share the same character and because multiple clients can use different characters at the same time, the server designates one client as the *input-active* client and sends mouse and voice input only to that client application. This maintains the orderly management of user input, so that an appropriate client responds to the input.

Typically, user interaction determines which client application becomes input-active. For example, if the user clicks a character, that character's client application becomes input-active. Similarly, if a user speaks the name of a character, it becomes input-active. Also, when the server processes a character's **Show** method, the client of that character becomes input-active.

When a character is hidden, the client of that character will no longer be input-active for that character. The server automatically makes the active client of any remaining character(s) input-active. When all characters are hidden, no client is input-active. However, in this situation, if the user presses the Listening hotkey, Agent will continue to listen for its commands (using the speech recognition engine matching the topmost character of the last input-active client).

If multiple clients are sharing the same character, the server will designate its *active client* as input-active client. The active character is the topmost in the client order. You can set your client to be the active or not-active client using the **Activate** method. You can also use the **Activate** method to explicitly make your client input-active; but to avoid disrupting other clients of the character, you should do so only when your client application is active. For example, if the user clicks your application's window, activating your application, you can call the **Activate** method to receive and process mouse and speech input directed to the character.

Pop-up Menu Support

Microsoft Agent includes a pop-up menu (also known as a contextual menu) for each character. The server displays this pop-up menu automatically when a user right-clicks the character. You can add commands for your client application to the menu by defining a **Commands** collection. For each command in the collection that you define, you can specify **Caption** and **Visible** properties. The **Caption** is the text that appears in the menu when the **Visible** property is set to **True**. You can also use the **Enabled** property to display the command in the menu as disabled and the **HelpContextID** to support Help support for the property. Define the access key for the menu text by including an ampersand (&) before the text character of the **Caption** text setting.

The server automatically adds to the menu commands for opening the Voice Commands Window and hiding the character as well as the **Commands** captions of other clients of the character to enable users to switch between clients. The server automatically adds a separator to the menu between its menu entries and those defined by the client. Separators appear only when there are items in the menu to separate.

To remove commands from a menu, use the **Remove** method. Note that menu entries do not change while the menu displays. If you add or remove commands or change their properties, the menu displays the changes when the user redisplays the menu.

If you prefer to provide your own pop-up menu services for a character, you can use the **AutoPopupMenu** property to turn off server handling of the right-click action. You can then use the **Click** event notification to create your own menu handling behavior.

When the user selects a command from a character's pop-up menu or the Voice Commands Window, the server triggers the **Command** event of the associated client and passes back the parameters of the input using the **UserInput** object.

The server also provides a pop-up menu for the character's taskbar icon. When the character is visible, right-clicking this menu displays the same commands as those displayed by right-clicking the character. However, when the character is hidden, only the server-supplied commands are included.

Speech Input Support

In addition to supporting mouse and keyboard interaction, Microsoft Agent includes direct support for speech input. Because Microsoft Agent's support for speech input is based on Microsoft SAPI (Speech Application Programming Interface), you can use Microsoft Agent with speech recognition command and control engines that include the SAPI-required support. For more information on speech engine requirements, see Appendix G, "Speech Engine Support Requirements."

Microsoft provides a command-and-control speech recognition engine you can use with Microsoft Agent. You can find further information about available speech engine support and how to use speech engines at the Microsoft Agent download.

The user can initiate speech input by pressing and holding the push-to-talk Listening hotkey. In this Listening mode, if the speech engine receives the beginning of spoken input, it holds the audio channel open until it detects the end of the utterance. However, when not receiving input, it does not block audio output. This enables the user to issue multiple voice commands while holding down the key, and the character can respond when the user isn't speaking.

The Listening mode times out once the user releases the Listening key. The user can adjust the time-out for this mode using the Advanced Character Options. You cannot set this time-out from your client application code.

If a character attempts to speak while the user is speaking, the character's audible output fails though text may still be displayed in its word balloon. If the character has the audio channel while the Listening key is pressed, the server automatically transfers control back to the user after processing the text in the **Speak** method. An optional MIDI tone is played to cue the user to begin speaking. This enables the user to provide input even if the application driving the character failed to provide logical pauses in its output.

You can also use the **Listen** method to initiate speech input. Calling this method turns on the speech recognition for a predefined period of time. If there is no input during this interval, Microsoft Agent automatically turns off the speech recognition engine and frees up the audio channel. This avoids blocking input to or output from the audio device and minimizes the processor overhead the speech recognition uses when it is on. You can also use the **Listen** method to turn off speech input. However, be aware that because the speech recognition engine operates asynchronously, the effect may not be immediate. As a result, it is possible to receive a **Command** event even after your code called **Listen** to turn off speech input.

To support speech input, you define a *grammar*, a set of words you want the speech recognition engine to listen and match for as the **Voice** setting for a **Command** in your **Commands** collection. You can include optional and alternative words and repeated sequences in your grammar. Note that Agent does not enable the Listening hotkey until one of its clients has successfully loaded a speech engine or has authored a **Voice** for one of its **Command** objects.

Whether the user presses the Listening hotkey or your client application calls the **Listen** method to initiate speech input, the speech recognition engine attempts to match an utterance's input to the grammar for the commands that have been defined, and passes the information back to the server. The server then notifies the client application using the **Command** event (**IAgentNotifySink::Command**); passing back the **UserInput** object that includes the command ID of the best match and next two alternative matches (if any), a confidence score, and the matching text for each match.

The server also notifies your client application when it matches the speech input to one of its supplied commands. While the command ID is NULL, you still get the confidence score and text matched. When in Listening mode, the server automatically plays the animation assigned to the character's **Listening** state. Then, when an utterance is actually detected, the server plays the character's **Hearing** state animation. The server will keep the character in an attentive state until the utterance has ended. This provides the appropriate social feedback to cue the user for input.

If the user disables speech input in Advanced Character Options, the Listening hotkey will also be disabled. Similarly, attempting to call the **Listen** method when speech input is disabled will cause the method to fail.

Speech Engine Selection

A character's language ID setting determines its default speech input language; Microsoft Agent requests SAPI for an installed engine that matches that language. If a client application does not specify a language preference, Microsoft Agent will attempt to find a speech recognition engine that matches the user default language ID (using the major language ID, then the minor language ID). If no engine is available matching this language, speech is disabled for that character.

You can also request a specific speech recognition engine by specifying its mode ID (using the character **SRModeID** property). However, if the language ID for that mode ID does not match the client's language setting, the call will fail (raise an error in the control). The speech recognition engine will then remain the last successfully set engine by the client, or if none, the engine that matches the current system language ID. If there is still no match, speech input is not available for that client.

Microsoft Agent automatically loads a speech recognition engine when speech input is initiated by a user pressing the Listening hotkey or the input-active client calls the **Listen** method. However, an engine may also be loaded when setting or querying its mode ID, setting or querying the properties of the Voice Commands Window, querying **SRStatus**, or when speech is enabled and the user displays the Speech Input page of the Advanced Character Options. However, Microsoft Agent only keeps loaded the speech engines that clients are using.

Speech Input Events

In addition to the **Command** event notification, Agent also notifies the input-active client when the server turns the Listening mode on or off, using the **ListenStart** and **ListenComplete** events (**IAgentNotifySinkEx::ListeningState**). However, if the user presses the Listening mode key and there is no matching speech recognition engine available for the topmost character of the input-active client, the server starts the Listening hotkey mode time-out, but does not generate a **ListenStart** event for the active client of the character. If, before the time-out completes, the user activates another character with speech recognition engine support, the server attempts to activate speech input and generates the **ListenStart** event.

Similarly, if a client attempts to turn on the Listening mode using the **Listen** method and there is no matching speech recognition engine available, the call fails and the server does not generate a **ListenStart** event. In the Microsoft Agent control, the **Listen** method returns **False**, but the call does not raise an error.

When the Listening key mode is on and the user switches to a character that uses a different speech recognition engine, the server switches to and activates that engine and triggers a **ListenComplete** and then a **ListenStart** event. If the activated character does not have an available speech recognition engine (because one is not installed or none match the activated character's language ID setting), the server will trigger the **ListenComplete** event for the previously activated character and passes back a value in the **Cause** parameter. However, the server does not generate **ListenStart** or **ListenComplete** events for the clients that do not have speech recognition support.

If a client successfully calls the **Listen** method and a character without speech recognition engine support becomes input-active before the Listening mode time-out completes, and then the user switches back to the character of the original client, the server will generate a **ListenStart** event for that client.

If the input-active client switches speech recognition engines by changing **SRModeID** while in Listening mode, the server switches to and activates that engine without re-triggering the **ListenStart** event. However, if the specified engine is not available, the call fails (raises an error in the control) and the server also calls the **ListenComplete** event.

The Voice Commands Window

The Voice Commands Window displays the current active voice commands available for the character. The window appears when the Open Commands Window command is chosen or the **Visible** property of the **CommandsWindow** object is set to **True**. If the speech engine has not yet been loaded, querying or setting this property will cause Microsoft Agent to attempt to initialize the engine. If the user disables speech, the window can still display; however, it will include a text message that informs the user that speech is currently disabled.

The input-active client's commands appear in the Voice Commands Window based on the **Voice Caption** and **Voice** property settings listed under the **Voice Caption** of their **Commands** collection.

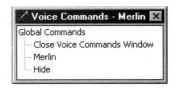

FIGURE 3-1. Voice Commands Window

The Voice Commands Window appears when the Open Commands Window command is chosen. The input-active client's commands appear in the Voice Commands Window based on the **Voice Caption** and **Voice** property settings listed under **Voice Caption** of the **Commands** collection.

The Voice Commands Window also lists the **Voice Caption** of the **Commands** collection for other clients of the character, and the following server-generated voice commands for general interaction under the Global Commands entry:

Voice Caption	Voice Grammar
Open	Close Voice Commands Window	((open | show) [the] commands [window]	what can I say [now]) toggles with: close [the] commands [window]
Hide	hide *
CharacterName	*CharacterName***
Global Commands	[show] [me] global commands

* A character is listed here only if it is currently visible.

** All loaded characters are listed.

Speaking the voice command for another client's **Commands** collection switches to that client, and the Voice Commands Window displays the commands of that client. No other entries are expanded. Similarly, if the user switches characters, the Voice Commands Window changes to display the commands of its input-active client. If the client is already input-active, speaking one of its voice commands has no effect. (However, if the user collapses the active client's subtree with the mouse, speaking the client name redisplays the client's subtree.)

If a client has voice commands, but no **Voice** setting for its **Commands** object (or no **Voice Caption**), the tree displays "(command undefined)" as the parent entry—but only when that client is input-active and the client has commands in its collection that have **Caption** and **Voice** settings.

The server automatically displays the commands of the current input-active client and, if necessary, scrolls the window to display as many of the client's commands as possible, based on the size of the window. If the character has no client entries, the Global Commands entry is expanded.

If the user speaks "Global Commands," the Voice Commands Window always displays its associated subtree entries. If they are already displayed, the command has no effect.

Although you can also display or hide the Voice Commands Window from your application's code using the **Visible** property, you cannot change the Voice Commands Window size or location. The server maintains the Voice Commands Window's properties based on the user's interaction with the window. Its initial location is immediately adjacent to the character's taskbar icon.

The Voice Commands Window is included in the ALT+TAB window order. This enables a user to switch to the window to scroll, resize, or reposition the window with the keyboard.

The Listening Tip

The Listening Tip is another speech input service provided by Microsoft Agent. When speech input is installed, Agent includes a special tooltip window that appears when the user presses the Listening hotkey or calls the Listen method. The Listening Tip appears only when the speech services are available. If no client has authored a voice command or successfully loads a speech engine, the Listening Tip does not appear. Further, both speech input and the Display Listening Tips option in the Advanced Character Options must be enabled for the tip to appear.

The following table summarizes the display of the Listening Tip when speech recognition is enabled.

Action	Result
User presses the Listening mode hotkey or input- active calls the **Listen** method	The Listening Tip appears below the active client's character and displays: -- *CharacterName* is listening -- for "*InputActiveClientCommandsVoiceCaption*" commands.
	If the client hasn't defined a **VoiceCaption** its **Commands** object, the value of its **Caption** property is used.
	The first line identifying the character is centered. The second line is left justified and breaks to a third line when it exceeds the Listening Tip's maximum width.
	If an input-active client of the character does not have a caption or defined voice parameters for its **Commands** object, the Listening Tip displays: -- *CharacterName* is listening -- for commands.
	If there are no visible characters, the Listening Tip appears adjacent to the character's taskbar icon and displays: -- *CharacterName* is listening -- Say the name of a character to display it.
	If the speech recognition is still initializing, the Listening Tip displays: -- *CharacterName* is preparing to listen -- Please wait to speak.
	If the audio channel is busy, as when the character is audibly speaking or some other application is using the audio channel, the Listening Tip displays: -- *CharacterName* is not listening -- for *InputActiveClientCommandsVoiceCaption* commands.
	If there is no language-compatible speech engine installed for the input-active client's character, the Listening Tip displays the following, where *Language* represents the selected language of the character: -- *CharacterName* is not listening -- Speech input is not available in *Language*.
	If the audio device is not available for other reasons, such as when it is busy or there is some error in attempting to open the audio device, the following tip appears when the Listening mode is activated: -- *CharacterName* is not listening -- Speech input not available.
	If the input-active client application has not defined any **Voice** settings for commands and has also disabled voice parameters for Agent's global commands, this tip appears: -- *CharacterName* is not listening -- No voice commands.
	If all characters are hidden, the Listening Tip displays the following text: -- *CharacterName* is listening -- Say the name of a character to display it.

Action	Result
User speaks a voice command	If the spoken text matches a client- or server-defined command, the Listening Tip appears below the active client's character and displays:

-- *CharacterName* is listening --

Heard *"CommandText"*

However, when a recognition is passed back and the Listening mode has timed out, but the Listening Tip time-out has not, or if the Listening mode is still in effect, but the audio channel is not yet available (for example, the user is still holding the Listening key or the Listening mode has not timed out, because the character is speaking), the Listening Tip displays:

-- *CharacterName* is not listening --

Heard *"text heard"*

When the spoken text matches a server-defined command, but the server does not act on it because the command has a low confidence score, the second line of the Listening Tip displays:

Didn't understand your request.

The first line is centered. The second line is left justified and breaks to a third line when it exceeds the Listening Tip's maximum width.

The Listening Tip automatically times out after being presented. If the "Heard" text time-out completes while the user is still holding down the hotkey, the tip reverts to the "listening" text unless the server receives another matching utterance. In this case, the tip displays the new "Heard" text and begins the time-out for that tip text. If the user releases the hotkey and the server is displaying the "Heard" text, the time-out continues and the Listening Tip window is hidden when the time-out interval elapses.

If the server has not yet attempted to load a speech recognition engine, the Listening Tip will not display. Similarly, if the user has disabled the display of the Listening Tip or disabled speech input in Advanced Character Options, the Listening Tip will not be displayed.

The Listening Tip does not appear when the pointer is over the character's taskbar icon. Instead, the standard notification tip window appears and displays the character's name.

Client applications cannot write directly to the Listening Tip, but you can specify alternative text that the server displays on recognition of a matching voice command. To do this, set the **Confidence** property and the new **ConfidenceText** property for the command. If spoken input matches the command, but the best match does not exceed the confidence setting, the server uses the text set in the **ConfidenceText** property in the tip window. If the client does not supply this value, the server displays the text (grammar) it matched.

The Listening Tip text appears in the language based on the input-active client's character language ID setting, regardless of whether there is a language-compatible speech recognition engine available.

The Advanced Character Options Window

The Advanced Character Options window provides options for users to adjust their interaction with all characters. For example, users can disable speech input or change input parameters. Users can also change the output settings for the word balloon. These settings override any set by a client application or set as part of the character definition. Your application cannot change or disable these options, because they apply to the general user preferences for operation of all characters. However, the server will notify your application (**DefaultCharacterChange**) when the user changes and applies an option. You can also display or close the window using the window's **Visible** property and access its location through its **Top** and **Left** properties.

Output Services

In addition to supporting the animation of a character, Microsoft Agent supports audio output for the character. This includes spoken output and sound effects. For spoken output, the server automatically lip-syncs the character's defined mouth images to the output. You can choose text-to-speech (TTS) synthesis, recorded audio, or only word balloon text output.

Synthesized Speech Support

If you use synthesized speech, your character has the ability to say almost anything, which provides the greatest flexibility. With recorded audio, you can give the character a specific or unique voice. To specify output, provide the spoken text as a parameter of the **Speak** method.

Because Microsoft Agent's architecture uses Microsoft SAPI for synthesized speech output, you can use any engine that conforms to this specification, and supports International Phonetic Alphabet (IPA) output using the **Visual** method of the **ITTSNotifySinkW** interface.

A character's language ID setting determines its TTS output. If a client does not specify a language ID for the character, the character's language ID is set to the user default language ID. If the character's definition includes a specific engine and that engine can be loaded and it matches the character's language setting, that engine will be used. Otherwise, Microsoft Agent enumerates the other available engines and requests a SAPI best match based on language, gender, and age (in that order). If there is no matching engine available, there is no TTS output for that client's use of the character. Agent attempts to load the TTS engine on the first **Speak** call or when you query or successfully set its mode ID.

A client application can also specify a TTS engine for its character (using the **TTSModeID** property). This overrides the server's attempt to automatically find a matching engine based on the character's preferred TTS mode ID or the character's current language ID setting. However, if that engine is not installed (or cannot otherwise be loaded), the call will fail (and raise an error in the control). The server then attempts to load another engine based on the language ID, compiled character TTS setting, and available TTS engines. If there is still no match, TTS is not available for that client, but the character can still speak into its word balloon.

Only the TTS engines in use by any client remain loaded. For example, if a character has a defined preference for a specific engine and that engine is available, but your client application has specified a different engine (by setting a character's language ID differently from the engine or specifying a different mode ID), only the engine specified by your application remains loaded. The engine matching the character's defined preference for a TTS setting is unloaded (unless another client is using the character's compiled engine setting).

Audio Output Support

Microsoft Agent enables you to use audio files for a character's spoken output. You can record audio files and use the **Speak** method to play that data. Microsoft Agent animation services automatically support lip-syncing the character mouth by using the audio characteristics of the audio file. Microsoft Agent also supports a special format for audio files, which includes additional phoneme and word-break information for more enhanced lip-sync support. You can generate this special format using the Microsoft Linguistic Information Sound Editing Tool.

Word Balloon Support

Spoken output can also appear as textual output in the form of a cartoon word balloon. This can be used to supplement the spoken output of a character or as an alternative to audio output when you use the **Speak** method.

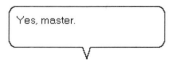

FIGURE 3-2. The Word Balloon

You can also use a word balloon to communicate what a character is "thinking" using the **Think** method. This displays the text you supply in a still "thought" balloon. The **Think** method also differs from the **Speak** method in that it produces no audio output.

Word balloons support only captioned communication from the character, *not* user input. Therefore, the word balloon does not support input controls. However, you can easily provide user input for a character, using interfaces from your programming language or the other input services provided by Microsoft Agent, such as the pop-up menu.

When you define a character, you can specify whether to include word balloon support. However, if you use a character that includes word balloon support, you cannot disable the support.

Animation Sound Effects

Microsoft Agent also enables you to include sound effects as a part of a character's animation. Using the Microsoft Agent Character Editor, you can specify the filename of standard Windows sound (.WAV) files to trigger on a given frame. Note that Microsoft Agent does not mix sound effects and spoken output, so spoken output does not begin until a sound effect completes. Therefore, avoid any long or looping sound effect as a part of a character's animation.

C H A P T E R   4

Programming the Microsoft Agent Control

Although applications can write directly to the Microsoft Agent services using its automation server interfaces, Microsoft Agent also includes an ActiveX (OLE) control. The control supports easy programming using a scripting language such as Microsoft Visual Basic Scripting Edition (VBScript) or other languages that support the ActiveX control interface.

Document Conventions

This documentation uses the following typographical conventions:

Convention	Description
Sub, Visible, Caption	Words in bold with initial letter capitalized indicate keywords.
agent, String, Now	Italic words indicate placeholders for information you supply.
ENTER, F1	Words in all capital letters indicate filenames, key names, and key sequences.
`Agent1.Commands.Enabled = True`	Words in this font indicate code samples.
`' This is a comment`	An apostrophe (') indicates a code comment.
`Agent1.Commands.Add "Test1", _` `"Test 1", "test one"`	A space and an underscore (_) continues a line of code.
`[words or expression]`	Items inside square brackets are optional.
`This	That`	A vertical bar indicates a choice between two or more items.
`agent`	The word "agent" in italics represents the name of the agent control you use.

The descriptions of programming interfaces in this document follow the conventions for Microsoft VBScript. However, they should be generally applicable to other languages as well.

Accessing the Control in Web Pages

To access the Microsoft Agent services from a Web page, use the HTML <OB-JECT> tag within the <HEAD> or <BODY> element of the page, specifying the Microsoft CLSID (class identifier) for the control. In addition, use a CODEBASE parameter to specify the location of the Microsoft Agent installation file and its version number.

If Microsoft Internet Explorer (version 3.02 or later) is installed on the system, but Microsoft Agent is not yet installed and the user accesses a Web page that has the <OBJECT> tag with the Agent CLSID, the browser will automatically attempt to download Agent from the Microsoft Web site. Then, the user will be asked whether to proceed with installation. For other browsers, contact the supplier for information regarding their support or third-party support for ActiveX controls.

The following example illustrates how to use the CODEBASE parameter to autodownload the English language version 2.0 of Microsoft Agent. For information about the current location of the Microsoft Agent installation file for specific language versions and the current release number available, see the Microsoft Agent Downloads for Developers page (http://www.microsoft.com/workshop/imedia/agent/agentdevdl.asp).

```
<OBJECT
classid="clsid: D45FD31B-5C6E-11D1-9EC1-00C04FD7081F"
CODEBASE = "#VERSION=2,0,0,0"
 id=Agent
>
</OBJECT>
```

Subject to a valid Microsoft Agent distribution license, Agent can also be installed from your own HTTP server or as part of an application's installation process. To support installation from your own HTTP server, you need to post the Microsoft Agent self-installing cabinet .Exe file and specify its URL in the CODEBASE tag.

```
<OBJECT
classid="clsid: D45FD31B-5C6E-11D1-9EC1-00C04FD7081F"
CODEBASE = "http://your server/msagent.exe#VERSION=2,0,0,0"
 id=Agent
>
</OBJECT>
```

To obtain Agent's self-installing cabinet file from the Microsoft Agent web site, simply download the Agent file, and choose the browser's Save option. This should save the file to your specified location.

To support autodownload of a Microsoft Agent language component from a Web page, include the language component's Object tag on the page before the Agent control Object tag:

```
<OBJECT width=0 height=0
CLASSID="CLSID:C348XXXX-A7F8-11D1-AA75-00C04FA34D72"
CODEBASE = "#VERSION=2,0,0,0">
</OBJECT>
```

where *XXXX* is replaced with a Language ID. For the languages currently supported, see the contents of your CD or check the Microsoft Agent Web site.

Note

- The <OBJECT> tag for a language component must precede the <OBJECT> tag for the Microsoft Agent core component.

- Multiple languages can be installed on the same client.

- Before setting the **LanguageID** of a character, we recommend that your script verify that the locale of the browser, available in the **navigator.userLanguage** property, matches the language being set.

To support other language versions of Agent, you use another Object tag specifying the language component. However, be aware that attempting to install multiple languages at the same time may require the user to reboot. The Agent language components can be obtained from the Agent web site using the same procedure as for the Agent core component. Distribution licensing for the language components are covered in the standard Agent distribution license. To begin using a character, you must load the character using the **Load** method. A character can be loaded from the user's local storage or an HTTP server. For more information about the syntax for loading a character, see the **Load** method. Once the character has been successful loaded you can use the methods, properties, and events exposed by the Agent control to program the character. You can also use the methods, properties, and events exposed by your programming language and the browser to program the character; for example, to program its reaction to a button click. Consult the documentation for your browser to determine what features it exposes in its scripting model. For Microsoft Internet Explorer, see the Scripting Object Model, which is available in the ActiveX SDK.

Agent's services remain loaded only when there is at least one client application with a connection. This means that when a user moves between Agent-enabled Web pages, Agent will shut down and any characters you loaded will disappear. To keep Agent running between pages (and thereby keep a character visible), create another client that remains loaded between page changes. For example, you can create an HTML frameset and declare an <OBJECT> tag for Agent in the parent frame. You can then script the pages you load into the child frame(s), to call into the parent's script. Alternatively, you can also include an <OBJECT> tag on each page you load into the child frame. In this case, remember that each page will be its own client. You may need to use the **Activate** method to set which client has control when the user interacts with the parent or child page.

Using VBScript

VBScript is a programming language included with Microsoft Internet Explorer. For other browsers, contact your vendor about support. VBScript 2.0 (or later) is recommended for use with Agent. Although earlier versions of VBScript may work with Agent, they lack certain functions that you may want to use. You can download VBScript 2.0 and obtain further information on VBScript at the Microsoft Downloads site and the Microsoft VBScript site.

To program Microsoft Agent from VBScript, use the HTML <SCRIPT> tags. To access the programming interface, use the name of the control you assign in the <OBJECT> tag, followed by the subobject (if any), the name of the method or property, and any parameters or values supported by the method or property:

```
agent[.object].Method parameter, [parameter]
agent[.object].Property = value
```

For events, include the name of the control followed by the name of the event and any parameters:

```
Sub agent_event (ByVal parameter[,ByVal parameter])
statements…
End Sub
```

You can also specify an event handler using the <SCRIPT> tag's **For...Event** syntax:

```
<SCRIPT LANGUAGE=VBScript For=agent Event=event[(parameter[,parameter])])>
statements…
</SCRIPT>
```

Although Microsoft Internet Explorer supports this latter syntax, not all browsers do. For compatibility, use only the former syntax for events.

With VBScript (2.0 or later), you can verify whether Microsoft Agent is installed by trying to create the object and checking to see if it exists. The following sample demonstrates how to check for the Agent control without triggering an auto-download of the control (as would happen if you included an <OBJECT> tag for the control on the page):

```
<!-- WARNING - This code requires VBScript 2.0.
It will always fail to detect the Agent control
in VbScript 1.x, because CreateObject doesn't work.
-->

<SCRIPT LANGUAGE=VBSCRIPT>
If HaveAgent() Then
      'Microsoft Agent control was found.
document.write "<H2 align=center>Found</H2>"
Else
      'Microsoft Agent control was not found.
document.write "<H2 align=center>Not Found</H2>"
End If

Function HaveAgent()
' This procedure attempts to create an Agent Control object.
' If it succeeds, it returns True.
'     This means the control is available on the client.
' If it fails, it returns False.
'     This means the control hasn't been installed on the client.

   Dim agent
   HaveAgent = False
   On Error Resume Next
   Set agent = CreateObject("Agent.Control.1")
   HaveAgent = IsObject(agent)

End Function

</SCRIPT>
```

Using JavaScript and JScript

If you use JavaScript or Microsoft JScript to access Microsoft Agent's programming interface, follow the conventions for this language for specifying methods or properties:

```
agent.object.Method (parameter)
agent.object.Property = value
```

JavaScript does not currently have event syntax for non-HTML objects. However, with Internet Explorer you can use the <SCRIPT> tag's **For…Event** syntax:

```
<SCRIPT LANGUAGE="JScript" FOR="object" EVENT="event()">
statements…
</SCRIPT>
```

Because not all browsers currently support this event syntax, you may want to use JScript only for pages that support Microsoft Internet Explorer or for code that does not require event handling.

To access Agent's object collections, use the JScript **Enumerator** function. However, versions of JScript included prior to Internet Explorer 4.0 do not support this function and do not support collections. To access methods and properties of the **Character** object, use the **Character** method. Similarly, to access the properties of a **Command** object, use the **Command** method.

Accessing Speech Services

Although Microsoft Agent's services include support for speech input, a compatible command-and-control speech recognition engine must be installed to access Agent's speech input services. Similarly, if you want to use Microsoft Agent's speech services to support synthesized speech output for a character, you must install a compatible text-to-speech (TTS) speech engine for your character.

To enable speech input support in your application, define a **Command** object and set its **Voice** property. Agent will automatically load speech services, so that when the user presses the Listening key or you call **Listen**, the speech recognition engine will be loaded. By default the character's **LanguageID** will determine which engine is loaded. Agent attempts to load the first engine that the Microsoft Speech API (SAPI) returns as matching this language. Use **SRModeID** if you want to load a specific engine.

To enable text-to-speech output, use the **Speak** method. Agent will automatically attempt to load an engine that matches the character's **LanguageID**. If the character's definition includes a specific TTS engine mode ID and that engine is available and matches the character's **LanguageID**, Agent loads that engine for the character. If it is not, it loads the first TTS engine that SAPI returns as matching the character's language setting. You can also use the **TTSModeID** to load a specific engine.

Typically, Agent loads speech recognition when the Listening mode is initiated and a text-to-speech engine when **Speak** is first called. However, if you want to preload the speech engine, you query the properties related to the speech interfaces. For example, querying **SRModeID** or **TTSModeID** will attempt to load that type of engine.

Because Microsoft Agent's speech services are based on the Microsoft Speech API, you can use any engines that support the required speech interfaces. Further information on the availability and use of speech recognition and text-to-speech engines at the Microsoft Agent Download page.

Accessing the Control from Visual Basic and Other Programming Languages

You can also use Microsoft Agent's control from Visual Basic and other programming languages. Make sure that the language fully supports the ActiveX control interface, and follow its conventions for adding and accessing ActiveX controls.

To access the control, Agent must already be installed on the target system. If you want to install Microsoft Agent as part of your application, you must have a valid distribution license for Agent. You can access the License Agreement from the Microsoft Agent web site, *http://www.microsoft.com/sitebuilder/workshop/imedia/agent/licensing.asp*.

You can then download Agent's self-installing cabinet file from the web site (using the Save rather than Run option). You can include this file in your installation setup program. Whenever it is executed, it will automatically install Agent on the target system. For further details on installation, see the Microsoft Agent distribution license agreement. Installation other than using Agent's self-installing cabinet file, such as attempting to copy and register Agent component files, is not supported. This ensures consistent and complete installation. Note that the Microsoft Agent self-installing file will not install on Microsoft Windows 2000 (NT5) because that version of the operating system already includes its own version of Agent.

To successfully install Agent on a target system, you must also ensure that the target system has a recent version of the Microsoft Visual C++ runtime (Msvcrt.dll), Microsoft registration tool (Regsvr32.dll), and Microsoft COM dlls. The easiest way to ensure that the necessary components are on the target system is to require that Microsoft Internet Explorer 3.02 or later is installed. Alternatively, you can install the first two components which are available as part of Microsoft Visual C++. The necessary COM dlls can be installed as part of the Microsoft DCOM update, available at the Microsoft web site. You can find further information and licensing information for these components at the Microsoft web site.

Agent's language components can be installed the same way. Similarly, you can use this technique to install the ACS format of the Microsoft characters available for distribution from the Microsoft Agent web site. The character files automatically install to the Microsoft Agent \Chars subdirectory.

Because Microsoft Agent's components are designed as operating system components, Agent may not be uninstalled. Similarly, where Agent is already installed as part of the Windows operating system, the Agent self-installing cabinet may not install.

Creating an Instance of the Control

Accessing Microsoft Agent's control requires that you first create an instance of the control. The easiest way to do this is to place an instance of the control on a form. You may have to add the control to your toolbox before adding it to your form. Depending on your programming language, you may also be able to create the control at runtime.

Accessing the Control's Methods, Properties, and Events

Using Microsoft Agent's control with Visual Basic is very similar to using the control with VBScript, except that events in Visual Basic must include the data type of passed parameters. Adding the Microsoft Agent control to a form will automatically include Microsoft Agent's events with their appropriate parameters. It will also automatically create a connection to the Agent server when the application runs.

You may also be able to use your programming language's object's creation syntax to create an instance of the control at runtime. For example, in Visual Basic (5.0 or later), if you include the Microsoft Agent 2.0 Control in your project's references, you can use a **With Events..New** declaration. If you do not include the reference, VB raises an error indicating that Microsoft Agent was unable to start (error code 80042502).

```
' Declare a global variable for the control
Dim WithEvents MyAgent as Agent

' Create an instance of the control using New
Set MyAgent = New Agent

' Load a character
MyAgent.Characters.Load "Genie", " Genie.acs"

' Display the character
MyAgent.Characters("Genie").Show
```

For versions of VB prior to 5.0, you can use the VB **New** keyword without **WithEvents** declaration or the VB **CreateObject** function, but these conventions will not expose the Agent control's events. You also need to use the **Connected** property before you reference any Agent methods or properties. If this is not done, VB will raise an error indicating that Microsoft Agent was unable to start (error code 80042502).

Similarly for other programming languages, you may have to use the **Connected** property to establish a connection to the Agent Component Object Model (COM) server before your code can call any of the Agent control's methods or properties. In addition, for some programming languages, Agent's methods and properties may not be directly exposed unless you declare the Agent control using its type. For example, in Microsoft Access 97, you will need to declare the object as type Agent (or **IAgentCtlEx**) to see the methods and properties display in the Auto List Members drop-down box when you type.

Most programming languages that support ActiveX controls follow conventions similar to Visual Basic. For programming languages that do not support object collections, you can use the **Character** method and **Command** method to access methods and properties of items in the collection.

Programming languages like Visual Basic, that provide access to the object types exposed by the Agent control, enable you to use these in your object declarations. For example, instead of declaring an object as a generic type:

```
Dim Genie as Object
```

You can declare an object as a specific type:

```
Dim Genie as IAgentCtlCharacterEx
```

This may improve the overall performance of your application.

For some object types, you may find two types that are the same except for the "Ex" suffix. Where both exist, use the "Ex" type because this provides the full functionality of Agent. The non-"Ex" counterparts are included only for backward compatibility.

Updating from Previous Version

Applications built and compiled with the previous 1.5 version of Microsoft Agent should run without modification under the new 2.0 version. The **Connected** property can no longer be set to **False**; certain properties of the SpeechInput object that have been replaced still exist, but no longer turn any values, and the server no longer fires the **Restart** and **Shutdown** events.

However, if you update your applications to use the Agent 2.0 control, you may have to modify your code. If you have installed the 2.0 version of Microsoft Agent and load a Visual Basic project use the earlier version of the Agent control, Visual Basic includes an option that will automatically display a message indicating that it detected a new version of the control. To ensure proper operation of your application, always choose to use the later version.

For other programming languages (such as Microsoft Office 97 VBA), to update the control, you may have to first remove the 1.5 Agent control and save your code. Then, quit the programming environment, restart the programming environment, reload your code and insert the new control. Avoid editing an Agent 2.0-enabled application in the same instance of the programming environment that you are editing an Agent 1.5-enabled application in. Some programming environments may not handle the differences between the two versions of controls.

You should be able to uninstall the Agent 1.5 release on your system after installing the Agent 2.0 release. However, if Agent 1.5 is installed over the 2.0 release, you may have to reinstall 2.0.

Accessing Microsoft Agent Services Directly

If you are using C, C++, or Java, you can access the Microsoft Agent server directly using its ActiveX (OLE) interfaces. For more information on these interfaces, see Chapter 5, "Programming the Microsoft Agent Server Interface."

The Agent Object Model

The Microsoft Agent Object Model consists of the following objects:

- Request
- Agent (control)
- Characters (collection)
- Character
- Commands (collection)
- Command
- Balloon
- AnimationNames (collection)
- SpeechInput
- AudioOutput
- CommandsWindow
- PropertySheet

These objects are organized in the following hierarchy. (The dotted line following an object indicates that multiple objects can exist.)

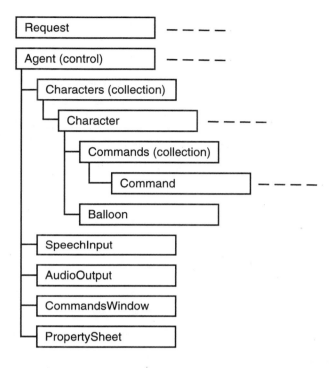

FIGURE 4-1. The Agent Object

The Request Object

The server processes some methods, such as **Load**, **Get**, **Play**, and **Speak**, asynchronously. This enables your application code to continue while the method is completing. When a client application calls one of these methods, the control creates and returns a **Request** object for the request. You can use the **Request** object to track the status of the method by assigning an object variable to the method. In Visual Basic, first declare an object variable:

```
Dim MyRequest as Object
```

In VBScript, you don't include the variable type in your declaration:

```
Dim MyRequest
```

and use Visual Basic's Set statement to assign the variable to the method call:

```
Set MyRequest = agent.Characters("CharacterID").method (parameter[s])
```

This adds a reference to the **Request** object. The **Request** object will be destroyed when there are no more references to it. Where you declare the **Request** object and how you use it determines its lifetime. If the object is declared local to a subroutine or function, it will be destroyed when it goes out of scope; that is, when the subroutine or function ends. If the object is declared globally, it will not be destroyed until either the program terminates or a new value (or a value set to "empty") is assigned to the object.

The **Request** object provides several properties you can query. For example, the **Status** property returns the current status of the request. You can use this property to check the status of your request:

```
Dim MyRequest

Set MyRequest = Agent1.Characters.Load ("Genie", _
    "http://agent.microsoft.com/characters/v2/genie/genie.acf")

If (MyRequest.Status = 2) then
    'do something

Else If (MyRequest.Status = 0) then
    'do something right away

End If
```

The **Status** property returns the status of a **Request** object as a Long integer value.

Status	Definition
0	Request successfully completed.
1	Request failed.
2	Request pending (in the queue, but not complete).
3	Request interrupted.
4	Request in progress.

The **Request** object also includes a Long integer value in the **Number** property that returns the error or cause of the **Status** code. If none, this value is zero (0). The **Description** property contains a string value that corresponds to the error number. If the string doesn't exist, **Description** contains "Application-defined or object-defined error".

For the values and meaning returned by the **Number** property, see **Error Codes**.

The server places animation requests in the specified character's queue. This enables the server to play the animation on a separate thread, and your application's code can continue while animations play. If you create a **Request** object reference, the server automatically notifies you when an animation request has started or completed through the **RequestStart** and **RequestComplete** events. Because methods that return **Request** objects are asynchronous and may not complete during the scope of the calling function, declare your reference to the **Request** object globally.

The following methods can be used to return a **Request** object: **GestureAt**, **Get**, **Hide**, **Interrupt**, **Load**, **MoveTo**, **Play**, **Show**, **Speak**, and **Wait**.

The Agent Control

Referencing the Agent control provides access to events and most other objects supported by Microsoft Agent. The Agent control also directly exposes its own set of properties.

Agent Control Methods

The following method is available from the Agent control.

ShowDefaultCharacterProperties Method

Description
Displays the default character's properties.

Syntax
agent.ShowDefaultCharacterProperties [*X* , *Y*]

Part	Description
X	Optional. A short integer value that indicates the horizontal (X) screen coordinate to display the window. This coordinate must be specified in pixels.
Y	Optional. A short integer value that indicates the vertical (Y) screen coordinate to display the window. This coordinate must be specified in pixels.

Remarks
Calling this method displays the default character properties window (not the Microsoft Agent property sheet). If you do not specify the X and Y coordinates, the window appears at the last location it was displayed.

See also DefaultCharacterChange event

Agent Control Properties

The following properties are directly accessed from the Agent control:

Connected, Name, RaiseRequestErrors

In addition, some programming environments may assign additional design-time or run-time properties. For example, Visual Basic adds **Left**, **Index**, **Tag**, and **Top** properties that define the location of the control on a form even though the control does not appear on the form's page at run time.

The **Suspended** property is still supported for backward compatibility, but always returns **False** because the server no longer supports a suspended state.

Connected Property

Description

Returns or sets whether the current control is connected to the Microsoft Agent server.

Syntax

*agent.***Connected** [= *boolean*]

Part	Description
boolean	A Boolean expression specifying whether the control is connected.
	True The control is connected.

Remarks

In many situations, specifying the control automatically creates a connection with the Microsoft Agent server. For example, specifying the Microsoft Agent control's CLSID in the <OBJECT> tag in a Web page automatically opens a server connection and exiting the page closes the connection. Similarly, for Visual Basic or other languages that enable you to drop a control on a form, running the program automatically opens a connection and exiting the program closes the connection. If the server isn't currently running, it automatically starts.

However, if you want to create an Agent control at run time, you may also need to explicitly open a new connection to the server using the **Connected** property. For example, in Visual Basic you can create an ActiveX object at run time using the Set statement with the **New** keyword (or **CreateObject** function). While this creates the object, it may not create the connection to the server. You can use the **Connected** property before any code that calls into Microsoft Agent's programming interface, as shown in the following example:

```
' Declare a global variable for the control
Dim MyAgent as Agent

' Create an instance of the control using New
Set MyAgent = New Agent

' Open a connection to the server
MyAgent.Connected = True

' Load a character
MyAgent.Characters.Load "Genie", " Genie.acs"

' Display the character
MyAgent.Characters("Genie").Show
```

Creating a control using this technique does not expose the Agent control's events. In Visual Basic 5.0 (and later), you can access the control's events by including the control in your project's references, and use the **WithEvents** keyword in your variable declaration:

```
Dim WithEvents MyAgent as Agent

' Create an instance of the control using New
Set MyAgent = New Agent
```

Using **WithEvents** to create an instance of the Agent control at run time automatically opens the connection with the Microsoft Agent server. Therefore, you don't need to include a **Connected** statement.

You can close your connection to the server by releasing all references you created to Agent objects, such as **IAgentCtlCharacterEx** and **IAgentCtlCommandEx**. You must also release your reference to the Agent control itself. In Visual Basic, you can release a reference to an object by setting its variable to **Nothing**. If you have loaded characters, unload them before releasing the character object.

```
Dim WithEvents MyAgent as Agent
Dim Genie as IAgentCtlCharacterEx

Sub Form_Load

' Create an instance of the control using New
Set MyAgent = New Agent

' Open a connection to the server
MyAgent.Connected = True
```

(continued)

(continued)

```
' Load the character into the Characters collection
MyAgent.Characters.Load "Genie", " Genie.acs"

' Create a reference to the character
Set Genie = MyAgent.Characters("Genie")

End Sub

Sub CloseConnection

' Unload the character
MyAgent.Characters.Unload "Genie"

' Release the reference to the character object
Set Genie = Nothing

' Release the reference to the Agent control
Set MyAgent = Nothing
End Sub
```

Note You cannot close your connection to the server by releasing references where the component has been added. For example, you cannot close your connection to the server on Web pages where you use the <OBJECT> tag to declare the control or in a Visual Basic application where you drop the control on a form. While releasing all Agent references will reduce Agent's working set, the connection remains until you navigate to the next page or exit the application.

Name Property

Description

Returns the name used in code to identify the control. This property is read-only at run time.

Syntax

agent.**Name**

Remarks

In some programming environments such as Visual Basic, adding the control automatically generates a default name for the control that can be changed at design time. For HTML scripts, you can define the name in the <OBJECT> tag. If you define the name, follow the conventions of the programming language for defining object names.

RaiseRequestErrors Property

Description

Returns or sets whether errors for requests are raised.

Syntax

agent.RaiseRequestErrors [= *boolean*]

Part	Description
boolean	A Boolean value that determines whether errors in requests are raised.
	True (Default) Request errors are raised.
	False Request errors are not raised.

Remarks

This property enables you to determine whether the server raises errors that occur with methods that support **Request** objects. For example, if you specify an animation name that does not exist in a **Play** method, the server raises an error (displaying the error message) unless you set this property to **False**.

It may be useful for programming languages that do not provide recovery when an error is raised. However, use care when setting this property to **False**, because it might be harder to find errors in your code.

Agent Control Events

The Microsoft Agent control provides several events that enable your client application to track the state of the server:

ActivateInput, ActiveClientChange, AgentPropertyChange, BalloonHide, BalloonShow, Bookmark, Click, Command, DblClick, DeactivateInput, DefaultCharacterChange, DragComplete, DragStart, HelpComplete, Hide, IdleComplete, IdleStart, ListenComplete, ListenStart, Move, RequestComplete, RequestStart, Show, Size

The **Restart** and **Shutdown** events are supported for backward compatibility, but the server no longer sends these events.

ActivateInput Event

Description

Occurs when a client becomes input-active.

Syntax

Sub *agent*_**ActivateInput (ByVal** *CharacterID*)

Part	Description
CharacterID	Returns the ID of the character through which the client becomes input-active.

Remarks

The input-active client receives mouse and speech input events supplied by the server. The server sends this event only to the client that becomes input-active.

This event can occur when the user switches to your **Commands** object, for example, by choosing your **Commands** object entry in the Commands Window or in the pop-up menu for a character. It can also occur when the user selects a character (by clicking or speaking its name), when a character becomes visible, and when the character of another client application becomes hidden. You can also call the **Activate** method (with **State** set to 2) to explicitly make the character topmost, which results in your client application becoming input-active and triggers this event. However, this event does not occur if you use the **Activate** method only to specify whether your client is the active client of the character.

See also **DeactivateInput, Activate**

ActiveClientChange Event

Description

Occurs when the active client of the character changes.

Syntax

Sub *agent.***ActiveClientChange (ByVal** *CharacterID*, **ByVal** *Active*)

Part	Description
CharacterID	Returns the ID of the character for which the event occurred.
Active	A Boolean value that indicates whether the client became active or not active.
	True The client application became the active client of the character.
	False The client application is no longer the active client of the character.

Remarks

When multiple client applications share the same character, the active client of the character receives mouse input (for example, Microsoft Agent control click or drag events). Similarly, when multiple characters are displayed, the active client of the topmost character (also known as the input-active client) receives **Command** events.

When the active client of a character changes, this event passes back the ID of that character and **True** if your application has become the active client of the character or **False** if it is no longer the active client of the character.

A client application may receive this event when the user selects a client application's entry in character's pop-up menu or by voice command, when the client application changes its active status, or when another client application quits its connection to Agent. Agent sends this event only to the client applications that are directly affected; that either become the active client or stop being the active client.

See also **ActivateInput** event, **Active** property, **DeactivateInput** event, **Activate** method

AgentPropertyChange Event

Description
Occurs when the user changes a property in the Advanced Character Options window.

Syntax
Sub *agent.***AgentPropertyChange**()

Remarks
This event indicates when the user has changed and applied any property included in the Advanced Character Option window.

In your code for this handling this event, you can query for the specific property settings of **AudioOutput** or **SpeechInput** objects.

See also **DefaultCharacterChange** event

BalloonHide Event

Description
Occurs when a character's word balloon is hidden.

Syntax
Sub *agent_***BalloonHide** (**ByVal** *CharacterID*)

Part	Description
CharacterID	Returns the ID of the character associated with the word balloon.

Remarks

The server sends this event only to the clients of the character (applications that have loaded the character) that uses the word balloon.

See also **BalloonShow** event

BalloonShow Event

Description

Occurs when a character's word balloon is shown.

Syntax

Sub *agent_***BalloonShow** (**ByVal** *CharacterID*)

Part	Description
CharacterID	Returns the ID of the character associated with the word balloon.

Remarks

The server sends this event only to the clients of the character (applications that have loaded the character) that uses the word balloon.

See also **BalloonHide** event

Bookmark Event

Description

Occurs when a bookmark in a speech text string that your application defined is activated.

Syntax

Sub *agent_***Bookmark**(**ByVal** *BookmarkID*)

Part	Description
BookmarkID	A Long integer identifying the bookmark number.

Remarks

To specify a bookmark event, use the **Speak** method with a **Mrk** tag in your supplied text.

See also Chapter 6, "Speech Output Tags."

Click Event

Description

Occurs when the user clicks a character or the character's icon.

Syntax

Sub *agent*_**Click (ByVal** *CharacterID*, **ByVal** *Button*, **ByVal** *Shift*, **ByVal** *X*, **ByVal** *Y*)

Part	Description
CharacterID	Returns the ID of the clicked character as a string.
Button	Returns an integer that identifies the button that was pressed and released to cause the event. The button argument is a bit field with bits corresponding to the left button (bit 0), right button (bit 1), and middle button (bit 2). These bits correspond to the values 1, 2, and 4, respectively. Only one of the bits is set, indicating the button that caused the event. If the character includes a taskbar icon, and bit 13 is also set, the click occurred on the taskbar icon.
Shift	Returns an integer that corresponds to the state of the SHIFT, CTRL, and ALT keys when the button specified in the button argument is pressed or released. A bit is set if the key is down. The shift argument is a bit field with the least-significant bits corresponding to the SHIFT key (bit 0), the CTRL key (bit 1), and the ALT key (bit 2). These bits correspond to the values 1, 2, and 4, respectively. The shift argument indicates the state of these keys. Some, all, or none of the bits can be set, indicating that some, all, or none of the keys are pressed. For example, if both CTRL and ALT were pressed, the value of shift would be 6.
X,Y	Returns an integer that specifies the current location of the mouse pointer. The X and Y values are always expressed in pixels, relative to the upper left corner of the screen.

Remarks

This event is sent only to the input-active client of a character. When the user clicks a character or its taskbar icon with no input-active client, the server sends the event to its active client. If the character is visible (**Visible = True**), the user's action also sets the character's last input-active client as the current input-active client, sending the **ActivateInput** event to that client, and then sending the **Click** event. If the character is hidden (**Visible = False**), and the user clicks the character's taskbar icon using button 1, the character is also automatically shown.

Note Clicking a character does not disable all other character output (all characters). However, pressing the Listening key does flush the input-active character's output and triggers the **RequestComplete** event, passing a **Request.Status** that indicates that the client's queue was interrupted.

Command Event

Description

Occurs when the user chooses a (client's) command.

Syntax

Sub *agent_***Command(ByVal** *UserInput***)**

Part	Description		
UserInput	Identifies the **Command** object returned by the server. The following properties can be accessed from the **Command** object:		
	CharacterID	A string value identifying the name (ID) of the character that received the command.
	Name	A string value identifying the name (ID) of the command.
	Confidence	A Long integer value indicating the confidence scoring for the command.
	Voice	A string value identifying the voice text for the command.
	Alt1Name	A string value identifying the name of the next (second) best command.
	Alt1Confidence	A Long integer value indicating the confidence scoring for the next (second) best command.
	Alt1Voice	A string value identifying the voice text for the next best alternative command match.
	Alt2Name	A string value identifying the name of third best command match.
	Alt2Confidence	A Long integer identifying the confidence scoring for the third best command match.
	Alt2Voice	A string value identifying the voice text for the third best command match.
	Count	Long integer value indicating the number of alternatives returned.

Remarks

The server notifies you with this event when your application is input-active and the user chooses a command by spoken input or character's pop-up menu. The event passes back the number of possible matching commands in **Count** as well as the name, confidence scoring, and voice text for those matches.

If voice input triggers this event, the server returns a string that identifies the best match in the **Name** parameter, and the second- and third-best match in

Alt1Name and **Alt2Name**. An empty string indicates that the input did not match any command your application defined; for example, it could be one of the server's defined commands. If the command was matched to the Agent's command; for example, Hide, an empty string would be returned in the **Name** parameter, but you would still receive the text heard in the **Voice** parameter.

You may get the same command name returned in more than one entry. **Confidence**, **Alt1Confidence**, and **Alt2Confidence** parameters return the relative scores, in the range of -100 to 100, that are returned by the speech recognition engine for each respective match. **Voice**, **Alt1Voice**, and **Alt2Voice** parameters return the voice text that the speech recognition engine matched for each alternative. If **Count** returns zero (0), the server detected spoken input, but determined that there was no matching command.

If voice input was not the source for the command, for example, if the user selected the command from the character's pop-up menu, the server returns the name (ID) of the command selected in the **Name** property. It also returns the value of the **Confidence** parameter as 100, and the value of the **Voice** parameters as the empty string (""). **Alt1Name** and **Alt2Name** also return empty strings. **Alt1Confidence** and **Alt2Confidence** return zero (0), and **Alt1Voice** and **Alt2Voice** return empty strings. **Count** returns 1.

Note Not all speech recognition engines may return all the values for all the parameters of this event. Check with your engine vendor to determine whether the engine supports the Microsoft Speech API interface for returning alternatives and confidence scores.

DblClick Event

Description
Occurs when the user double-clicks a character.

Syntax
Sub *agent*_**DblClick (ByVal** *CharacterID*, **ByVal** *Button*, **ByVal** *Shift*, **ByVal** *X*, **ByVal** *Y*)

Part	Description
CharacterID	Returns the ID of the double-clicked character as a string.
Button	Returns an integer that identifies the button that was pressed and released to cause the event. The button argument is a bit field with bits corresponding to the left button (bit 0), right button (bit 1), and middle button (bit 2). These bits correspond to the values 1, 2, and 4, respectively. Only one of the bits is set, indicating the button that caused the event. If the character includes a taskbar icon, if bit 13 is also set, the click occurred on the taskbar icon.

Part	Description
Shift	Returns an integer that corresponds to the state of the SHIFT, CTRL, and ALT keys when the button specified in the button argument is pressed or released. A bit is set if the key is down. The shift argument is a bit field with the least-significant bits corresponding to the SHIFT key (bit 0), the CTRL key (bit 1), and the ALT key (bit 2). These bits correspond to the values 1, 2, and 4, respectively. The shift argument indicates the state of these keys. Some, all, or none of the bits can be set, indicating that some, all, or none of the keys are pressed. For example, if both CTRL and ALT were pressed, the value of shift would be 6.
X,Y	Returns an integer that specifies the current location of the mouse pointer. The X and Y values are always expressed in pixels, relative to the upper left corner of the screen.

Remarks

This event is sent only to the input-active client of a character. When the user double-clicks a character or its taskbar icon with no input-active client, the server sends the event to its last input-active client. If the character is visible (**Visible = True**), then it also sets the active client as the current input-active client, sending the **ActivateInput** event to that client, and then sending the **DblClick** event. If the character is hidden (**Visible = False**) and the user double-clicks the character's taskbar icon using button 1, it also automatically shows the character.

DeactivateInput Event

Description

Occurs when a client becomes non-input-active.

Syntax

Sub *agent*_**DeactivateInput** (**ByVal** *CharacterID*)

Part	Description
CharacterID	Returns the ID of the character that makes the client become non-input-active.

Remarks

A non-input-active client no longer receives mouse or speech events from the server (unless it becomes input-active again). The server sends this event only to the client that becomes non-input-active.

This event occurs when your client application is input-active and the user chooses the caption of another client in a character's pop-up menu or the Voice Commands Window or you call the **Activate** method and set the **State** parameter to 0. It may also occur when the user selects the name of another character by clicking or speaking. You also get this event when your character is hidden or another character becomes visible.

See also ActivateInput event

DefaultCharacterChange Event

Description
Occurs when the user changes the default character.

Syntax
Sub *agent.***DefaultCharacterChange (ByVal** *GUID***)**

Part	Description
GUID	Returns the unique identifier for the character.

Remarks
This event indicates when the user has changed the character assigned as the user's default character. The server sends this only to clients that have loaded the default character.

When the new character appears, it assumes the same size as any already loaded instance of the character or the previous default character (in that order).

See also ShowDefaultCharacterProperties method, **Load** method

DragComplete Event

Description
Occurs when the user completes dragging a character.

Syntax
Sub *agent*_**DragComplete (ByVal** *CharacterID*, **ByVal** *Button*, **ByVal** *Shift*, **ByVal** *X*, **ByVal** *Y*)

Part	Description
CharacterID	Returns the ID of the dragged character as a string.
Button	Returns an integer that identifies the button that was pressed and released to cause the event. The button argument is a bit field with bits corresponding to the left button (bit 0), right button (bit 1), and middle button (bit 2). These bits correspond to the values 1, 2, and 4, respectively. Only one of the bits is set, indicating the button that caused the event.

Part	Description
Shift	Returns an integer that corresponds to the state of the SHIFT, CTRL, and ALT keys when the button specified in the button argument is pressed or released. A bit is set if the key is down. The shift argument is a bit field with the least-significant bits corresponding to the SHIFT key (bit 0), the CTRL key (bit 1), and the ALT key (bit 2). These bits correspond to the values 1, 2, and 4, respectively. The shift argument indicates the state of these keys. Some, all, or none of the bits can be set, indicating that some, all, or none of the keys are pressed. For example, if both CTRL and ALT were pressed, the value of shift would be 6.
X,Y	Returns an integer that specifies the current location of the mouse pointer. The X and Y values are always expressed in pixels, relative to the upper left corner of the screen.

Remarks

This event is sent only to the input-active client of a character. When the user drags a character with no input-active client, the server sets its last input-active client as the current input-active client, sending the **ActivateInput** event to that client, and then sending the **DragStart** and **DragComplete** events.

See also **DragStart** event

DragStart Event

Description

Occurs when the user begins dragging a character.

Syntax

Sub *agent_***DragStart** (**ByVal** *CharacterID*, **ByVal** *Button*, **ByVal** *Shift*, **ByVal** *X*, **ByVal** *Y*)

Part	Description
CharacterID	Returns the ID of the clicked character as a string.
Button	Returns an integer that identifies the button that was pressed and released to cause the event. The button argument is a bit field with bits corresponding to the left button (bit 0), right button (bit 1), and middle button (bit 2). These bits correspond to the values 1, 2, and 4, respectively. Only one of the bits is set, indicating the button that caused the event.

Part	Description
Shift	Returns an integer that corresponds to the state of the SHIFT, CTRL, and ALT keys when the button specified in the button argument is pressed or released. A bit is set if the key is down. The shift argument is a bit field with the least-significant bits corresponding to the SHIFT key (bit 0), the CTRL key (bit 1), and the ALT key (bit 2). These bits correspond to the values 1, 2, and 4, respectively. The shift argument indicates the state of these keys. Some, all, or none of the bits can be set, indicating that some, all, or none of the keys are pressed. For example, if both CTRL and ALT were pressed, the value of shift would be 6.
X,Y	Returns an integer that specifies the current location of the mouse pointer. The X and Y values are always expressed in pixels, relative to the upper left corner of the screen.

Remarks

This event is sent only to the input-active client of a character. When the user drags a character with no input-active client, the server sets its last input-active client as the current input-active client, sending the **ActivateInput** event to that client, and then sending the **DragStart** event.

See also **DragComplete** event

HelpComplete Event

Description

Indicates that context-sensitive Help mode has been exited.

Syntax

Sub *agent.***HelpComplete (ByVal** *CharacterID*, **ByVal** *Name*, **ByVal** *Cause*)

Part	Description
CharacterID	Returns the ID of the clicked character as a string.
Name	Returns a string value identifying the name (ID) of the command.
Cause	Returns a value that indicates what caused the Help mode to complete.
	The user selected a command supplied by your application.
	The user selected the **Commands** object of another client.
	The user selected the Open Voice Commands command.
	The user selected the Close Voice Commands command.
	The user selected the Show CharacterName command.
	The user selected the Hide CharacterName command.
	The user selected (clicked) the character.

Remarks

Typically, Help mode completes when the user clicks or drags the character or selects a command from the character's pop-up menu. Clicking on another character or elsewhere on the screen does not cancel Help mode. The client that set Help mode for the character can cancel Help mode by setting **HelpModeOn** to **False**. (This does not trigger the **HelpComplete** event.)

When the user selects a command from the character's pop-up menu in Help mode, the server removes the menu, calls Help with the command's specified **HelpContextID**, and sends this event. The context-sensitive (also known as What's This?) Help window is displayed at the pointer location. If the user selects the command by voice input, the Help window is displayed over the character. If the character is off-screen, the window is displayed on-screen nearest to the character's current position.

If the server returns Name as an empty string (""), it indicates that the user selected a server-supplied command.

This event is sent only to the client application that places the character in Help mode.

See also **HelpModeOn** property, **HelpContextID** property

Hide Event

Description

Occurs when a character is hidden.

Syntax

Sub *agent_***Hide** (**ByVal** *CharacterID*, **ByVal** *Cause*)

Part	Description
CharacterID	Returns the ID of the hidden character as a string.
Cause	Returns a value that indicates what caused the character to hide.
	1 User hid the character by selecting the command on the character's taskbar icon pop-up menu or using speech input.
	3 Your client application hid the character.
	5 Another client application hid the character.
	7 User hid the character by selecting the command on the character's pop-up menu.

Remarks

The server sends this event to all clients of the character. To query the current state of the character, use the **Visible** property.

See also **Show** event, **VisibilityCause** property

IdleComplete Event

Description

Occurs when the server ends the **Idling** state of a character.

Syntax

Sub *agent_***IdleComplete (ByVal** *CharacterID*)

Part	Description
CharacterID	Returns the ID of the idling character as a string.

Remarks

The server sends this event to all clients of the character.

See also **IdleStart** event

IdleStart Event

Description

Occurs when the server sets a character to the **Idling** state.

Syntax

Sub *agent_***IdleStart (ByVal** *CharacterID*)

Part	Description
CharacterID	Returns the ID of the idling character as a string.

Remarks

The server sends this event to all clients of the character.

See also **IdleComplete** event

ListenComplete Event

Description

Occurs when Listening mode (speech recognition) has ended.

Syntax

Sub *agent.***ListenComplete** (**ByVal** *CharacterID*, **ByVal** *Cause*)

Part	Description
CharacterID	Returns the ID of the listening character as a string.
Cause	Returns the cause of the complete event as an integer that may be one of the following:

    1   Listening mode was turned off by program code.

    2   Listening mode (turned on by program code) timed out.

    3   Listening mode (turned on by the Listening key) timed out.

    4   Listening mode was turned off because the user released the Listening key.

    5   Listening mode ended because the user finished speaking.

    6   Listening mode ended because the input-active client was deactivated.

    7   Listening mode ended because the default character was changed.

    8   Listening mode ended because the user disabled speech input.

Remarks

This event is sent to all clients when the Listening mode time-out ends, after the user releases the Listening key, when the input active client calls the **Listen** method with **False**, or the user finished speaking. You can use this event to determine when to resume character spoken (audio) output.

If you turn on Listening mode using the **Listen** method and then the user presses the Listening key, the Listening mode resets and continues until the Listening key time-out completes, the Listening key is released, or the user finishes speaking, whichever is later. In this situation, you will not receive a **ListenComplete** event until the listening key's mode completes.

The event returns the character to the clients that currently have this character loaded. All other clients receive a null character (empty string).

See also **ListenStart** event, **Listen** method

ListenStart Event

Description
Occurs when Listening mode (speech recognition) begins.

Syntax
Sub *agent.***ListenStart (ByVal** *CharacterID***)**

Part	Description
CharacterID	Returns the ID of the listening character as a string.

Remarks
This event is sent to all clients when Listening mode begins because the user pressed the Listening key or the input-active client called the **Listen** method with **True**. You can use this event to avoid having your character speak while the Listening mode is on.

If you turn on Listening mode with the **Listen** method and then the user presses the Listening key, the Listening mode resets and continues until the Listening key time-out completes, the Listening key is released, or the user finishes speaking, whichever is later. In this situation, when Listening mode is already on, you will not get an additional **ListenStart** event when the user presses the Listening key.

The event returns the character to the clients that currently have this character loaded. All other clients receive a null character (empty string).

See also ListenComplete event, **Listen** method

Move Event

Description
Occurs when a character is moved.

Syntax
Sub *agent_***Move (ByVal** *CharacterID*, **ByVal** *X*, **ByVal** *Y*, **ByVal** *Cause***)**

Part	Description
CharacterID	Returns the ID of the character that moved.
X	Returns the x-coordinate (in pixels) of the top edge of character frame's new location as an integer.
Y	Returns the y-coordinate (in pixels) of the left edge of character frame's new location as an integer.

Part	Description
Cause	Returns a value that indicates what caused the character to move.

1   The user dragged the character.

2   Your client application moved the character.

3   Another client application moved the character.

4   The Agent server moved the character to keep it onscreen after a screen resolution change.

Remarks
This event occurs when the user or an application changes the character's position. Coordinates are relevant to the upper left corner of the screen. This event is sent only to the clients of the character (applications that have loaded the character).

See also **MoveCause** property, **Size** event

RequestComplete Event

Description
Occurs when the server completes a queued request.

Syntax
Sub *agent*_**RequestComplete** (**ByVal** *Request*)

Part	Description
Request	Returns the **Request** object.

Remarks
This event returns a **Request** object. Because requests are processed asynchronously, you can use this event to determine when the server completes processing a request (such as a **Get**, **Play**, or **Speak** method) to synchronize this event with other actions generated by your application. The server sends the event only to the client that created the reference to the **Request** object and only if you defined a global variable for the request reference:

```
Dim MyRequest
Dim Genie

Sub window_Onload

Agent1.Characters.Load "Genie",_
    "http://agent.microsoft.com/characters/v2/genie/genie.acf"
```

```
Set Genie = Agent.Characters("Genie")

' This syntax will generate RequestStart and RequestComplete events.
Set MyRequest = Genie.Get("state", "Showing")
' This syntax will not generate RequestStart and RequestComplete events.
Genie.Get "state", "Hiding"

End Sub

Sub Agent1_RequestComplete(ByVal Request)

If Request = MyRequest Then
    Status = "Showing animation is now loaded"

End Sub
```

Because animation **Request** objects don't get assigned until the server processes the request, make sure that the **Request** object exists before you attempt to evaluate it. For example, in Visual Basic, if you use a conditional to test whether a specific request was completed, you can use the **Nothing** keyword:

```
Sub Agent1_RequestComplete (ByVal Request)

If Not (MyRequest Is Nothing) Then
    If Request = MyRequest Then
    '-- Do whatever
    End If
End If

End Sub
```

Note In VBScript 1.0, this event fires even if you don't define references to a **Request** object. This has been fixed in VBScript 2.0, which can be downloaded from *http://microsoft.com/msdownload/scripting.htm*.

See also **RequestStart** event

RequestStart Event

Description
Occurs when the server begins a queued request.

Syntax
Sub *agent*_**RequestStart** (**ByVal** *Request*)

Part	Description
Request	Returns the **Request** object.

Remarks

The event returns a **Request** object. Because requests are processed asynchronously, you can use this event to determine when the server begins processing a request (such as a **Get**, **Play**, or **Speak** method) and thereby synchronize this with other actions generated by your application. The event is sent only to the client that created the reference to the **Request** object and only if you defined a global variable for the request reference:

```
Dim MyRequest
Dim Genie

Sub window_Onload

Agent1.Characters.Load "Genie", _
    "http://agent.microsoft.com/characters/v2/genie/genie.acf"

Set Genie = Agent1.Characters("Genie")

' This syntax will generate RequestStart and RequestComplete events.
Set MyRequest = Genie.Get("state", "Showing")

' This syntax will not generate RequestStart and RequestComplete events.
Genie.Get ("state", "Hiding")

End Sub

Sub Agent1_RequestStart(ByVal Request)

If Request = MyRequest Then
    Status = "Loading the Showing animation"

End Sub
```

The **Status** returns 4 (request in progress) for the **Request** object returned.

Because animation **Request** objects don't get assigned until the server processes the request, make sure that the **Request** object exists before you attempt to evaluate it. For example, in Visual Basic, if you use a conditional to test whether a specific request was completed, you can use the **Nothing** keyword:

```
Sub Agent1_RequestStart (ByVal Request)

If Not (MyRequest Is Nothing) Then
    If Request = MyRequest Then
    '-- Do whatever
    End If
End If

End Sub
```

Note In VBScript 1.0, this event fires even if you don't define references to a **Request** object. This has been fixed in VBScript 2.0, which can be downloaded from *http://microsoft.com/msdownload/scripting.htm*.

See also RequestComplete event

Show Event

Description
Occurs when a character is displayed.

Syntax
Sub *agent_***Show (ByVal** *CharacterID*, **ByVal** *Cause*)

Part	Description
CharacterID	Returns the ID of the character shown as a string.
Cause	Returns a value that indicates what caused the character to display.
	2 The user showed the character (using the menu or voice command).
	4 Your client application showed the character.
	6 Another client application showed the character.

Remarks
The server sends this event to all clients of the character. To query the current state of the character, use the **Visible** property.

See also Hide event, **VisibilityCause** property

Size Event

Description
Occurs when a character's size changes.

Syntax
Sub *agent_***Size (ByVal** *CharacterID*, **ByVal** *Width*, **ByVal** *Height*)

Part	Description
CharacterID	Returns the ID of the character that moved.
Width	Returns the character frame's new width (in pixels) as an integer.
Height	Returns the character frame's new height (in pixels) as an integer.

Remarks

This event occurs when an application changes the size of a character. This event is sent only to the clients of the character (applications that have loaded the character).

See also **Move** event

The Characters Object

Your client application can support one or more characters. In addition, you can share a character among several applications. Microsoft Agent defines the **Characters** object as a collection of characters. To access a character, load the character's data into the **Characters** collection and specify that that item in the collection uses the methods and properties supported for that character.

Characters Object Methods

The **Characters** object supports methods for accessing, loading, and unloading characters into its collection:

Character, Load, Unload

Character Method

Description

Returns a **Character** object in a **Characters** collection.

Syntax

agent.**Characters.Character** *"CharacterID"*

Remarks

You can use this method to access a **Character** object's methods and properties.

Note This method may be required for some programming languages that do not support collections. It is not required for VBScript or Visual Basic. For further information on specifying **Character** methods, see the section on character object methods later in this chapter.

Load Method

Description

Loads a character into the **Characters** collection.

Syntax

agent.**Characters.Load** *"CharacterID", Provider*

Part	Description
CharacterID	Required. A string value that you will use to refer to the character data to be loaded.
Provider	Required. A variant data type that must be one of the following:
Filespec	The local file location of the specified character's definition file.
URL	The HTTP address for the character's definition file.

Remarks

You can load characters from the Agent subdirectory by specifying a relative path (one that does not include a colon or leading slash character). This prefixes the path with Agent's characters directory (located in the localized Windows\msagent directory). For example, specifying the following would load Genie.acs from Agent's Chars directory:

```
Agent.Character.Load "genie", "genie.acs"
```

You can also specify your own directory in Agent's Chars directory.

```
Agent.Character.Load "genie", "MyCharacters\genie.acs"
```

You can load the character currently set as the current user's default character by not including a path as the second parameter of the **Load** method.

```
Agent.Character.Load "character"
```

You cannot load the same character (a character having the same GUID) more than once from a single instance of the control. Similarly, you cannot load the default character and other characters at the same time from a single instance of the control because the default character could be the same as the other character. If you attempt to do this, the server raises an error. However, you can create another instance of the Agent control and load the same character.

The Microsoft Agent Data Provider supports loading character data stored either as a single structured file (.ACS) with character data and animation data together or as separate character data (.ACF) and animation (.ACA) files. Use the single structured .ACS file to load a character that is stored on a local disk or network and accessed using a conventional file protocol (such as UNC pathnames). Use the separate .ACF and .ACA files when you want to load the animation files individually from a remote site where they are accessed using the HTTP protocol.

For .ACS files, using the **Load** method provides access a character's animations. For .ACF files, you also use the **Get** method to load animation data. The **Load** method does not support downloading .ACS files from an HTTP site.

Loading a character does not automatically display the character. Use the **Show** method first to make the character visible.

If you use the **Load** method to load a character file stored on the local machine and the call fails; for example, because the file is not found, Agent raises an error. You can use the support in your programming language to provide an error handling routine to catch and process the error.

```
Sub Form_Load
    On Error GoTo ErrorHandler
    Agent1.Characters.Load "mychar", "genie.acs"
    ' Successful load
    . . .
    Exit Sub
ErrorHandler:
    ' Unsuccessful load
    . . .
    Resume Next
End Sub
```

You can also handle the error by setting **RaiseRequestErrors** to **False**, declaring an object, and assigning the **Load** request to it. Then follow the **Load** call with a statement that checks the status of the **Request** object.

```
Dim LoadRequest as Object

Sub Form_Load
    Agent1.RaiseRequestErrors = False
    Set LoadRequest = Agent1.Characters.Load _
        ("mychar", "c:\some directory\some character.acs")
    If LoadRequest.Status Not 0 Then
        ' Unsuccessful load
        . . .
        Exit Sub
    Else
        ' Successful load
        . . .
End Sub
```

If you load a character that is not local; for example, using HTTP protocol, you can also check for a **Load** failure by assigning a **Request** object to the **Load** method. However, because this method of loading a character is handled asynchronously, check its status in the **RequestComplete** event. This technique will not work loading a character using the UNC protocol because the **Load** method is processed synchronously.

To load a character from the Microsoft Agent site, consult the Character Data page at *http://www.microsoft.com/workshop/imedia/agent/characterdata.asp* for the latest information on the location of the character files.

Unload Method

Description

Unloads the character data for the specified character.

Syntax

*agent.***Characters.Unload** *"CharacterID"*

Remarks

Use this method when you no longer need a character, to free up memory used to store information about the character. If you access the character again, use the **Load** method.

This method does not return a **Request** object.

Character Object Methods

The server also exposes methods for each character in a **Characters** collection. The following methods are supported:

Activate, GestureAt, Get, Hide, Interrupt, Listen MoveTo, Play, Show, ShowPopupMenu, Speak, Stop, StopAll, Think, Wait

To use a method, reference the character in the collection. In VBScript and Visual Basic, you do this by specifying the ID for a character:

```
Sub FormLoad

'Load the genie character into the Characters collection
Agent1.Characters.Load "Genie", "Genie.acs"

'Display the character
Agent1.Characters("Genie").Show
Agent1.Characters("Genie").Play "Greet"
Agent1.Characters("Genie").Speak "Hello. "

End Sub
```

To simplify the syntax of your code, you can define an object variable and set it to reference a character object in the **Characters** collection; then you can use your variable to reference methods or properties of the character. The following example demonstrates how you can do this using the Visual Basic Set statement:

```
'Define a global object variable
Dim Genie as Object

Sub FormLoad

'Load the genie character into the Characters collection
Agent1.Characters.Load "Genie", " Genie.acs"

'Create a reference to the character
Set Genie = Agent1.Characters("Genie")

'Display the character
Genie.Show

'Get the Restpose animation
Genie.Get "animation", "RestPose"

'Make the character say Hello
Genie.Speak "Hello."

End Sub
```

In Visual Basic 5.0, you can also create your reference by declaring your variable as a **Character** object:

```
Dim Genie as IAgentCtlCharacterEx

Sub FormLoad

'Load the genie character into the Characters collection
Agent1.Characters.Load "Genie", "Genie.acs"

'Create a reference to the character
Set Genie = Agent1.Characters("Genie")

'Display the character
Genie.Show

End Sub
```

Declaring your object of type **IAgentCtlCharacterEx** enables early binding on the object, which results in better performance.

In VBScript, you cannot declare a reference as a particular type. However, you can simply declare the variable reference:

```
<SCRIPT LANGUAGE = "VBSCRIPT">
<!---

    Dim Genie
```

```
Sub window_OnLoad

'Load the character
AgentCtl.Characters.Load "Genie", _
   "http://agent.microsoft.com/characters/v2/genie/genie.acf"

'Create an object reference to the character in the collection
set Genie= AgentCtl.Characters ("Genie")

'Get the Showing state animation
Genie.Get "state", "Showing"

'Display the character
Genie.Show

End Sub

-->
</SCRIPT>
```

Some programming languages do not support collections. However, you can access a **Character** object's methods with the **Character** method:

```
agent.Characters.Character("CharacterID").method
```

In addition, you can also create a reference to the **Character** object to make your script code easier to follow:

```
<SCRIPT LANGUAGE="JScript" FOR="window" EVENT="onLoad()">
<!--

   //Load the character's data
   AgentCtl.Characters.Load ("Genie", _
      "http://agent.microsoft.com/characters/v2/genie/genie.acf");

   //Create a reference to this object
   Genie = AgentCtl.Characters.Character("Genie");

   //Get the Showing state animation
   Genie.Get("state", "Showing");

   //Display the character
   Genie.Show();

-->
</SCRIPT>
```

Activate Method

Description
Sets the active client or character.

Syntax

agent.**Characters** (*"CharacterID"*).**Activate** [*State*]

Part	Description
State	Optional. You can specify the following values for this parameter:
	0 Not the active client.
	1 The active client.
	2 (Default) The topmost character.

Remarks
When multiple characters are visible, only one of the characters receives speech input at a time. Similarly, when multiple client applications share the same character, only one of the clients receives mouse input (for example, Microsoft Agent control click or drag events). The character set to receive mouse and speech input is the topmost character and the client that receives the input is the active client of that character. (The topmost character's window also appears at the top of the character window's z-order.) Typically, the user determines the topmost character by explicitly selecting the character. However, topmost activation also changes when a character is shown or hidden (the character becomes or is no longer topmost, respectively.)

You can also use this method to explicitly manage when your client receives input directed to the character such as when your application itself becomes active. For example, setting **State** to 2 makes the character topmost and your client receives all mouse and speech input events generated from user interaction with the character. Therefore, it also makes your client the input-active client of the character.

However, you can also set yourself to be the active client for a character without making the character topmost, by setting **State** to 1. This enables your client to receive input directed to that character when the character becomes topmost. Similarly, you can set your client to not be the active client (not to receive input) when the character becomes topmost, by setting **State** to 0.

Avoid calling this method directly after a **Show** method. **Show** automatically sets the input-active client. When the character is hidden, the **Activate** call may fail if it gets processed before the **Show** method completes.

If you call this method to a function, it returns a Boolean value that indicates whether the method succeeded. Attempting to call this method with the **State** parameter set to 2 when the specified character is hidden will fail. Similarly, if you set **State** to 0 and your application is the only client, this call fails because a character must always have a topmost client.

```
Dim Genie as Object

Sub FormLoad()

Agent1.Characters.Load "Genie", "Genie.acs"

Set Genie = Agent1.Characters ("Genie")

If (Genie. Activate = True) Then
    'I'm active

Else
    'I must be hidden or something

End If

End Sub
```

Note Calling this method with **State** set to 1 does not typically generate an **ActivateInput** event unless there are no other characters loaded or your application is already input-active.

See also **ActivateInput** event, **DeactivateInput** event

GestureAt Method

Description
Plays the gesturing animation for the specified character at the specified location.

Syntax
agent.**Characters** (*"CharacterID"*).**GestureAt** *x,y*

Part	Description
x,y	Required. An integer value that indicates the horizontal (*x*) screen coordinate and vertical (*y*) screen coordinate to which the character will gesture. These coordinates must be specified in pixels.

Remarks
The server automatically plays the appropriate animation to gesture toward the specified location. The coordinates are always relative to the screen origin (upper left).

If you declare an object reference and set it to this method, it returns a **Request** object. In addition, if the associated animation has not been loaded on the local machine, the server sets the **Request** object's **Status** property to "failed" with an appropriate error number. Therefore, if you are using the HTTP protocol to access character animation data, use the **Get** method to load the **Gesturing** state animations before calling the **GestureAt** method.

Get Method

Description
Retrieves specified animation data for the specified character.

Syntax
agent.**Characters** (*"CharacterID"*).**Get** *Type*, *Name*, [*Queue*]

Part	Description	
Type	Required. A string value that indicates the animation data type to load.	
	"**Animation**"	A character's animation data.
	"**State**"	A character's state data.
	"**WaveFile**"	A character's audio (for spoken output) file.
Name	Required. A string that indicates the name of the animation type.	
	"*name*"	The name of the animation or state.
	For animations, the name is based on that defined for the character when saved using the Microsoft Agent Character Editor.	
	For states, the following values can be used:	
	"**Gesturing**"	To get all **Gesturing** state animations.
	"**GesturingDown**"	To get the **GesturingDown** animation.
	"**GesturingLeft**"	To get the **GesturingLeft** animation.
	"**GesturingRight**"	To get the **GesturingRight** animation.
	"**GesturingUp**"	To get the **GesturingUp** animation.
	"**Hiding**"	To get the **Hiding** state animation.
	"**Hearing**"	To get the **Hearing** state animation.
	"**Idling**"	To get all **Idling** state animations.
	"**IdlingLevel1**"	To get all **IdlingLevel1** animations.
	"**IdlingLevel2**"	To get all **IdlingLevel2** animations.
	"**IdlingLevel3**"	To get all **IdlingLevel3** animations.
	"**Listening**"	To get the **Listening** state animation.

Part	Description	
	"Moving"	To get all **Moving** state animations.
	"MovingDown"	To get the **MovingDown** animation.
	"MovingLeft"	To get the **MovingLeft** animation.
	"MovingRight"	To get the **MovingRight** animation.
	"MovingUp"	To get the **MovingUp** animation.
	"Showing"	To get the **Showing** state animation.
	"Speaking"	To get the **Speaking** state animation.

You can specify multiple animations and states by separating them with commas. However, you cannot mix types in the same **Get** statement.

	"URL or filespec"	The specification for the sound (.WAV or .LWV) file. If the specification is not complete, it is interpreted as being relative to the specification used in the **Load** method.
Queue	Optional. A Boolean expression specifying whether the server queues the **Get** request.	
	True	(Default) Queues the **Get** request. Any animation request that follows the **Get** request (for the same character) waits until the animation data is loaded.
	False	Does not queue the **Get** request.

Remarks

If you load a character using the HTTP protocol (an .ACF file), you must use the **Get** method to retrieve animation data before you can play the animation. You do not use this method if you loaded the character using the UNC protocol (an .ACS file). You also cannot retrieve HTTP data for a character using **Get** if you loaded that character using the UNC protocol (.ACS character file).

If you declare an object reference and set it to this method, it returns a **Request** object. If the associated animation fails to load, the server sets the **Request** object's **Status** property to "failed" with an appropriate error number. You can use the **RequestComplete** event to check the status and determine what action to take.

Animation or sound data retrieved with the **Get** method is stored in the browser's cache. Subsequent calls will check the cache, and if the animation data is already there, the control loads the data directly from the cache. Once loaded, the animation or sound data can be played with the **Play** or **Speak** methods.

See also **Load** method

Hide Method

Description

Hides the specified character.

Syntax

agent.**Characters** (*"CharacterID"*).**Hide** [*Fast*]

Part	Description
Fast	Optional. A Boolean value that indicates whether to skip the animation associated with the character's Hiding state
	True Does not play the **Hiding** animation.
	False (Default) Plays the **Hiding** animation.

Remarks

The server queues the actions of the **Hide** method in the character's queue, so you can use it to hide the character after a sequence of other animations. You can play the action immediately by using the **Stop** method before calling this method.

If you declare an object reference and set it to this method, it returns a **Request** object. In addition, if the associated **Hiding** animation has not been loaded and you have not specified the **Fast** parameter as **True**, the server sets the **Request** object **Status** property to "failed" with an appropriate error number. Therefore, if you are using the HTTP protocol to access character or animation data, use the **Get** method and specify the **Hiding** state to load the animation before calling the **Hide** method.

Hiding a character can also result in triggering the **ActivateInput** event of another client.

Note Hidden characters cannot access the audio channel. The server will pass back a failure status in the **RequestComplete** event if you generate an animation request and the character is hidden.

See also **Show** method

Interrupt Method

Description

Interrupts the animation for the specified character.

Syntax

agent.**Characters** (*"CharacterID"*).**Interrupt** *Request*

Part	Description
Request	A **Request** object for a particular animation call.

Remarks

You can use this to sync up animation between characters. For example, if another character is in a looping animation, this method will stop the loop and move to the next animation in the character's queue. You cannot interrupt a character animation that you are not using (that you have not loaded).

To specify the request parameter, you must create a variable and assign the animation request you want to interrupt:

```
Dim GenieRequest as Object
Dim RobbyRequest as Object
Dim Genie as Object
Dim Robby as Object

Sub FormLoad()

    MyAgent1.Characters.Load "Genie", "Genie.acs"

    MyAgent1.Characters.Load "Robby", "Robby.acs"

    Set Genie = MyAgent1.Characters ("Genie")
    Set Robby = MyAgent1.Characters ("Robby")

    Genie.Show

    Genie.Speak "Just a moment"

    Set GenieRequest = Genie.Play ("Processing")

    Robby.Show
    Robby.Play "confused"
    Robby.Speak "Hey, Genie. What are you doing?"
    Robby.Interrupt GenieRequest

    Genie.Speak "I was just checking on something."

End Sub
```

You cannot interrupt the animation of the same character you specify in this method because the server queues the **Interrupt** method in that character's animation queue. Therefore, you can only use **Interrupt** to halt the animation of another character you have loaded.

If you declare an object reference and set it to this method, it returns a **Request** object.

Note Interrupt does not flush the character's queue; it halts the existing animation and moves on to the next animation in the character's queue. To halt and flush a character's queue, use the **Stop** method.

See also Stop method

Listen Method

Description
Turns on Listening mode (speech recognition) for a timed period.

Syntax
*agent.***Characters** (*"CharacterID"*)**.Listen** *State*

Part	Description
State	Required. A Boolean value that determines whether to turn Listening mode on or off.
	True Turns Listening mode on.
	False Turns Listening mode off.

Remarks
Setting this method to **True** enables Listening mode (turns on speech recognition) for a fixed period of time (10 seconds). While you cannot set the value of the time-out, you can turn off Listening mode before the time-out expires. If you (or another client) successfully set Listening mode on and you attempt to set this property to **True** before the time-out expires, the method succeeds and resets the time-out. However, if the Listening mode is on because the user is pressing the Listening key, the method succeeds, but the time-out is ignored and the Listening mode ends based on the user's interaction with the Listening key.

This method succeeds only when called by the input-active client and if speech services have been started. To ensure that speech services have been started, query or set the **SRModeID** or set the **Voice** setting for a **Command** before you call **Listen**—otherwise the method will fail. To detect the success of this method, call it as a function and it will return a Boolean value indicating whether the method succeeded.

```
If Genie.Listen(True) Then
   'The method succeeded
```

```
Else
   ' The method failed

End If
```

The method also fails if the user is pressing the Listening key and you attempt to set **Listen** to **False**. However, if the user has released the Listening key and Listening mode has not timed out, it will succeed.

Listen also fails if there is no compatible speech engine available that matches the character's **LanguageID** setting, the user has disabled speech input using the Microsoft Agent property sheet, or the audio device is busy.

When you successfully set this method to **True**, the server triggers the **ListenStart** event. The server sends **ListenComplete** when the Listening mode time-out completes or when you set **Listen** to **False**.

This method does not automatically call **Stop** and play a Listening state animation as the server does when the Listening key is pressed. This enables you to determine whether to interrupt the current animation using the **ListenStart** animation by calling **Stop** and playing your own appropriate animation. However, the server does call **Stop** and plays a Hearing state animation when a user utterance is detected.

See also **LanguageID** property, **ListenComplete** event, **ListenStart** event

MoveTo Method

Description
Moves the specified character to the specified location.

Syntax
agent.**Characters** (*"CharacterID"*).**MoveTo** *x,y,* [*Speed*]

Part	Description
x,y	Required. An integer value that indicates the left edge (*x*) and top edge (*y*) of the animation frame. Express these coordinates in pixels.
Speed	Optional. A Long integer value specifying in milliseconds how quickly the character's frame moves. The default value is 1000. Specifying zero (0) moves the frame without playing an animation.

Remarks

The server automatically plays the appropriate animation assigned to the **Moving** states. The location of a character is based on the upper left corner of its frame.

If you declare an object variable and set it to this method, it returns a **Request** object. In addition, if the associated animation has not been loaded on the local machine, the server sets the **Request** object's **Status** property to "failed" with an appropriate error number. Therefore, if you are using the HTTP protocol to access character or animation data, use the **Get** method to load the **Moving** state animations before calling the **MoveTo** method.

Even if the animation is not loaded, the server still moves the frame.

Note If you call **MoveTo** with a non-zero value before the character is shown, it will return a failure status if you assigned it a **Request** object, because the non-zero value indicates that you are attempting to play an animation when the character is not visible.

Note The **Speed** parameters actual effect may vary based on the speed of the processor of the computer and the priority of other tasks running on the system.

Play Method

Description

Plays the specified animation for the specified character.

Syntax

agent.**Characters** (*"CharacterID"*).**Play** *"AnimationName"*

Part	Description
AnimationName	Required. A string that specifies the name of an animation sequence.

Remarks

An animation's name is defined when the character is compiled with the Microsoft Agent Character Editor. Before playing the specified animation, the server attempts to play the **Return** animation for the previous animation, if one has been assigned.

When accessing a character's animations using a conventional file protocol, you can simply use the **Play** method specifying the name of the animation. However, if you are using the HTTP protocol to access character animation data, use the **Get** method to load the animation before calling the **Play** method.

See also **Get** method

To simplify your syntax, you can declare an object reference and set it to reference the **Character** object in the **Characters** collection and use the reference as part of your **Play** statements:

```
Dim Genie
Agent1.Characters.Load "Genie", _
    "http://agent.microsoft.com/characters/v2/genie/genie.acf"

Set Genie = Agent1.Characters ("Genie")

Genie.Get "state", "Showing"
Genie.Show

Genie.Get "animation", "Greet, GreetReturn"
Genie.Play "Greet"
Genie.Speak "Hello."
```

If you declare an object reference and set it to this method, it returns a **Request** object. In addition, if you specify an animation that is not loaded or if the character has not been successfully loaded, the server sets the **Status** property of **Request** object to "failed" with an appropriate error number. However, if the animation does not exist and the character's data has already been successfully loaded, the server raises an error.

The **Play** method does not make the character visible. If the character is not visible, the server plays the animation invisibly, and sets the **Status** property of the **Request** object.

Show Method

Description

Makes the specified character visible and plays its associated **Showing** animation.

Syntax

agent.**Characters** (*"CharacterID"*).**Show** [*Fast*]

Part	Description
Fast	Optional. A Boolean expression specifying whether the server plays the **Showing** animation.
	True Skips the **Showing** state animation.
	False (Default) Does not skip the **Showing** state animation.

Remarks

If you declare an object reference and set it to this method, it returns a **Request** object. In addition, if the associated **Showing** animation has not been loaded and you have not specified the **Fast** parameter as **True**, the server sets the **Request** object's **Status** property to "failed" with an appropriate error number. Therefore, if you are using the HTTP protocol to access character animation data, use the **Get** method to load the **Showing** state animation before calling the **Show** method.

Avoid setting the **Fast** parameter to **True** without first playing an animation beforehand; otherwise, the character frame may display with no image. In particular, note that if you call **MoveTo** when the character is not visible, it does not play any animation. Therefore, if you call the **Show** method with **Fast** set to **True**, no image will display. Similarly, if you call **Hide** then **Show** with **Fast** set to **True**, there will be no visible image.

See also **Hide** method

ShowPopupMenu Method

Description

Displays the character's pop-up menu at the specified location.

Syntax

*agent.***Characters** (*"CharacterID"*).**ShowPopupMenu** *x, y*

Part	Description
x	Required. An integer value that indicates the horizontal (*x*) screen coordinate to display the menu. These coordinates must be specified in pixels.
y	Required. An integer value that indicates the vertical (*y*) screen coordinate to display the menu. These coordinates must be specified in pixels.

Remarks

Agent automatically displays the character's pop-up menu when the user right-clicks the character. If you set **AutoPopupMenu** to **False**, you can use this method to display the menu.

The menu remains displayed until the user selects a command or displays another menu. Only one pop-up menu can be displayed at a time; therefore, calls to this method will cancel (remove) the former menu.

This method should be called only when your client application is the active client of the character; otherwise it fails. To determine the success of this method you can call it as a function and it will return a Boolean value indicating whether the method succeeded.

```
If Genie.ShowPopupMenu (10,10) = True Then
   ' The menu will be displayed

Else
   ' The menu will not be displayed

End If
```

See also **AutoPopupMenu** property

Speak Method

Description

Speaks the specified text or audio file for the specified character.

Syntax

agent.**Characters** (*"CharacterID"*).**Speak** [*Text*], [*Url*]

Part	Description
Text	Optional. A string that specifies what the character says.
Url	Optional. A string expression specifying the specification for an audio file. The specification can be a file specification or URL.

Remarks

Although the *Text* and *Url* parameters are optional, one of them must be supplied. To use this method with a character configured to speak only in its word balloon or using a text-to-speech (TTS) engine, simply provide the *Text* parameter. Include a space between words to define appropriate word breaks in the word balloon, even for languages that do not traditionally include spaces.

You can also include vertical bar characters (|) in the *Text* parameter to designate alternative strings, so that the server randomly chooses a different string each time it processes the method.

Character support of TTS output is defined when the character is compiled using the Microsoft Agent Character Editor. To generate TTS output, a compatible TTS engine must already be installed before calling this method. For further information, see Accessing Speech Services on page 43.

If you use recorded sound-file output for the character, specify the file's location in the *Url* parameter. (The filename cannot include any characters not included in the US codepage 1252.) However, if you are using the HTTP protocol to access the character animation data, use the **Get** method to load the animation before calling the **Speak** method. When doing so, you still use the *Text* parameter to specify the words that appear in the character's word balloon. However, if you specify a linguistically enhanced sound file (.LWV) for the *Url* parameter and do not specify text for the word balloon, the *Text* parameter uses the text stored in the file.

You can also vary parameters of the speech output with special tags that you include in the *Text* parameter. For more information, see Chapter 6, "Speech Output Tags."

If you declare an object reference and set it to this method, it returns a **Request** object. You can use this to synchronize other parts of your code with the character's spoken output, as in the following example:

```
Dim SpeakRequest as Object
...
Set SpeakRequest = Genie.Speak ("And here it is.")
...
Sub Agent1_RequestComplete (ByVal Request as Object)
' Make certain the request exists
If SpeakRequest Not Nothing Then
   ' See if it was this request
   If Request = SpeakRequest Then
      ' Display the message box
      Msgbox "Ta da!"
   End If
End If
End Sub
```

You can also use a **Request** object to check for certain error conditions. For example, if you use the **Speak** method to speak and do not have a compatible TTS engine installed, the server sets the **Request** object's **Status** property to "failed" with its **Description** property to "Class not registered" or "Unknown or object returned error". To determine if you have a TTS engine installed, use the **TTSModeID** property.

Similarly, if you have the character attempt to speak a sound file, and if the file has not been loaded or there is a problem with the audio device, the server also sets the **Request** object's **Status** property to "failed" with an appropriate error code number.

You can also include bookmark speech tags in your Speak text to synchronize your code:

```
Dim SpeakRequest as Object
...
Set SpeakRequest = Genie.Speak ("And here \mrk=100\it is.")
...
Sub Agent1_Bookmark (ByVal BookmarkID As Long)
If BookmarkID = 100 Then
   ' Display the message box
      Msgbox "Tada!"
   End If
End Sub
```

See also Chapter 6, "Speech Output Tags."

The **Speak** method uses the last action played to determine which speaking animation to play. For example, if you preceded the **Speak** command with a **Play** "GestureRight", the server will play **GestureRight** and then the **GestureRight** speaking animation. If the last animation played has no speaking animation, Agent plays the animation assigned to the character's **Speaking** state.

If you call **Speak** and the audio channel is busy, the character's audio output will not be heard, but the text will display in the word balloon.

Agent's automatic word breaking in the word balloon breaks words using whitespace characters (for example, Space or Tab). However, if it cannot, it may break a word to fit the balloon. In languages like Japanese, Chinese, and Thai, where spaces are not used to break words, insert a Unicode zero-width space character (0x200B) between characters to define logical word breaks.

Note The word balloon's **Enabled** property must also be **True** for text to display.

Note Set the character's language ID (by setting the character's **LanguageID** before using the **Speak** method to ensure appropriate text display within the word balloon.

See also **Bookmark** event, **RequestStart** event, **RequestComplete** event

Stop Method

Description
Stops the animation for the specified character.

Syntax
agent.**Characters** ("*CharacterID*").**Stop** [*Request*]

Part	Description
Request	Optional. A **Request** object specifying a particular animation call.

Remarks

To specify the request parameter, you must create a variable and assign the animation request you want to stop. If you don't set the **Request** parameter, the server stops all animations for the character, including queued **Get** calls, and clears its animation queue unless the character is currently playing its **Hiding** or **Showing** animation. This method does not stop non-queued **Get** calls.

To stop a specific animation or **Get** call, declare an object variable and assign your animation request to that variable:

```
Dim MyRequest
Dim Genie

Agent1.Characters.Load "Genie", _
    "http://agent.microsoft.com/characters/v2/genie/genie.acf"

Set Genie = Agent1.Characters ("Genie")

Genie.Get "state", "Showing"
Genie.Get "animation", "Greet, GreetReturn"

Genie.Show

'This animation will never play
Set MyRequest = Genie.Play ("Greet")

Genie.Stop MyRequest
```

This method will not generate a **Request** object.

See also **StopAll** method

StopAll Method

Description

Stops all animation requests or specified types of requests for the specified character.

Syntax

agent.**Characters** (*"CharacterID"*).**StopAll** [*Type*]

Part	Description
Type	Optional. To use this parameter you can use any of the following values. You can also specify multiple types by separating them with commas.

"**Get**"		To stop all queued **Get** requests.
"**NonQueuedGet**"		To stop all non-queued **Get** requests (**Get** method with **Queue** parameter set to **False**).
"**Move**"		To stop all queued **MoveTo** requests.
"**Play**"		To stop all queued **Play** requests.
"**Speak**"		To stop all queued **Speak** requests.

Remarks

If you don't set the **Type** parameter, the server stops all animations for the character, including queued and non-queued **Get** requests, and clears its animation queue. It also stops playing a character's Hiding or Showing animation.

This method will not generate a **Request** object.

See also **Stop** method

Think Method

Description

Displays the specified text for the specified character in a "thought" word balloon.

Syntax

agent.**Characters** (**"***CharacterID***"**).**Think** [*Text*]

Part	Description
Text	Optional. A string that specifies the character's thought output.

Remarks

Like the **Speak** method, the **Think** method is a queued request that displays text in a word balloon, except that the **Think** word balloon differs visually. In addition, the balloon supports only the Bookmark speech control tag (**\Mrk**) and ignores any other speech control tags. Unlike **Speak**, the **Think** method does not change the character's animation state.

The **Balloon** object's properties affect the output of both the **Speak** and **Think** methods. For example, the **Balloon** object's **Enabled** property must be **True** for text to display.

If you declare an object reference and set it to this method, it returns a **Request** object. In addition, if the file has not been loaded, the server sets the **Request** object's **Status** property to "failed" with an appropriate error code number.

Agent's automatic word breaking in the word balloon breaks words using white-space characters (for example, Space or Tab). However, if it cannot, it may break a word to fit the balloon. In languages like Japanese, Chinese, and Thai where spaces are not used to break words, insert a Unicode zero-width space character (0x200B) between characters to define logical word breaks.

Note Set the character's language ID before using the **Speak** method to ensure appropriate text display within the word balloon.

Wait Method

Description

Causes the animation queue for the specified character to wait until the specified animation request completes.

Syntax

agent.**Characters** (*"CharacterID"*).**Wait** *Request*

Part	Description
Request	A **Request** object specifying a particular animation..

Remarks

Use this method only when you support multiple (simultaneous) characters and are trying to sequence the interaction of characters. (For a single character, each animation request is played sequentially—after the previous request completes.) If you have two characters and you want a character's animation request to wait until the other character's animation completes, set the **Wait** method to the other character's animation **Request** object. To specify the request parameter, you must create a variable and assign the animation request you want to interrupt:

```
Dim GenieRequest
Dim RobbyRequest
Dim Genie
Dim Robby

Sub window_Onload

Agent1.Characters.Load "Genie", _
    "http://agent.microsoft.com/characters/v2/genie/genie.acf"
```

```
Agent1.Characters.Load "Robby", _
   "http://agent.microsoft.com/characters/v2/robby/robby.acf"

Set Genie = Agent1.Characters("Genie")
Set Robby = Agent1.Characters("Robby")

Genie.Get "State", "Showing"
Robby.Get "State", "Showing"

Genie.Get "Animation", "Announce, AnnounceReturn, Pleased, " + _
   "PleasedReturn"

Robby.Get "Animation", "Confused, ConfusedReturn, Sad, SadReturn"

Set Genie = Agent1.Characters ("Genie")
Set Robby = Agent1.Characters ("Robby")

Genie.MoveTo 100,100
Genie.Show

Robby.MoveTo 250,100
Robby.Show

Genie.Play "Announce"
Set GenieRequest = Genie.Speak ("Why did the chicken cross the road?")

Robby.Wait GenieRequest
Robby.Play "Confused"
Set RobbyRequest = Robby.Speak _
   ("I don't know. Why did the chicken cross the road?")

Genie.Wait RobbyRequest
Genie.Play "Pleased"
Set GenieRequest = Genie.Speak ("To get to the other side.")

Robby.Wait GenieRequest
Robby.Play "Sad"
Robby.Speak "I never should have asked."

End Sub
```

You can also streamline your code by just calling **Wait** directly, using a specific animation request.

```
Robby.Wait Genie.Play "GestureRight"
```

This avoids having to explicitly declare a **Request** object.

Character Object Properties

The **Character** object exposes the following properties:

Active, AutoPopupMenu, Description, ExtraData, GUID, HasOtherClients, Height, HelpContextID, HelpFile, HelpModeOn, IdleOn, LanguageID, Left, MoveCause, Name, OriginalHeight, OriginalWidth, Pitch, SoundEffectsOn, Speed, SRModeID, SRStatus, Top, TTSModeID, Version, VisibilityCause, Visible, Width

Note that the **Height**, **Left**, **Top**, and **Width** properties of a character differ from those that may be supported by the programming environment for the placement of the control. The **Character** properties apply to the visible presentation of a character, not the location of the Microsoft Agent control.

As with **Character** object methods, you can access a character's properties using the **Characters** collection, or simplify your syntax by declaring an object variable and setting it to a character in the collection. In the following example, Test1 and Test2 will be set to the same value:

```
Dim Genie
Dim MyRequest

Sub window_Onload

Agent.Characters.Load "Genie", _
   "http://agent.microsoft.com/characters/v2/genie/genie.acf"

Set Genie = Agent.Characters("Genie")

Genie.MoveTo 15,15
Set MyRequest = Genie.Show()

End Sub

Sub Agent_RequestComplete(ByVal Request)

If Request = MyRequest Then
   Test1 = Agent.Characters("Genie").Top
   Test2 = Genie.Top
   MsgBox "Test 1 is " + cstr(Test1) + "and Test 2 is " + cstr(Test2)
End If

End Sub
```

Because the server loads a character asynchronously, ensure that the character has been loaded before querying its properties, for example, using the **RequestComplete** event. Otherwise, the properties may return incorrect values.

Active Property

Description

Returns whether your application is the active client of the character and whether the character is topmost.

Syntax

*agent.***Characters** (*"CharacterID"*)**.Active** [= *State*]

Part	Description
state	An integer expression specifying the state of your client application.
	0 Not the active client.
	1 The active client.
	2 The input-active client. (The topmost character.)

Remarks

When multiple client applications share the same character, the active client of the character receives mouse input (for example, Microsoft Agent control **Click** or **Drag** events). Similarly, when multiple characters are displayed, the active client of the topmost character (also known as the input-active client) receives Command events.

You can use the **Activate** method to set whether your application is the active client of the character or to make your application the input active client (which also makes the character topmost).

See also **Activate** method

AutoPopupMenu Property

Description

Returns or sets whether right-clicking the character or its taskbar icon automatically displays the character's pop-up menu.

Syntax

*agent.***Characters** (*"CharacterID"*)**.AutoPopupMenu** [= *boolean*]

Part	Description
boolean	A Boolean expression specifying whether the server automatically displays the character's pop-up menu on right-click.
	True (Default) Displays the menu on right-click.
	False Does not display the menu on right-click.

Remarks

By setting this property to **False**, you can create your own menu-handling behavior. To display the menu after setting this property to **False**, use the **ShowPopupMenu** method.

This property applies only to your client application's use of the character; the setting does not affect other clients of the character or other characters of your client application.

See also **ShowPopupMenu** method

Description Property

Description

Returns or sets a string that specifies the description for the specified character.

Syntax

agent.**Characters(**"*CharacterID*"**).Description** [= *string*]

Part	Description
string	A string value corresponding to the character's description (in the current language setting).

Remarks

A character's **Description** may depend on the character's **LanguageID** setting. A character's name in one language may be different or use different characters than in another. The character's default **Description** for a specific language is defined when the character is compiled with the Microsoft Agent Character Editor.

Note The **Description** property setting is optional and may not be supplied for all characters.

ExtraData Property

Description

Returns a string that specifies additional data stored as part of the character.

Syntax

agent.**Characters(**"*CharacterID*"**).ExtraData**

Remarks

The default value for the **ExtraData** property for a character is defined when the character is compiled with the Microsoft Agent Character Editor. It cannot be changed or specified at run time.

Note The **ExtraData** property setting is optional and may not be supplied for all characters.

GUID Property

Description

Returns the unique identifier for the character.

Syntax

agent.**Characters** (*"CharacterID"*).**GUID**

Remarks

This property returns a string representing the internal identifier that the server uses to refer to uniquely identify the character. A character identifier is set when it is compiled with the Microsoft Agent Character Editor. The property is read-only.

HasOtherClients Property

Description

Returns whether the specified character is in use by other applications.

Syntax

agent.**Characters**(*"CharacterID"*).**HasOtherClients**

Value	Description
True	The character has other clients.
False	The character does not have other clients.

Remarks

You can use this property to determine whether your application is the only or last client of the character, when more than one application is sharing (has loaded) the same character.

Height Property

Description
Returns or sets the height of the specified character's frame.

Syntax
agent.**Characters** ("*CharacterID*").**Height** [= *value*]

Part	Description
value	A Long integer that specifies the character's frame height.

Remarks
The **Height** property is always expressed in pixels, relative to screen coordinates (upper left). This property's setting applies to all clients of the character.

Even though the character appears in an irregularly shaped region window, the height of the character is based on the external dimensions of the rectangular animation frame used when the character was compiled with the Microsoft Agent Character Editor.

HelpContextID Property

Description
Returns or sets an associated context number for the character. Used to provide context-sensitive Help for the character.

Syntax
agent.**Characters** ("*CharacterID*").**HelpContextID** [= *Number*]

Part	Description
Number	An integer specifying a valid context number.

Remarks
To support context-sensitive Help for the character, assign the context number to the character you use for the associated Help topic when you compile your Help file. This property applies only to the client of the character; the setting does not affect other clients of the character or other characters of the client.

If you've created a Windows Help file for your application and set the character's **HelpFile** property, Agent automatically calls Help when **HelpModeOn** is set to **True** and the user clicks the character. If there is a context number in the **HelpContextID**, Agent calls Help and searches for the topic identified by the

current context number. The current context number is the value of
HelpContextID for the character.

Note Building a Help file requires the Microsoft Windows Help Compiler.

See also **HelpFile** property, **HelpModeOn** property

HelpFile Property

Description
Returns or sets the path and filename for a Microsoft Windows context-sensitive
Help file supplied by the client application.

Syntax
*agent.***Characters** (*"CharacterID"*)**.Helpfile** [= *Filename*]

Part	Description
Filename	A string expression specifying the path and filename of the Windows Help file.

Remarks
If you've created a Windows Help file for your application and set the character's
HelpFile property, Agent automatically calls Help when **HelpModeOn** is set to
True and the user clicks the character or selects a command from its pop-up
menu. If you specified a context number in the **HelpContextID** property of the
selected command, Help displays a topic corresponding to the current Help context; otherwise it displays "No Help topic associated with this item."

This property applies only to your client application's use of the character; the
setting does not affect other clients of the character or other characters of your
client application.

See also **HelpModeOn** property, **HelpContextID** property

HelpModeOn Property

Description
Returns or sets whether context-sensitive Help mode is on for the character.

Syntax
*agent.***Characters** (*"CharacterID"*)**.HelpModeOn** [= *boolean*]

Part	Description
boolean	A Boolean expression specifying whether context-sensitive Help mode is on.
	True Help mode is on.
	False (Default) Help mode is off.

Remarks

When you set this property to **True**, the mouse pointer changes to the context-sensitive Help image when moved over the character or over the pop-up menu for the character. When the user clicks or drags the character or clicks an item in the character's pop-up menu, the server triggers the **HelpComplete** event and exits Help mode.

In Help mode, the server does not send the **Click**, **DragStart**, **DragComplete**, and **Command** events, unless you set the **AutoPopupMenu** property to **True**. In that case, the server will send the **Click** event (does not exit Help mode), but only for the right mouse button to enable you to display the pop-up menu.

This property applies only to your client application's use of the character; the setting does not affect other clients of the character or other characters of your client application.

See also **HelpComplete** event

IdleOn Property

Description

Returns or sets a Boolean value that determines whether the server manages the specified character's **Idling** state animations.

Syntax

agent.**Characters** (*"CharacterID"*).**IdleOn** [= *boolean*]

Part	Description
boolean	A Boolean expression specifying whether the server manages idle mode.
	True (Default) Server handling of the idle state is enabled.
	False Server handling of the idle state is disabled.

Remarks

The server automatically sets a time-out after the last animation played for a character. When this timer's interval is complete, the server begins the **Idling** state for a character, playing its associated **Idling** animations at regular intervals. If you want to disable the server from automatically playing the **Idling** state animations, set the property to **False** and play an animation or call the **Stop** method. Setting this value does not affect the current animation state of the character.

This property applies only to your client application's use of the character; the setting does not affect other clients of the character or other characters of your client application.

LanguageID Property

Description
Returns or sets the language ID for the character.

Syntax
*agent.***Characters** (*"CharacterID"*)**.LanguageID** [= *LanguageID*]

Part	Description
LanguageID	A Long integer specifying the language ID for the character. The language ID (LANGID) for a character is a 16-bit value defined by Windows, consisting of a primary language ID and a secondary language ID. The following examples are values for languages supported by Microsoft Agent. To determine the value for other languages, see the Win32 SDK documentation.

Arabic	&H0401	Italian	&H0410
Basque	&H042D	Japanese	&H0411
Chinese (Simplified)	&H0804	Korean	&H0412
Chinese (Traditional)	&H0404	Norwegian	&H0414
Croatian	&H041A	Polish	&H0415
Czech	&H0405	Portuguese	&H0816
Danish	&H0406	Portuguese (Brazilian)	&H0416
Dutch	&H0413	Romanian	&H0418
English (British)	&H0809	Russian	&H0419
English (US)	&H0409	Slovakian	&H041B
Finnish	&H040B	Slovenian	&H0424
French	&H040C	Spanish	&H0C0A
German	&H0407	Swedish	&H041D
Greek	&H0408	Thai	&H041E
Hebrew	&H040D	Turkish	&H041F
Hungarian	&H040E		

Remarks
If you do not set the **LanguageID** for the character, its language ID will be the current system language ID if the corresponding Agent language DLL is installed, otherwise, the character's language will be English (US).

This property also determines the language for word balloon text, the commands in the character's pop-up menu, and the speech recognition engine. It also determines the default language for TTS output.

If you try to set the language ID for a character and the Agent language DLL for that language is not installed or a display font for the language ID is not available, Agent raises an error and **LanguageID** remains at its last setting.

Setting this property does not raise an error if there are no matching speech engines for the language. To determine if there is a compatible speech engine available for the **LanguageID**, check **SRModeID** or **TTSModeID**. If you do not set **LanguageID**, it will be set to the user default language ID setting.

This property applies only to your client application's use of the character; the setting does not affect other clients of the character or other characters of your client application.

Note If you set **LanguageID** to a language that supports bidirectional text (such as Arabic or Hebrew), but the system running your application does not have bidirectional support installed, text in the word balloon will appear in logical rather than display order.

See also **SRModeID** property, **TTSModeID** property

Left Property

Description
Returns or sets the left edge of the specified character's frame.

Syntax
agent.**Characters** ("*CharacterID*").**Left** [= *value*]

Part	Description
value	A Long integer that specifies the left edge of the character's frame.

Remarks
The **Left** property is always expressed in pixels, relative to screen origin (upper left). This property's setting applies to all clients of the character.

Even though the character appears in an irregularly shaped region window, the location of the character is based on the external dimensions of the rectangular animation frame used when the character was compiled with the Microsoft Agent Character Editor.

MoveCause Property

Description

Returns an integer value that specifies what caused the character's last move.

Syntax

agent.**Characters(**"*CharacterID*"**).MoveCause**

Value	Description
0	The character has not been moved.
1	The user moved the character.
2	Your application moved the character.
3	Another client application moved the character.
4	The Agent server moved the character to keep it onscreen after a screen resolution change.

Remarks

You can use this property to determine what caused the character to move, when more than one application is sharing (has loaded) the same character. These values are the same as those returned by the **Move** event.

See also **Move** event, **MoveTo** method

Name Property

Description

Returns or sets a string that specifies the default name of the specified character.

Syntax

agent.**Characters (**"*CharacterID*"**).Name** [= *string*]

Part	Description
string	A string value corresponding to the character's name (in the current language setting).

Remarks

A character's **Name** may depend on the character's **LanguageID** setting. A character's name in one language may be different or use different characters than in another. The character's default **Name** for a specific language is defined when the character is compiled with the Microsoft Agent Character Editor.

Avoid renaming a character, especially when using it in a scenario where other client applications may use the same character. Agent uses the character's **Name** to automatically create commands for hiding and showing the character.

OriginalHeight Property

Description
Returns an integer value that specifies the character's original height.

Syntax
*agent.***Characters** (**"***CharacterID***").OriginalHeight**

Remarks
This property returns the character's frame height as built with the Microsoft Agent Character Editor.

See also **Height** property, **OriginalWidth** property

OriginalWidth Property

Description
Returns an integer value that specifies the character's original width.

Syntax
*agent.***Characters** (**"***CharacterID***").OriginalWidth**

Remarks
This property returns the character's frame width as built with the Microsoft Agent Character Editor.

See also **Width** property, **OriginalHeight** property

Pitch Property

Description
Returns a Long integer for the specified character's speech output (TTS) pitch setting.

Syntax
*agent.***Characters** (**"***CharacterID***").Pitch**

Remarks

This property applies only to characters configured for TTS output. If the character does not support TTS output, this property returns zero (0).

Although your application cannot write this value, you can include **Pit** (pitch) tags in your output text that will temporarily increase the pitch for a particular utterance. However, using the **Pit** tag to change the pitch will not change the **Pitch** property setting.

See also Chapter 6, "Speech Output Tags."

SoundEffectsOn Property

Description

Returns or sets whether sound effects are enabled for your character.

Syntax

agent.**Characters("***CharacterID***").SoundEffectsOn** [= *boolean*]

Part	Description
boolean	A Boolean expression specifying whether sound effects are enabled.
	True Sound effects are enabled.
	False Sound effects are disabled.

Remarks

This property determines whether sound effects included as a part of a character's animations will play when an animation plays. This property's setting applies to all clients of the character.

See also SoundEffects property

Speed Property

Description

Returns a Long integer that specifies the current speed of the character's speech output.

Syntax

agent.**Characters ("***CharacterID***").Speed**

Remarks

This property returns the current speaking output speed setting for the character. For characters using TTS output, the property returns the actual TTS output setting for the character. If TTS is not enabled or the character does not support TTS output, the setting reflects the user setting for output speed.

Although your application cannot write this value, you can include **Spd** (speed) tags in your output text that will temporarily speed up the output for a particular utterance. However, using the **Spd** tag to change the character's spoken output does not affect the **Speed** property setting.

See also Chapter 6, "Speech Output Tags."

SRModelID Property

Description

Returns or sets the speech recognition engine the character uses.

Syntax

*agent.***Characters** (*"CharacterID"*)**.SRModeID** [= *ModeID*]

Part	Description
ModeID	A string expression that corresponds to the mode ID of a speech engine.

Remarks

The property determines the speech recognition engine used by the character for speech input. The mode ID for a speech recognition engine is a formatted string defined by the speech vendor that uniquely identifies the engine. For more information, see Microsoft Speech Engines.

If you specify a mode ID for a speech engine that isn't installed, if the user has disabled speech recognition (in the Microsoft Agent property sheet), or if the language of the specified speech engine doesn't match the character's **LanguageID** setting, the server raises an error.

If you query this property and haven't already (successfully) set the speech recognition engine, the server returns the mode ID of the engine that SAPI returns based on the character's **LanguageID** setting. If you haven't set the character's **LanguageID**, then Agent returns the mode ID of the engine that SAPI returns based on the user's default language ID setting. If there is no matching engine, the server returns an empty string (""). Querying this property does not require that **SpeechInput.Enabled** be set to **True**. However, if you query the property when speech input is disabled, the server returns an empty string.

When speech input is enabled (in the Advanced Character Options window), querying or setting this property will load the associated engine (if it is not already loaded), and start speech services. That is, the Listening key is available, and the Listening Tip is displayable. (The Listening key and Listening Tip are enabled only if they are also enabled in Advanced Character Options.) However, if you query the property when speech is disabled, the server does not start speech services.

This property applies only to your client application's use of the character; the setting does not affect other clients of the character or other characters of your client application.

Microsoft Agent's speech engine requirements are based on the Microsoft Speech API. Engines supporting Microsoft Agent's SAPI requirements can be installed and used with Agent.

Note This property also returns the empty string if you have no compatible sound support installed on your system.

Note Querying this property does not typically return an error. However, if the speech engine takes an abnormally long time to load, you may get an error indicating that the query timed out.

See also LanguageID property

SRStatus Property

Description
Returns whether speech input can be started for the character.

Syntax
*agent.***Characters** (*"CharacterID"*)**.SRStatus**

Value	Description
0	Conditions support speech input.
1	There is no audio input device available on this system. (Note that this does not detect whether or not a microphone is installed; it can only detect whether the user has a properly installed input-enabled sound card with a working driver.)
2	Another client is the active client of this character, or the current character is not topmost.
3	The audio input or output channel is currently busy, an application is using audio.

Value	Description
4	An unspecified error occurred in the process of initializing the speech recognition subsystem. This includes the possibility that there is no speech engine available matching the character's language setting.
5	The user has disabled speech input in the Advanced Character Options.
6	An error occurred in checking the audio status, but the cause of the error was not returned by the system.

Remarks

This property returns the conditions necessary to support speech input, including the status of the audio device. You can check this property before you call the **Listen** method to better ensure its success.

When speech input is enabled in the Agent property sheet (Advanced Character Options), querying this property will load the associated engine, if it is not already loaded, and start speech services. That is, the Listening key is available, and the Listening Tip is automatically displayable. (The Listening key and Listening Tip are only enabled if they are also enabled in Advanced Character Options.) However, if you query the property when speech is disabled, the server does not start speech services.

This property only applies to your client application's use of the character; the setting does not affect other clients of the character or other characters of your client application.

See also Listen method

Top Property

Description

Returns or sets the top edge of the specified character's frame.

Syntax

*agent.***Characters** (*"CharacterID"*)**.Top** [= *value*]

Part	Description
value	A Long integer that specifies the character's top edge.

Remarks

The **Top** property is always expressed in pixels, relative to screen origin (upper left). This property's setting applies to all clients of the character.

Even though the character appears in an irregularly shaped region window, the location of the character is based on the external dimensions of the rectangular animation frame used when the character was compiled with the Microsoft Agent Character Editor.

Use the **MoveTo** method to change the character's location.

See also **Left** property, **MoveTo** method

TTSModelID Property

Description
Returns or sets the TTS engine mode used for the character.

Syntax
*agent.***Characters** (*"CharacterID"*)**.TTSModelID** [= *ModeID*]

Part	Description
ModeID	A string expression that corresponds to the mode ID of a speech engine.

Remarks
This property determines the TTS (text-to-speech) engine mode ID for a character's spoken output. The mode ID for a TTS engine is a formatted string defined by the speech vendor that uniquely identifies the engine's mode.

See also Appendix E, "Microsoft Speech Engines for Microsoft Agent."

Setting this property overrides the server's attempt to load an engine based on the character's compiled TTS setting and the character's current **LanguageID** setting. However, if you specify a mode ID for an engine that isn't installed or if the user has disabled speech output in the Microsoft Agent property sheet (**AudioOutput.Enabled = False**), the server raises an error.

If you do not (or have not successfully) set a TTS mode ID for the character, the server checks to see if the character's compiled TTS mode setting matches the character's **LanguageID** setting, and that the associated TTS engine is installed. If so, the TTS mode used by the character for spoken output and this property returns that mode ID. If not, the server requests a compatible SAPI speech engine that matches the **LanguageID** of the character, as well as the gender and age set for the character's compiled mode ID. If you have not set the character's **LanguageID**, its **LanguageID** is the current user language. If no matching engine can be found, querying for this property returns an empty string for the engine's mode ID. Similarly, if you query this property when the user has disabled speech output in the Microsoft Agent property sheet (**AudioOutput.Enabled = False**), the value will be an empty string.

Querying or setting this property will load the associated engine (if it is not already loaded). However, if the engine specified in the character's compiled TTS setting is installed and matches the character's language ID setting, the engine will be loaded when the character loads.

This property applies only to your client application's use of the character; the setting does not affect other clients of the character or other characters of your client application.

Microsoft Agent's speech engine requirements are based on the Microsoft Speech API. Engines supporting Microsoft Agent's SAPI requirements can be installed and used with Agent.

Note This property also returns the empty string if you have no compatible sound support installed on your system.

Note Setting the **TTSModeID** can fail if Speech.dll is not installed and the engine you specify does not match the character's compiled TTS mode setting.

Note Querying this property does not typically return an error. However, if the speech engine takes an abnormally long time to load, you may get an error indicating that the query timed out.

See also   LanguageID property

Version Property

Description
Returns version of the character.

Syntax
*agent.***Characters** (*"CharacterID"*)**.Version**

Remarks
The **Version** property returns a string that corresponds to the version of the standard animation set definition for which the character was compiled. The character's version number is automatically set when you build it with the Microsoft Agent Character Editor.

VisibilityCause Property

Description
Returns an integer value that specifies what caused the character's visible state.

Syntax
agent.**Characters("***CharacterID***").VisibilityCause**

Value	Description
0	The character has not been shown.
1	User hid the character using the command on the character's taskbar icon pop-up menu or using speech input.
2	The user showed the character.
3	Your application hid the character.
4	Your application showed the character.
5	Another client application hid the character.
6	Another client application showed the character.
7	The user hid the character using the command on the character's pop-up menu.

Remarks
You can use this property to determine what caused the character to move when more than one application is sharing (has loaded) the same character. These values are the same as those returned by the **Show** and **Hide** events.

See also **Hide** event, **Show** event, **Hide** method, **Show** method

Visible Property

Description
Returns a Boolean indicating whether the character is visible.

Syntax
agent.**Characters ("***CharacterID***").Visible**

Value	Description
True	The character is displayed.
False	The character is hidden (not visible).

Remarks

This property indicates whether the character's frame is being displayed. It does not necessarily mean that there is an image on the screen. For example, this property returns **True** even when the character is positioned off the visible display area or when the current character frame contains no images. This property's setting applies to all clients of the character.

This property is read-only. To make a character visible or hidden, use the **Show** or **Hide** methods.

Width Property

Description

Returns or sets the width of the frame for the specified character.

Syntax

*agent.***Characters** (*"CharacterID"*)**.Width** [= *value*]

Part	Description
value	A Long integer that specifies the character's frame width.

Remarks

The **Width** property is always expressed in pixels. This property's setting applies to all clients of the character.

Even though the character appears in an irregularly shaped region window, the location of the character is based on the external dimensions of the rectangular animation frame used when the character was compiled with the Microsoft Agent Character Editor.

The Commands Collection Object

The Microsoft Agent server maintains a list of commands that are currently available to the user. This list includes commands that the server defines for general interaction (such as Hide and Open The Voice Commands Window), the list of available (but non-input-active) clients, and the commands defined by the current active client. The first two sets of commands are global commands; that is, they are available at any time, regardless of the input-active client. Client-defined commands are available only when that client is input-active and the character is visible.

Each client application can define a collection of commands called the **Commands** collection. To add a command to the collection, use the **Add** or **Insert** method. Although you can specify a command's properties with separate statements, for optimum code performance, specify all of a command's properties in the **Add** or **Insert** method statement. For each command in the collection, you can determine whether user access to the command appears in the character's pop-up menu, in the Voice Commands Window, in both, or in neither. For example, if you want a command to appear on the pop-up menu for the character, set the command's **Caption** and **Visible** properties. To display the command in the Voice Commands Window, set the command's **VoiceCaption** and **Voice** properties.

A user can access the individual commands in your **Commands** collection only when your client application is input-active. Therefore, when you may be sharing the character with other client applications you'll typically want to set the **Caption**, **VoiceCaption**, and **Voice** properties for the **Commands** collection object as well as for the commands in the collection. This places an entry for your **Commands** collection in a character's pop-up menu and in the Voice Commands Window.

When the user switches to your client by choosing its **Commands** entry, the server automatically makes your client input-active, notifying your client application using the **ActivateInput** event and makes the commands in its collection available. The server also notifies the client that it is no longer input-active with the **DeActivateInput** event. This enables the server to present and accept only the commands that apply to the current input-active client's context. It also serves to avoid command-name collisions between clients.

A client can also explicitly request to make itself the input-active client using the **Activate** method. This method also supports setting your application to not be the input-active client. You may want to use this method when you are sharing a character with another application, setting your application to be input-active when your application window gets focus and not input-active when it loses focus.

Similarly, you can use the **Activate** method to set your application to be (or not be) the active client of the character. The active client is the client that receives input when its character is the topmost character. When this status changes, the server notifies your application with the **ActiveClientChange** event.

When a character's pop-up menu displays, changes to the properties of a **Commands** collection or the commands in its collection do not appear until the user redisplays the menu. However, the Commands Window does display changes as they happen.

Commands Object Methods

The server supports the following methods for the **Commands** collection object:

AddCommand, Insert, Remove, RemoveAll

Add Method

Description

Adds a **Command** object to the **Commands** collection.

Syntax

agent.**Characters** (*"CharacterID"*).**Commands.Add** *Name, Caption, Voice,* _
Enabled, Visible

Part	Description
Name	Required. A string value corresponding to the ID you assign for the command.
Caption	Optional. A string value corresponding to the name that will appear in the character's pop-up menu and in the Commands Window when the client application is input-active. For more information, see the Command object's **Caption** property.
Voice	Optional. A string value corresponding to the words or phrase to be used by the speech engine for recognizing this command. For more information on formatting alternatives for the string, see the **Command** object's **Voice** property.
Enabled	Optional. A Boolean value indicating whether the command is enabled. The default value is **True**. For more information, see the **Command** object's **Enabled** property.
Visible	Optional. A Boolean value indicating whether the command is visible in the character's pop-up menu for the character when the client application is input-active. The default value is **True**. For more information, see the **Command** object's **Visible** property.

Remarks

The value of a **Command** object's **Name** property must be unique within its **Commands** collection. You must remove a **Command** before you can create a new **Command** with the same **Name** property setting. Attempting to create a **Command** with a **Name** property that already exists raises an error.

This method also returns a **Command** object. This enables you to declare an object and assign a **Command** to it when you call the **Add** method.

```
Dim Cmd1 as IAgentCtlCommandEx
Set Cmd1 = Genie.Commands.Add("my first command", "Test", "Test", True, True)
Cmd1.VoiceCaption = "this is a test"
```

See also Insert **method**, Remove **method**, RemoveAll **method**

Command Method

Description

Returns a **Command** object in a **Commands** collection.

Syntax

agent.**Characters** (**"***CharacterID***"**).**Commands.Command** *"Name"*

Remarks

You can use this method to access a **Command** object's properties.

Note This method may be required for some programming languages. It is not required for VBScript or Visual Basic. For further information on specifying **Command** methods, see Command Object Properties.

Insert Method

Description

Inserts a **Command** object in the **Commands** collection.

Syntax

agent.**Characters** (**"***CharacterID***"**).**Commands.Insert** *Name, RefName, Before, _ Caption, Voice, Enabled, Visible*

Part	Description
Name	Required. A string value corresponding to the ID you assign to the **Command**.
RefName	Required. A string value corresponding to the name (ID) of the command just above or below where you want to insert the new command.
Before	Optional. A Boolean value indicating whether to insert the new command before the command specified by RefName.
	True (Default). The new command will be inserted before the referenced command.
	False The new command will be inserted after the referenced command.
Caption	Optional. A string value corresponding to the name that will appear in the character's pop-up menu and in the Commands Window when the client application is input-active. For more information, see the Command object's **Caption** property.

Part	Description
Voice	Optional. A string value corresponding to the words or phrase to be used by the speech engine for recognizing this command. For more information on formatting alternatives for the string, see the **Command** object's **Voice** property.
Enabled	Optional. A Boolean value indicating whether the command is enabled. The default value is **True**. For more information, see the **Command** object's **Enabled** property.
Visible	Optional. A Boolean value indicating whether the command is visible in the Commands Window when the client application is input-active. The default value is **True**. For more information, see the **Command** object's **Visible** property.

Remarks

The value of a **Command** object's **Name** property must be unique within its **Commands** collection. You must remove a **Command** before you can create a new **Command** with the same **Name** property setting. Attempting to create a **Command** with a **Name** property that already exists raises an error.

This method also returns a **Command** object. This enables you to declare an object and assign a **Command** to it when you call the **Insert** method.

```
Dim Cmd2 as IAgentCtlCommandEx
Set Cmd2 = Genie.Commands.Insert _
   ("my second command", "my first command",_ True, "Test", "Test", True, True)
Cmd2.VoiceCaption = "this is a test"
```

See also **Add** method, **Remove** method, **RemoveAll** method

Remove Method

Description

Removes a **Command** object from the **Commands** collection.

Syntax

agent.**Characters** (*"CharacterID"*).**Commands.Remove** *Name*

Part	Description
Name	Required. A string value corresponding to the ID for the command.

Remarks

When a **Command** object is removed from the collection, it no longer appears when the character's pop-up menu is displayed or in the Commands Window when your client application is input-active.

See also **RemoveAll** method

RemoveAll Method

Description

Removes all **Command** objects from the **Commands** collection.

Syntax

agent.**Characters** (*"CharacterID"*)**.Commands.RemoveAll**

Remarks

When a **Command** object is removed from the collection, it no longer appears when the character's pop-up menu is displayed or in the Commands Window when your client application is input-active.

See also **Remove** method

Commands Object Properties

The server supports the following properties for the **Commands** collection:

Caption, Count, DefaultCommand, FontName, FontSize, GlobalVoiceCommandsEnabled, HelpContextID, Visible, Voice, VoiceCaption

An entry for the **Commands** collection can appear in both the pop-up menu and the Voice Commands Window for a character. To make this entry appear in the pop-up menu, set its **Caption** property. To include the entry in the Voice Commands Window, set its **VoiceCaption** property. (For backward compatibility, if there is no **VoiceCaption**, the **Caption** setting is used)

The following table summarizes how the properties of a **Commands** object affect the entry's presentation:

Caption Property	Voice-Caption Property	Voice Property	Visible Property	Appears in Character's Pop-up Menu	Appears in Commands Voice Window
Yes	Yes	Yes	True	Yes, using **Caption**	Yes, using **VoiceCaption**
Yes	Yes	No[1]	True	Yes, using **Caption**	No
Yes	Yes	Yes	False	No	Yes, using **VoiceCaption**
Yes	Yes	No[1]	False	No	No
No[1]	Yes	Yes	True	No	Yes, using **VoiceCaption**
No[1]	Yes	Yes	False	No	Yes, using **VoiceCaption**
No[1]	Yes	No[1]	True	No	No
No[1]	Yes	No[1]	False	No	No
Yes	No[1]	Yes	True	Yes, using **Caption**	Yes, using **Caption**
Yes	No[1]	No[1]	True	Yes	No
Yes	No[1]	Yes	False	No	Yes, using **Caption**
Yes	No[1]	No[1]	False	No	No
No[1]	No[1]	Yes	True	No	No[2]
No[1]	No[1]	Yes	False	No	No[2]
No[1]	No[1]	No[1]	True	No	No
No[1]	No[1]	No[1]	False	No	No

[1] If the property setting is null. In some programming languages, an empty string may not be interpreted as the same as a null string.

[2] The command is still voice-accessible, and appears in the Voice Commands Window as "(command undefined)".

Caption Property

Description
Determines the text displayed for the **Commands** object in the character's pop-up menu.

Syntax
agent.**Characters** ("*CharacterID*").**Commands.Caption** [= *string*]

Part	Description
string	A string expression that evaluates to the text displayed as the caption.

Remarks

Setting the **Caption** property for your **Commands** collection defines how it will appear on the character's pop-up menu when its **Visible** property is set to **True** and your application is not the input-active client. To specify an access key (unlined mnemonic) for your **Caption**, include an ampersand (&) character before that character.

If you define commands for a **Commands** collection that has a **Caption**, you typically also define a **Caption** for its associated **Commands** collection.

Count Property

Description

Returns a Long integer (read-only property) that specifies the count of **Command** objects in the **Commands** collection.

Syntax

agent.**Characters** (*"CharacterID"*).**Commands.Count**

Remarks

Count includes only the number of **Command** objects you define in your **Commands** collection. Server or other client entries are not included.

DefaultCommand Property

Description

Returns or sets the default command of the **Commands** object.

Syntax

agent.**Characters** (*"CharacterID"*).**Commands.DefaultCommand** [= *string*]

Part	Description
string	A string value identifying the name (ID) of the **Command**.

Remarks

This property enables you to set a **Command** in your **Commands** collection as the default command, rendering it bold. This does not actually change command handling or double-click events.

This property applies only to your client application's use of the character; the setting does not affect other clients of the character or other characters of your client application.

FontName Property

Description
Returns or sets the font used in the character's pop-up menu.

Syntax
*agent.***Characters** (*"CharacterID"*)**.Commands.FontName** [= *Font*]

Part	Description
Font	A string value corresponding to the font's name.

Remarks
The **FontName** property defines the font used to display text in the character's pop-up menu. The default value for the font setting is based on the menu font setting for the character's **LanguageID** setting, or—if that's not set—the user default language ID setting.

This property applies only to your client application's use of the character; the setting does not affect other clients of the character or other characters of your client application.

FontSize Property

Description
Returns or sets the font size used in the character's pop-up menu.

Syntax
*agent.***Characters** (*"CharacterID"*)**.Commands.FontSize** [= *Points*]

Part	Description
Points	A Long integer value specifying the font size in points.

Remarks
The **FontSize** property defines the point size of the font used to display text in the character's pop-up menu. The default value for the font setting is based on the menu font setting for the character's **LanguageID** setting, or—if that's not set—the user default language setting.

This property applies only to your client application's use of the character; the setting does not affect other clients of the character or other characters of your client application.

GlobalVoiceCommandsEnabled Property

Description

Returns or sets whether voice is enabled for Agent's global commands.

Syntax

*agent.***Characters** (*"CharacterID"*)**.Commands.GlobalVoiceCommandsEnabled**
[= *boolean*]

Part	Description
boolean	A Boolean expression that indicates whether voice parameters for Agent's global commands are enabled.
	True (Default) Voice parameters are enabled.
	False Voice parameters are disabled.

Remarks

Microsoft Agent automatically adds voice parameters (grammar) for opening and closing the Voice Commands Window and for showing and hiding the character. If you set **GlobalVoiceCommandsEnabled** to **False**, Agent disables any voice parameters for these commands as well as the voice parameters for the **Caption** of other client's **Commands** objects. This enables you to eliminate these from your client's current active grammar. However, because this potentially blocks voice access to other clients, reset this property to **True** after processing the user's voice input.

Disabling the property does not affect the character's pop-up menu. The global commands added by the server will still appear. You cannot remove them from the pop-up menu.

HelpContextID Property

Description

Returns or sets an associated context number for the **Commands** object. Used to provide context-sensitive Help for the **Commands** object.

Syntax

*agent.***Characters** (*"CharacterID"*)**.Commands.HelpContextID** [= *Number*]

Part	Description
Number	An integer specifying a valid context number.

Remarks

If you've created a Windows Help file for your application and set the character's **HelpFile** property, Agent automatically calls Help when **HelpModeOn** is set to **True** and the user selects the **Commands** object. If you set a context number for **HelpContextID**, Agent calls Help and searches for the topic identified by that context number.

This property applies only to your client application's use of the character; the setting does not affect other clients of the character or other characters of your client application.

Note Building a Help file requires the Microsoft Windows Help Compiler.

See also **HelpFile** property

Visible Property

Description

Returns or sets a value that determines whether your **Commands** collection's caption appears in the character's pop-up menu.

Syntax

agent.**Characters** (*"CharacterID"*).**Commands.Visible** [= *boolean*]

Part	Description
boolean	A Boolean expression specifying whether your **Commands** object appears in the character's pop-up menu.
	True The **Caption** for your **Commands** collection appears.
	False The **Caption** for your **Commands** collection does not appear.

Remarks

For the caption to appear in the character's pop-up menu when your application is not the input-active client, this property must be set to **True** and the **Caption** property set for your Commands collection. In addition, this property must be set to **True** for commands in your collection to appear in the pop-up menu when your application is input-active.

Voice Property

Description

Returns or sets the text that is passed to the speech engine (for recognition).

Syntax

agent.**Characters** (*"CharacterID"*).**Commands.Voice** [= *string*]

Part	Description
string	A string value corresponding to the words or phrase to be used by the speech engine for recognizing this command.

Remarks

If you do not supply this parameter, the **VoiceCaption** for your **Commands** object will not appear in the Voice Commands Window.

The string expression you supply can include square bracket characters ([ ]) to indicate optional words and vertical bar characters, (|) to indicate alternative strings. Alternates must be enclosed in parentheses. For example, "(hello [there] | hi)" tells the speech engine to accept "hello," "hello there," or "hi" for the command. Remember to include appropriate spaces between the text that's in brackets or parentheses and the text that's not in brackets or parentheses. You can use the star (*) operator to specify zero or more instances of the words included in the group or the plus (+) operator to specify one or more instances. For example, the following results in a grammar that supports "try this", "please try this", "please please try this", with unlimited iterations of "please":

```
"please* try this"
```

The following grammar format excludes "try this" because the + operator defines at least one instance of "please":

```
"please+ try this"
```

The repetition operators follow normal rules of precedence and apply to the immediately preceding text item. For example, the following grammar results in "New York" and "New York York", but not "New York New York":

```
"New York+"
```

Therefore, you typically want to use these operators with the grouping characters. For example, the following grammar includes both "New York" and "New York New York":

```
"(New York)+"
```

Repetition operators are useful when you want to compose a grammar that includes a repeated sequence such as a phone number or specification of a list of items:

```
"call (one|two|three|four|five|six|seven|eight|nine|zero|oh)*"
"I'd like (cheese|pepperoni|pineapple|canadian bacon|mushrooms|and)+"
```

Although the operators can also be used with the optional square-brackets grouping character, doing so may reduce the efficiency of Agent's processing of the grammar.

You can also use an ellipsis (...) to support *word spotting*, that is, telling the speech recognition engine to ignore words spoken in this position in the phrase (sometimes called *garbage* words). When you use ellipses, the speech engine recognizes only specific words in the string regardless of when spoken with adjacent words or phrases. For example, if you set this property to "[...] check mail [...]", the speech recognition engine will match phrases like "please check mail" or "check mail please" to this command. Ellipses can be used anywhere within a string. However, be careful using this technique as voice settings with ellipses may increase the potential of unwanted matches.

When defining the word grammar for your command, include at least one word that is required; that is, avoid supplying only optional words. In addition, make sure that the word includes only pronounceable words and letters. For numbers, it is better to spell out the word than use an ambiguous representation. For example, "345" is not a good grammar form. Similarly, instead of "IEEE", use "I triple E". also, omit any punctuation or symbols. For example, instead of "the #1 $10 pizza!", use "the number one ten dollar pizza". Including non-pronounceable characters or symbols for one command may cause the speech engine to fail to compile the grammar for all your commands. Finally, make your voice parameter as distinct as reasonably possible from other voice commands you define. The greater the similarity between the voice grammar for commands, the more likely the speech engine will make a recognition error. You can also use the confidence scores to better distinguish between two commands that may have similar or similar-sounding voice grammar.

You can include in your grammar words in the form of "*text\pronunciation*", where *text* is the text displayed and *pronunciation* is text that clarifies the pronunciation. For example, the grammar, "1st\first", would be recognized when the user says "first", but the **Command** event will return the text, "1st\first". You can also use IPA (International Phonetic Alphabet) to specify a pronunciation by beginning the pronunciation with a pound sign character ("#"), then the text representing the IPA pronunciation.

For Japanese speech recognition engines, you can define grammar in the form "*kana\kanji*", reducing the alternative pronunciations and increasing the accuracy. (The ordering is reversed for backward compatibility.) This is particularly important for the pronunciation of proper names in Kanji. However, you can just pass in Kanji, without the Kana, in which case the engine should listen for all acceptable pronunciations for the Kanji. You can also pass in just Kana.

Also note that for languages such as Japanese, Chinese, and Thai, that do not use space characters to designate word breaks, insert a Unicode zero-width space character (0x200B) to indicate logical word breaks.

Except for errors using the grouping or repetition formatting characters, Agent will not report errors in your grammar, unless the engine itself reports the error. If you pass text in your grammar that the engine fails to compile, but the engine does not handle and return as an error, Agent cannot report the error. Therefore, the client application must be carefully define grammar for the **Voice** property.

Note The grammar features available may depend on the speech recognition engine. You may want to check with the engine's vendor to determine what grammar options are supported. Use the **SRModeID** to use a specific engine.

VoiceCaption Property

Description
Returns or sets the text displayed for the **Commands** object in the Voice Commands Window.

Syntax
*agent.***Characters** (*"CharacterID"*)**.Commands.VoiceCaption** [= *string*]

Part	Description
string	A string expression that evaluates to the text displayed.

Remarks
If you set the **Voice** property of your **Commands** collection, you will typically also set its **VoiceCaption** property. The **VoiceCaption** text setting appears in the Voice Commands Window when your client application is input-active and the character is visible. If this property is not set, the setting for the **Commands** collection's **Caption** property determines the text displayed. When neither the **VoiceCaption** or **Caption** property is set, then commands in the collection appear in the Voice Commands Window under "(undefined command)" when your client application becomes input-active.

The **VoiceCaption** setting also determines the text displayed in the Listening Tip to indicate the commands for which the character listens.

See also **Caption** property

The Command Object

A **Command** object is an item in a **Commands** collection. The server provides the user access to your **Command** objects when your client application becomes input-active.

To access the property of a **Command** object, you reference it in its collection using its **Name** property. In VBScript and Visual Basic you can use the **Name** property directly:

```
agent.Characters("CharacterID").Commands("Name").property [= value]
```

For programming languages that don't support collections, use the **Command** method:

```
agent.Characters("CharacterID").Commands.Command("Name").property [= value]
```

You can also reference a Command object by creating a reference to it. In Visual Basic, declare an object variable and use the Set statement to create the reference:

```
Dim Cmd1 as Object
...
Set Cmd1 = Agent.Characters("MyCharacterID").Commands("SampleCommand")
...
Cmd1.Enabled = True
```

In Visual Basic 5.0, you can also declare the object as type **IAgentCtlCommandEx** and create the reference. This convention enables early binding, which results in better performance:

```
Dim Cmd1 as IAgentCtlCommandEx
...
Set Cmd1 = Agent.Characters("MyCharacterID").Commands("SampleCommand")
...
Cmd1.Enabled = True
```

In VBScript, you can declare a reference as a particular type, but you can still declare the variable and set it to the **Command** in the collection:

```
Dim Cmd1
...
Set Cmd1 = Agent.Characters("MyCharacterID").Commands("SampleCommand")
...
Cmd1.Enabled = True
```

A command may appear in either the character's pop-up menu and the Commands Window, or in both. To appear in the pop-up menu it must have a caption and have the **Visible** property set to **True**. In addition, its Commands collection object **Visible** property must also be set to **True**. To appear in the Commands

Window, a **Command** must have its **Caption** and **Voice** properties set. Note that a character's pop-up menu entries do not change while the menu displays. If you add or remove commands or change their properties while the character's pop-up menu is displayed, the menu displays those changes whenever the user next displays it. However, the Commands Window dynamically reflects any changes you make.

The following table summarizes how the properties of a **Command** affect its presentation:

Caption Property	Voice-Caption Property	Voice Property	Visible Property	Enabled Property	Appears in Character's Pop-up Menu	Appears in Commands Voice Window
Yes	Yes	Yes	True	True	Normal, using **Caption**	Yes, using **VoiceCaption**
Yes	Yes	Yes	True	False	Disabled, using **Caption**	No
Yes	Yes	Yes	False	True	Does not appear	Yes, using **VoiceCaption**
Yes	Yes	Yes	False	False	Does not appear	No
Yes	Yes	No[1]	True	True	Normal, using **Caption**	No
Yes	Yes	No[1]	True	False	Disabled, using **Caption**	No
Yes	Yes	No[1]	False	True	Does not appear	No
Yes	Yes	No[1]	False	False	Does not appear	No
No[1]	Yes	Yes	True	True	Does not appear	Yes, using **VoiceCaption**
No[1]	Yes	Yes	True	False	Does not appear	No
No[1]	Yes	Yes	False	True	Does not appear	Yes, using **VoiceCaption**
No[1]	Yes	Yes	False	False	Does not appear	No
No[1]	Yes	No[1]	True	True	Does not appear	No
No[1]	Yes	No[1]	True	False	Does not appear	No
No[1]	Yes	No[1]	False	True	Does not appear	No
No[1]	Yes	No[1]	False	False	Does not appear	No
Yes	No[1]	Yes	True	True	Normal, using **Caption**	Yes, using **Caption**
Yes	No[1]	Yes	True	False	Disabled, using **Caption**	No

[1] If the property setting is null. In some programming languages, an empty string may not be interpreted the same as a null string.

Caption Property	Voice-Caption Property	Voice Property	Visible Property	Enabled Property	Appears in Character's Pop-up Menu	Appears in Commands Voice Window
Yes	No[1]	Yes	False	True	Does not appear	Yes, using **Caption**
Yes	No[1]	Yes	False	False	Does not appear	No
Yes	No[1]	No[1]	True	True	Normal, using **Caption**	No
Yes	No[1]	No[1]	True	False	Disabled, using **Caption**	No
Yes	No[1]	No[1]	False	True	Does not appear	No
Yes	No[1]	No[1]	False	False	Does not appear	No
No[1]	No[1]	Yes	True	True	Does not appear	No[2]
No[1]	No[1]	Yes	True	False	Does not appear	No
No[1]	No[1]	Yes	False	True	Does not appear	No[2]
No[1]	No[1]	Yes	False	False	Does not appear	No
No[1]	No[1]	No[1]	True	True	Does not appear	No
No[1]	No[1]	No[1]	True	False	Does not appear	No
No[1]	No[1]	No[1]	False	True	Does not appear	No
No[1]	No[1]	No[1]	False	False	Does not appear	No

[1]   If the property setting is null. In some programming languages, an empty string may not be interpreted the same as a null string.

[2]   The command is still voice-accessible.

When the server receives input for one of your commands, it sends a **Command** event, and passes back the name of the **Command** as an attribute of the **UserInput** object. You can then use conditional statements to match and process the **Command**.

Command Object Properties

The following **Command** properties are supported:

Caption, Confidence, ConfidenceText, Enabled, HelpContextID, Visible, Voice, VoiceCaption

Caption Property

Description

Determines the text displayed for a **Command** in the specified character's pop-up menu.

Syntax

agent.**Characters** (*"CharacterID"*).**Commands**(*"name"*).**Caption** [= *string*]

Part	Description
string	A string expression that evaluates to the text displayed as the caption for the **Command**.

Remarks

To specify an access key (unlined mnemonic) for your **Caption**, include an ampersand (&) character before that character.

If you don't define a **VoiceCaption** for your command, your **Caption** setting will be used.

Confidence Property

Description

Returns or sets whether the client's **ConfidenceText** appears in the Listening Tip.

Syntax

agent.**Characters** (*"CharacterID"*).**Commands**(*"name"*).**Confidence** [= *Number*]

Part	Description
Number	A numeric expression that evaluates to a Long integer that identifies confidence value for the **Command**.

Remarks

If the returned confidence value of the best match (**UserInput.Confidence**) does not exceed value you set for the **Confidence** property, the text supplied in **ConfidenceText** is displayed in the Listening Tip.

ConfidenceText Property

Description

Returns or sets the client's **ConfidenceText** that appears in the Listening Tip.

Syntax

agent.**Characters** (*"CharacterID"*).**Commands**(*"name"*).**ConfidenceText** [= *string*]

Part	Description
string	A string expression that evaluates to the text for the **ConfidenceText** for the **Command**.

Remarks

When the returned confidence value of the best match (**UserInput.Confidence**) does not exceed the **Confidence** setting, the server displays the text supplied in **ConfidenceText** in the Listening Tip.

Enabled Property

Description

Returns or sets whether the **Command** is enabled in the specified character's pop-up menu.

Syntax

agent.**Characters** (*"CharacterID"*).**Commands**(*"name"*).**Enabled** [= *boolean*]

Part	Description
boolean	A Boolean expression specifying whether the **Command** is enabled.
	True The **Command** is enabled.
	False The **Command** is disabled.

Remarks

If the **Enabled** property is set to **True**, the **Command** object's caption appears as normal text in the character's pop-up menu when the client application is input-active. If the **Enabled** property is **False**, the caption appears as unavailable (disabled) text. A disabled **Command** is also not accessible for voice input.

HelpContextID Property

Description

Returns or sets an associated context number for the **Command** object. Used to provide context-sensitive Help for the **Command** object.

Syntax

agent.**Characters** (*"CharacterID"*).**Commands**(*"name"*).**HelpContextID** [= *Number*]

Part	Description
Number	An integer specifying a valid context number.

Remarks

If you've created a Windows Help file for your application and set the character's **HelpFile** property to the file, Agent automatically calls Help when **HelpModeOn** is set to **True** and the user selects the command. If you set a context number in the **HelpContextID**, Agent calls Help and searches for the topic identified by the current context number. The current context number is the value of **HelpContextID** for the command.

This property applies only to your client application's use of the character; the setting does not affect other clients of the character or other characters of your client application.

Note Building a Help file requires the Microsoft Windows Help Compiler.

See also **HelpFile** property

Visible Property

Description

Returns or sets whether the **Command** is visible in the character's pop-up menu.

Syntax

agent.**Characters** ("*CharacterID*").**Commands**("*name*").**Visible** [= *boolean*]

Part	Description
boolean	A Boolean expression specifying whether the **Command**'s caption appears in the character's pop-up menu.
	True (Default) The caption appears.
	False The caption does not appear.

Remarks

Set this property to **False** when you want to include voice input for your own interfaces without having them appear in the pop-up menu for the character. If you set a **Command** object's **Caption** property to the empty string (""), the caption text will not appear in the pop-up menu (for example, as a blank line), regardless of its **Visible** property setting.

The **Visible** property setting of a **Command** object's parent **Commands** collection does not affect the **Visible** property setting of the **Command**.

Voice Property

Description

Returns or sets the text that is passed to the speech engine grammar (for recognition) for matching this **Command** for the character.

Syntax

agent.**Characters** (*"CharacterID"*).**Commands** (*"name"*).**Voice** [= *string*]

Part	Description
string	A string expression corresponding to the words or phrase to be used by the speech engine for recognizing this **Command**.

Remarks

If you do not supply this parameter, the **VoiceCaption** for your **Commands** object will not appear in the Voice Commands Window. If you specify a **Voice** parameter but not a **VoiceCaption** (or **Caption**), the command will not appear in the Voice Commands Window, but it will be voice-accessible when the client application becomes input-active.

Your string expression can include square bracket characters ([ ]) to indicate optional words and vertical bar characters (|) to indicate alternative strings. Alternates must be enclosed in parentheses. For example, "(hello [there] | hi)" tells the speech engine to accept "hello," "hello there," or "hi" for the command. Remember to include appropriate spaces between the text that's in brackets or parentheses and the text that's not in brackets or parentheses.

You can use the star (*) operator to specify zero or more instances of the words included in the group or the plus (+) operator to specify one or more instances. For example, the following results in a grammar that supports "try this", "please try this", "please please try this", with unlimited iterations of "please":

```
"please* try this"
```

The following grammar format excludes "try this" because the + operator defines at least one instance of "please":

```
"please+ try this"
```

The repetition operators follow normal rules of precedence and apply to the immediately preceding text item. For example, the following grammar results in "New York" and "New York York", but not "New York New York":

```
"New York+"
```

Therefore, you typically want to use these operators with the grouping characters. For example, the following grammar includes both "New York" and "New York New York":

```
"(New York)+"
```

Repetition operators are useful when you want to compose a grammar that includes a repeated sequence such as a phone number or specification of a list of items.

```
"call (one|two|three|four|five|six|seven|eight|nine|zero|oh)*"
"I'd like (cheese|pepperoni|pineapple|canadian bacon|mushrooms|and)+"
```

Although the operators can also be used with the optional square-brackets grouping character, doing so may reduce the efficiency of Agent's processing of the grammar.

You can also use an ellipsis (…) to support *word spotting*, that is, telling the speech recognition engine to ignore words spoken in this position in the phrase (sometimes called *garbage* words). Therefore, the speech engine recognizes only specific words in the string regardless of when spoken with adjacent words or phrases. For example, if you set this property to "[…] check mail […]", the speech recognition engine will match phrases like "please check mail" or "check mail please" to this command. Ellipses can be used anywhere within a string. However, be careful using this technique as it may increase the potential of unwanted matches.

When defining the word grammar for your command, include at least one word that is required; that is, avoid supplying only optional words. In addition, make sure that the word includes only pronounceable words and letters. For numbers, it is better to spell out the word rather than using an ambiguous representation. For example, "345" is not a good grammar form. Similarly, instead of "IEEE", use "I triple E". Also, omit any punctuation or symbols. For example, instead of "the #1 $10 pizza!", use "the number one ten dollar pizza". Including non-pronounceable characters or symbols for one command may cause the speech engine to fail to compile the grammar for all your commands. Finally, make your voice parameter as distinct as reasonably possible from other voice commands you define. The greater the similarity between the voice grammar for commands, the more likely the speech engine will make a recognition error. You can also use the confidence scores to better distinguish between two commands that may have similar or similar-sounding voice grammar.

You can include in your grammar words in the form of "*text\pronunciation*", where *text* is the text displayed and *pronunciation* is text that clarifies the pronunciation. For example, the grammar, "1st\first", would be recognized when the user says "first", but the **Command** event will return the text, "1st\first". You can also use IPA (International Phonetic Alphabet) to specify a pronunciation by beginning the pronunciation with a pound sign character ("#"), then include the text representing the IPA pronunciation.

For Japanese speech recognition engines, you can define grammar in the form "*kana\kanji*", reducing the alternative pronunciations and increasing the accuracy. (The ordering is reversed for backward compatibility.) This is particularly important for the pronunciation of proper names in Kanji. However, you can just pass in Kanji without the Kana, in which case the engine should listen for all acceptable pronunciations for the Kanji. You can also pass in just Kana.

Also note that for languages such as Japanese, Chinese, and Thai, that do not use space characters to designate word breaks, insert a Unicode zero-width space character (0x200B) to indicate logical word breaks.

Except for errors using the grouping or repetition formatting characters, Agent will not report errors in your grammar, unless the engine itself reports the error. If you pass text in your grammar that the engine fails to compile, but the engine does not handle and return as an error, Agent cannot report the error. Therefore, the client application must be carefully define grammar for the **Voice** property.

Note The grammar features available may depend on the speech recognition engine. You may want to check with the engine's vendor to determine what grammar options are supported. Use the **SRModeID** to use a specific engine.

The operation of this property depends on the state of the server's speech recognition property. For example, if speech recognition is disabled or not installed, this property has no effect.

VoiceCaption Property

Description
Sets or returns the text displayed for the **Command** object in the Voice Commands Window.

Syntax
agent.**Characters** ("*CharacterID*").**Commands**("*Name*").**VoiceCaption** [= *string*]

Part	Description
string	A string expression that evaluates to the text displayed.

Remarks

If you define a **Command** object in a **Commands** collection and set its **Voice** property, you will typically also set its **VoiceCaption** property. This text will appear in the Voice Commands Window when your client application is input-active and the character is visible. If this property is not set, the setting for the **Caption** property determines the text displayed. When neither the **VoiceCaption** nor **Caption** property is set, the command does not appear in the Voice Commands Window.

See also Caption property

The Balloon Object

Microsoft Agent supports textual captioning of **Speak** method using a cartoon word balloon. The **Think** method enables you to display text without audio output in a "thought" word balloon.

A character's initial word balloon window defaults are defined and compiled in the Microsoft Agent Character Editor. Once running, the balloon's **Enabled** and **Font** properties may be overridden by the user. If a user changes the word balloon's properties, they affect all characters. Both the **Speak** and **Think** word balloons use the same property settings for size. You can access the properties for a character's word balloon through the **Balloon** object, which is a child of the **Character** object.

The **Balloon** object supports the following properties:

BackColor, BorderColor, CharsPerLine, Enabled, FontCharSet, FontName, FontItalic, FontSize, FontStrikeThru, FontUnderline, ForeColor, NumberOfLines, Style, Visible

BackColor Property

Description

Returns the background color currently displayed in the word balloon window for the specified character.

Syntax

*agent.***Characters** (*"CharacterID"*)**.Balloon.BackColor**

Remarks

The valid range for a normal RGB color is 0 to 16,777,215 (&HFFFFFF). The high byte of a number in this range equals 0; the lower 3 bytes, from least to most significant byte, determine the amount of red, green, and blue, respectively. The red, green, and blue components are each represented by a number between 0 and 255 (&HFF).

BorderColor Property

Description

Returns the border color currently displayed for the word balloon window for the specified character.

Syntax

agent.**Characters** (*"CharacterID"*).**Balloon.BorderColor**

Remarks

The valid range for a normal RGB color is 0 to 16,777,215 (&HFFFFFF). The high byte of a number in this range equals 0; the lower 3 bytes, from least to most significant byte, determine the amount of red, green, and blue, respectively. The red, green, and blue components are each represented by a number between 0 and 255 (&HFF).

CharsPerLine Property

Description

Returns the characters per line supported for the word balloon for the specified character.

Syntax

agent.**Characters** (*"CharacterID"*).**Balloon.CharsPerLine**

Remarks

The **CharsPerLine** property returns the average number of characters (letters) being displayed in the word balloon as a Long integer value. You can set the value using the **Style** property.

See also **Style** property

Enabled Property

Description

Returns whether the word balloon is enabled for the specified character.

Syntax

agent.**Characters** (*"CharacterID"*).**Balloon.Enabled**

Value	Description
True	The balloon is enabled.
False	The balloon is disabled.

Remarks

The **Enabled** property returns a Boolean value specifying whether the balloon is enabled. The word balloon default state is set as part of a character's definition when the character is compiled in the Microsoft Agent Character Editor. If a character is defined to not support the word balloon, this property will always be **False** for the character.

FontBold Property

Description

Returns the font style currently displayed in the word balloon window for the specified character.

Syntax

agent.**Characters** (*"CharacterID"*).**Balloon.FontBold**

Value	Description
True	The balloon font is bold.
False	The balloon font is not bold.

Remarks

The default value for the font settings of a character's word balloon are set in the Microsoft Agent Character Editor. In addition, the user can override font settings for all characters in the Microsoft Agent property sheet.

FontCharSet Property

Description
Returns or sets the character set for the font displayed in the specified character's word balloon.

Syntax
agent.**Characters** (*"CharacterID"*).**Balloon.FontCharSet** [= *value*]

Part	Description
value	An integer value that specifies the character set used by the font. The following are some common settings for value:
0	Standard Windows characters (ANSI).
1	Default character set.
2	The symbol character set.
128	Double-byte character set (DBCS) unique to the Japanese version of Windows.
129	Double-byte character set (DBCS) unique to the Korean version of Windows.
134	Double-byte character set (DBCS) unique to the Simplified Chinese version of Windows.
136	Double-byte character set (DBCS) unique to the Traditional Chinese version of Windows.
255	Extended characters normally displayed by MS-DOS® applications.
	For other character set values, consult the Microsoft Win32 documentation.

Remarks
The default value for the character set of a character's word balloon is set in the Microsoft Agent Character Editor. In addition, the user can override the character-set settings for all characters in the Microsoft Agent property sheet.

This property applies only to your client application's use of the character; the setting does not affect other clients of the character or other characters of your client application.

Note If you are using a character that you did not compile, check the **FontName** and **FontCharSet** properties for the character to determine whether they are appropriate for your locale. You may need to set these values before using the **Speak** method to ensure appropriate text display within the word balloon.

See also FontNam property

FontItalic Property

Description

Returns the font style currently displayed in the word-balloon window for the specified character.

Syntax

agent.**Characters** (*"CharacterID"*).**Balloon.FontItalic**

Value	Description
True	The balloon font is italic.
False	The balloon font is not italic.

Remarks

The default value for the font settings of a character's word balloon are set in the Microsoft Agent Character Editor. In addition, the user can override font settings for all characters in the Microsoft Agent property sheet.

FontName Property

Description

Returns or sets the font used in the word balloon for the specified character.

Syntax

agent.**Characters** (*"CharacterID"*).**Balloon.FontName** [= *font*]

Part	Description
font	A string value corresponding to the font's name.

Remarks

The **FontName** property defines the font used to display text in the word balloon window as a string. The default value for the font settings of a character's word balloon are set in the Microsoft Agent Character Editor. In addition, the user can override font settings for all characters in the Microsoft Agent property sheet.

This property applies only to your client application's use of the character; the setting does not affect other clients of the character or other characters of your client application.

Note If you are using a character that you did not compile, check the **FontName** and **FontCharSet** properties for the character to determine whether they are appropriate for your locale. You may need to set these values before using the **Speak** method to ensure appropriate text display within the word balloon.

See also FontCharSet property

FontSize Property

Description
Returns or sets the font size supported for the word balloon for the specified character.

Syntax
agent.**Characters** (*"CharacterID"*).**Balloon.FontSize** [= *Points*]

Part	Description
Points	A Long integer value specifying the font size in points.

Remarks
The **FontSize** property returns a Long integer value specifying the current font size in points. The maximum value for **FontSize** is 2160 points.

The default value for the font settings of a character's word balloon are set in the Microsoft Agent Character Editor. In addition, the user can override font settings for all characters in the Microsoft Agent property sheet.

FontStrikeThru Property

Description
Returns the font style currently displayed in the word balloon window for the specified character.

Syntax
agent.**Characters** (*"CharacterID"*).**Balloon.FontStrikeThru**

Value	Description
True	The balloon font uses the strikethrough effect.
False	The balloon font does not use the strikethrough effect.

Remarks

The default value for the font settings of a character's word balloon are set in the Microsoft Agent Character Editor. In addition, the user can override font settings for all characters in the Microsoft Agent property sheet.

FontUnderline Property

Description

Returns the font style currently displayed in the word balloon window for the specified character.

Syntax

agent.**Characters** (*"CharacterID"*).**Balloon.FontUnderline**

Value	Description
True	The balloon font is underlined.
False	The balloon font is not underlined.

Remarks

The default value for the font settings of a character's word balloon are set in the Microsoft Agent Character Editor. In addition, the user can override font settings for all characters in the Microsoft Agent property sheet.

ForeColor Property

Description

Returns the foreground color currently displayed in the word balloon window for the specified character.

Syntax

agent.**Characters** (*"CharacterID"*).**Balloon.ForeColor**

Remarks

The **ForeColor** property returns a value that specifies the color of text in the word balloon. The valid range for a normal RGB color is 0 to 16,777,215 (&HFFFFFF). The high byte of a number in this range equals 0; the lower 3 bytes, from least to most significant byte, determine the amount of red, green, and blue, respectively. The red, green, and blue components are each represented by a number between 0 and 255 (&HFF).

NumberOfLines Property

Description

Returns the number of lines supported for the word balloon for the specified character.

Syntax

agent.**Characters** (*"CharacterID"*).**Balloon.NumberOfLines**

Remarks

The **NumberOfLines** property returns the number of lines of text as a Long integer value.

Style Property

Description

Returns or sets the character's word balloon output style.

Syntax

agent.**Characters** (*"CharacterID"*).**Balloon.Style** [= *Style*]

Part	Description
Style	An integer that represents the balloon's output style. The style setting is a bit field with bits corresponding to: balloon-on (bit 0), size-to-text (bit 1), auto-hide (bit 2), auto-pace (bit 3), number of characters per lines (bits 16-23), and number of lines (bits 24-31).

Remarks

When the balloon-on style bit is set to 1, the word balloon appears when a **Speak** or **Think** method is used, unless the user overrides this setting in the Microsoft Agent property sheet. When set to 0, a balloon does not appear.

When the size-to-text style bit is set to 1, the word balloon automatically sizes the height of the balloon to the current size of the text for the **Speak** or **Think** statement. When set to 0, the balloon's height is based on the **NumberOfLines** property setting. If this style bit is set to 1 and you attempt to set the **NumberOfLines** property, Agent raises an error.

When the auto-hide style bit is set to 1, the word balloon automatically hides when spoken output completes. When set to 0, the balloon remains displayed until the next **Speak** or **Think** call, the character is hidden, or the user clicks or drags the character.

When the auto-pace style bit is set to 1, the word balloon paces the output based on the current output rate, for example, one word at a time. When output exceeds the size of the balloon, the former text is automatically scrolled. When set to 0, all text included in a **Speak** or **Think** statement is displayed at once.

To retrieve just the value of the bottom four bits, **And** the value returned by **Style** with 255. To set a bit value, **Or** the value returned with the value of the bits you want set. To turn a bit off, **And** the value returned with one's complement of the bit:

```
Const BalloonOn = 1

' Turn the word balloon off
Genie.Balloon.Style = Genie.Balloon.Style And (Not BalloonOn)
Genie.Speak "No balloon"

' Turn the word balloon on
Genie.Balloon.Style = Genie.Balloon.Style Or BalloonOn
Genie.Speak "Balloon"
```

The **Style** property also returns the number of characters per line in the lower byte of the upper word and the number of lines in the high byte of the upper word. While this can be more easily read using the **CharsPerLine** and **NumberOfLines** properties, the **Style** property also enables you to set those values. For example, to change the number of lines, **OR** the existing value of the **Style** property with the product of the new value times 2^{24}. To set the number of characters per line, **OR** the existing value with the product of the new value times 2^{16}.

```
' Set the number of lines to 4
Genie.Balloon.Style = Genie.Balloon.Style OR (4*(2^24))
' Set the number of characters per line to 16
Genie.Balloon.Style = Genie.Balloon.Style OR (16*(2^16))
```

The **Style** property can be set even if the user has disabled balloon display using the Microsoft Agent property sheet. However, the values for the number of lines must be between 1 and 128 and the number characters per line must be between 8 and 255. If you provide an invalid value for the **Style** property, Agent will raise an error.

This property applies only to your client application's use of the character; the setting does not affect other clients of the character or other characters of your client application.

The defaults for these style bits are based on their settings when the character is compiled with the Microsoft Agent Character Editor.

Visible Property

Description
Returns or sets the visible setting for the word balloon for the specified character.

Syntax
agent.**Characters** (*"CharacterID"*).**Balloon.Visible** [= *boolean*]

Part	Description
boolean	A Boolean expression specifying whether the word balloon is visible.
	True The balloon is visible.
	False The balloon is hidden.

Remarks
If you follow a **Speak** or **Think** call with a statement to attempt to change the balloon's property, it may not affect the balloon's Visible state because the **Speak** or **Think** call gets queued, but the call setting the balloon's visible state does not. Therefore, only set this value when no **Speak** or **Think** calls are in the character's queue.

If you attempt to set this property while the character is speaking, moving, or being dragged, the property setting does not take effect until the preceding operation is completed.

Calling the **Speak** and **Think** methods automatically makes the balloon visible, setting the **Visible** property to **True**. If the character's balloon AutoHide property is enabled, the balloon is automatically hidden after the output text is spoken. Clicking or dragging a character that is not currently speaking also automatically hides the balloon even if its AutoHide setting is disabled. You can change the character's AutoHide setting using the balloon's **Style** property.

See also **Style** property

The AnimationNames Collection

The **AnimationNames** collection is a special collection that contains the list of animation names compiled for a character. You can use the collection to enumerate the names of the animations for a character. For example, in Visual Basic or VBScript (2.0 or later) you can access these names using the **For Each**...**Next** statements:

```
For Each Animation in Genie.AnimationNames
   Genie.Play Animation
Next
```

Items in the collection have no properties, so individual items cannot be accessed directly.

For .ACF characters, the collection returns all the animations that have been defined for the character, not just the ones that have been retrieved with the **Get** method.

The AudioOutput Object

The **AudioOutput** object provides access to audio output properties maintained by the server. The properties are read-only, but the user can change them in the Microsoft Agent property sheet.

If you declare an object variable of type **IAgentCtlAudioObjectEx**, you will not be able to access all properties for the **AudioOutput** object. While Agent also supports **IAgentCtlAudioObject**, this latter interface is provided only for backward compatibility and supports only those properties in previous releases:

Enabled, **SoundEffects**, **Status**

Enabled Property

Description
Returns a Boolean indicating whether audio (spoken) output is enabled.

Syntax
agent.**AudioOutput.Enabled**

Value	Description
True	(Default) Spoken audio output is enabled.
False	Spoken audio output is disabled.

Remarks
This property reflects the Play Audio Output option on the Output page of the Agent property sheet (Advanced Character Options). When the **Enabled** property returns **True**, the **Speak** method produces audio output if a compatible TTS engine is installed or you use sound files for spoken output. When it returns **False**, it means that speech output is not installed or has been disabled by the user. The property setting applies to all Agent characters and is read-only; only the user can set this property value.

See also AgentPropertyChange event

SoundEffects Property

Description

Returns a Boolean indicating whether sound effects (.WAV) files configured as part of a character's actions will play.

Syntax

agent.**AudioOutput.SoundEffects**

Value	Description
True	Character sound effects are enabled.
False	Character sound effects are disabled.

Remarks

This property reflects the Play Character Sound Effects option on the Output page of the Agent property sheet (Advanced Character Options). When the **SoundEffects** property returns **True**, sound effects included in a character's definition will be played. When **False**, the sound effects will not be played. The property setting affects all characters and is read-only; only the user can set this property value.

See also AgentPropertyChange event

Status Property

Description

Returns the status of the audio output channel.

Syntax

agent.**AudioOutput.Status**

Value	Description
0	The audio output channel is available (not busy).
1	There is no support for audio output; for example, because there is no sound card.
2	The audio output channel can't be opened (is busy); for example, because some other application is playing audio.
3	The audio output channel is busy because the server is processing user speech input.

Value	Description
4	The audio output channel is busy because a character is currently speaking.
5	The audio output channel is not busy, but it is waiting for user speech input.
6	There was some other (unknown) problem in attempting to access the audio output channel.

Remarks

This setting enables your client application to query the audio output channel, returning an Integer value that indicates the status of the audio output channel. You can use this to determine whether it is appropriate to have your character speak or whether it is appropriate to try to turn on Listening mode (using the **Listen** method).

See also **ListenComplete** event

The SpeechInput Object

The **SpeechInput** object provides access to the speech input properties maintained by the Agent server. The properties are read-only for client applications, but the user can change them in the Microsoft Agent property sheet. The server returns values only if a compatible speech engine has been installed and is enabled.

The **Engine**, **Installed**, and **Language** properties are no longer supported, but (for backward compatibility) return null values if queried. To query or set a speech recognition's mode, use the **SRModeID** property.

SpeechInput Properties

If a speech recognition engine is installed and enabled, accessing these properties will start the speech engine:

Enabled, **HotKey**, **ListeningTip**

Enabled Property

Description

Returns a Boolean value indicating whether speech input is enabled.

Syntax

agent.**SpeechInput.Enabled**

Value	Description
True	Speech input is enabled.
False	Speech input is disabled.

Remarks

The **Enabled** property reflects the Characters Listen For Input option on the Speech Input page of the Agent property sheet (Advanced Character Options). The property setting affects all Agent characters and is read-only; only the user can change this property.

See also **AgentPropertyChange** event

HotKey Property

Description

Returns a string that specifies the user's current setting for the Listening key.

Syntax

agent.**SpeechInput.HotKey**

Remarks

The **HotKey** property reflects the current setting of the Listening key on the Speech Input page of the Agent property sheet (Advanced Character Options). The property is read-only; only the user can change the setting.

See also **AgentPropertyChange** event

ListeningTip Property

Description

Returns a Boolean indicating the current user setting for the Listening Tip.

Syntax

agent.**SpeechInput.ListeningTip**

Value	Description
True	The Listening Tip is enabled.
False	The Listening Tip is disabled.

Remarks

The **ListeningTip** property indicates whether the Display Listening Tip option in the Microsoft Agent property sheet (Advanced Character Options) is enabled. When **ListeningTip** returns **True** and speech input is enabled, the server displays the tip window when the user presses the Listening key.

See also **AgentPropertyChange** event

The CommandsWindow Object

The **CommandsWindow** object provides access to properties of the Voice Commands Window. The Voice Commands Window is a shared resource primarily designed to enable users to view voice-enabled commands. If speech recognition is disabled, the Voice Commands Window still displays, with the text "Speech input disabled" (in the language of the character). If no speech engine is installed that matches the character's language setting the window displays, "Speech input not available." If the input-active client has not defined voice parameters for its commands and has disabled global voice commands, the window displays, "No voice commands." You can also query the properties of the Voice Commands Window regardless of whether speech input is disabled or a compatible speech engine is installed.

CommandsWindow Properties

Height, Left, Top, Visible, Width

Height Property

Description

Returns an integer value specifying the current height, in pixels, of the Voice Commands Window.

Syntax

agent.**CommandsWindow.Height**

Remarks

The server displays the Voice Commands Window based on the position and size set by the user.

Left Property

Description

Returns an integer value specifying the left edge, in pixels, of the Voice Commands Window.

Syntax

agent.**CommandsWindow.Left**

Remarks

The server displays the Voice Commands Window based on the position and size set by the user.

Top Property

Description

Returns an integer value specifying the top edge, in pixels, of the Voice Commands Window.

Syntax

agent.**CommandsWindow.Top**

Remarks

The server displays the Voice Commands Window based on the position and size set by the user.

Visible Property

Description

Returns or sets whether the Voice Commands Window is visible (open).

Syntax

agent.**CommandsWindow.Visible** [= *boolean*]

Part	Description
boolean	A Boolean expression specifying whether the Voice Commands Window is visible.
	True The window is visible.
	False The window is hidden (closed).

Remarks

The server displays the window based on the position and size set by the user.

Note The user can override this property.

Width Property

Description

Returns an integer value specifying the width, in pixels, of the Voice Commands Window.

Syntax

agent.**CommandsWindow.Width**

Remarks

The server displays the Voice Commands Window based on the position and size set by the user.

The PropertySheet Object

The **PropertySheet** object provides several properties you can use if you want to manipulate the character relative to the Microsoft Agent property sheet (also known as the Advanced Character Options window).

Height, Left, Page, Top, Visible, Width

If you query **Height, Left, Top,** and **Width** properties before the property sheet has ever been shown, their values return as zero (0). Once shown, these properties return the last position and size of the window (relative to your current screen resolution).

Height Property

Description

Returns an integer value specifying the current height, in pixels, of the Microsoft Agent property sheet window.

Syntax

agent.**PropertySheet.Height**

Remarks

The server displays the window based on the location set by the user.

Left Property

Description

Returns an integer value specifying the current left edge, in pixels, of the Microsoft Agent property sheet window.

Syntax

agent.**PropertySheet.Left**

Remarks

The server displays the window based on the location set by the user.

Page Property

Description

Returns or sets the page displayed in the Microsoft Agent property sheet window.

Syntax

agent.**PropertySheet.Page** [= *string*]

Part	Description
string	A string expression with one of the following values.
	"**Speech**" Displays the Speech Input page.
	"**Output**" Displays the Output page.
	"**Copyright**" Displays the Copyright page.

Remarks

If no speech engine is installed, setting **Page** to "**Speech**" has no effect. Also, the window's **Visible** property must be set to **True** for the user to see the page.

Note The user can override this property.

Top Property

Description

Returns an integer value specifying the current top edge, in pixels, of the Microsoft Agent property sheet window.

Syntax

agent.**PropertySheet.Top**

Remarks

The server displays the window based on the location set by the user.

Visible Property

Description

Returns or sets whether the Microsoft Agent property sheet window is visible (open).

Syntax

agent.**PropertySheet.Visible** [= *boolean*]

Part	Description
boolean	A Boolean expression specifying whether the window is visible.
	True The window is visible.
	False The window is hidden (closed).

Remarks

The server displays the window based on the location and size set by the user.

Note The user can override this property.

Width Property

Description

Returns an integer value specifying the current width, in pixels, of the Microsoft Agent property sheet window.

Syntax

agent.**PropertySheet.Width**

Remarks

The server displays the window based on the location set by the user.

C H A P T E R   5

Programming the
Microsoft Agent Server Interface

Introduction

Microsoft Agent provides services that enable you to program animated characters from an application. These services are implemented as an OLE Automation server. OLE Automation enables an application to control another application's object programmatically. This chapter assumes an understanding of the Component Object Model (COM) and OLE. For an introduction of these services, see Chapter 3, "Microsoft Agent Programming Interface Overview." Sample programs are available at the Microsoft Agent Web site at *http://www.microsoft.com/ msagent* and on the book's CD.

Adding Microsoft Agent
Functionality to Your Application

To access Microsoft Agent's server interfaces, Agent must already be installed on the target system. If you want to install Microsoft Agent as part of your application, you must have a valid distribution license for Agent. You can access the license agreement from the Microsoft Agent web site at *http://www.microsoft.com/ sitebuilder/workshop/imedia/agent/licensing.asp*. You can then download Agent's self-installing cabinet file from the web site (using the Save rather than Run option). You can include this file in your installation setup program. Whenever it is executed, it will automatically install Agent on the target system. For further details on installation, see the Microsoft Agent distribution license agreement. Installation other than using Agent's self-installing cabinet file, such as attempting to copy and register Agent component files, is not supported. This ensures consistent and complete installation. Note that the Microsoft Agent self-installing file will not install on Microsoft Windows 2000 (NT5) because that version of the operating system already includes its own version of Agent.

To successfully install Agent on a target system, you must also ensure that the target system has a recent version of the Microsoft Visual C++ run time (Msvcrt.dll), Microsoft registration tool (Regsvr32.dll), and Microsoft COM dlls. The easiest way to ensure that the necessary components are on the target system is to require that Microsoft Internet Explorer 3.02 or later is installed. Alternatively, you can install the first two components which are available as part of Microsoft Visual C++. The necessary COM dlls can be installed as part of the Microsoft DCOM update, available at the Microsoft web site. You can find further information and licensing information for these components at the Microsoft web site.

Agent's language components can be installed the same way. Similarly, you can use this technique to install the ACS format of the Microsoft characters available for distribution from the Microsoft Agent web site. The character files automatically install to the Microsoft Agent\Chars subdirectory.

Because Microsoft Agent's components are designed as operating system components, Agent may not be uninstalled. Similarly, where Agent is already installed as part of the Windows operating system, the Agent self-installing cabinet may not install.

Once installed, to call Agent's interfaces, create an instance of the server and request a pointer to a specific interface that the server supports using the standard COM convention. In particular, the COM library provides an API function, **CoCreateInstance**, that creates an instance of the object and returns a pointer to the requested interface of the object. Request a pointer to the **IAgent** or **IAgentEx** interface in your **CoCreateInstance** call or in a subsequent call to **QueryInterface**.

The following code illustrates this in C/C++:

```
hRes = CoCreateInstance(CLSID_AgentServer,
                  NULL,
                  CLSCTX_SERVER,
                  IID_IAgentEx,
                  (LPVOID *)&pAgentEx);
```

If the Microsoft Agent server is running, this function connects to the server; otherwise, it starts up the server.

Note that the Microsoft Agent server interfaces often include extended interfaces that include an "Ex" suffix. These interfaces are derived from, and therefore include all the functionality of, their non-Ex counterparts. If you want to use any of the extended features, use the Ex interfaces.

Functions that take pointers to BSTRs allocate memory using **SysAllocString**. It is the caller's responsibility to free this memory using **SysFreeString**.

Loading Character and Animation Data

Once you have a pointer to the **IAgentEx** interface, you can use the **Load** method to load a character and retrieve its **IAgentCharacterEx** interface. There are three different possibilities for the Load path of a character. The first is compatible with Microsoft Agent 1.5 where the specified path is the full path and filename of a character file. The second possibility is to specify the filename only, in which case, Agent looks in its Chars directory. The last possibility is to supply an empty Variant parameter that causes the default character to be loaded.

```
// Create a variant to store the filename of the character to load

const LPWSTR kpwszCharacter = L"merlin.acs";

VariantInit(&vPath);

vPath.vt = VT_BSTR;
vPath.bstrVal = SysAllocString(kpwszCharacter);

// Load the character

hRes = pAgentEx->Load(vPath, &lCharID, &lRequestID);

// Get its IAgentCharacterEx interface

hRes = pAgentEx->GetCharacterEx(lCharID, &pCharacterEx);
```

You can use this interface to access the character's methods:

```
// Show the character.  The first parameter tells Microsoft
// Agent to show the character by playing an animation.

hRes = pCharacterEx->Show(FALSE, &lRequestID);

// Make the character speak

bszSpeak = SysAllocString(L"Hello World!");

hRes = pCharacterEx->Speak(bszSpeak, NULL, &lRequestID);

SysFreeString(bszSpeak);
```

When you no longer need Microsoft Agent services, such as when your client application shuts down, release its interfaces. Note that releasing the character interface does not unload the character. Call the **Unload** method to do this before releasing the **IAgentEx** interface:

```
// Clean up

if (pCharacterEx) {

    // Release the character interface

    pCharacterEx->Release();

    // Unload the character.  NOTE:  releasing the character
    // interface does NOT make the character go away.  You must
    // call Unload.

    pAgentEx->Unload(lCharID);
}

// Release the Agent

pAgentEx->Release();

VariantClear(&vPath);
```

Creating a Notification Sink

To be notified of events by Microsoft Agent, you must implement either the **IAgentNotifySink** or the **IAgentNotifySinkEx** interface, and create and register an object of that type following COM conventions:

```
// Create a notification sink

pSinkEx = new AgentNotifySinkEx;

pSinkEx->AddRef();

// And register it with Microsoft Agent

hRes = pAgentEx->Register((IUnknown *)pSinkEx, &lNotifySinkID);
```

Remember to unregister your notification sink when your application shuts down and releases Microsoft Agent's interfaces.

Accessing Services Using Java

You can also access Microsoft Agent services from a Java applet. Many of the functions accessible through the Microsoft Agent interfaces return values through parameters passed by reference. In order to pass these parameters from Java, it is necessary to create single-element arrays in your code and pass them as parameters to the appropriate function. If you're using Microsoft Visual J++ and have run the Java Type Library Wizard on the Microsoft Agent server, refer to the summary.txt file to review which functions require array arguments. The procedure is similar to that in C; you use the **IAgentEx** interface to create an instance of the server, then load the character:

```
private IAgentEx            m_AgentEx = null;
private IAgentCharacterEx   m_Merlin[] = {null};
private int                 m_MerlinID[] = {-1};
private int                 m_RequestID[] = {0};
private final String        m_CharacterPath = "merlin.acs";

public void start()
{
    // Start the Microsoft Agent Server

    m_AgentEx = (IAgentEx) new AgentServer();

    try
    {

        Variant characterPath = new Variant();
        characterPath.putString(m_CharacterPath);

        // Load the character

        m_AgentEx.Load(characterPath,
                m_MerlinID,
                m_RequestID);
    }
```

The procedure is slightly different when loading characters from a HTTP remote location such as a Web site. In this case the **Load** method is asynchronous and will raise a COM exception of E_PENDING (0x8000000a). You will need to catch this exception and handle it correctly as is done in the following functions:

```
// Constants used in asynchronous character loads

private final int E_PENDING = 0x8000000a;
private final int NOERROR = 0;


// This function loads a character from the specified path.
// It correctly handles the loading of characters from
// remote sites.

// This sample doesn't care about the request id returned
// from the Load call.  Real production code might use the
// request id and the RequestComplete callback to check for
// a successful character load before proceeding.
```

```
public int LoadCharacter(Variant path, int[] id)
{
    int requestid[] = {-1};
    int hRes = 0;

    try
    {
        // Load the character

        m_AgentEx.Load(path, id, requestid);
    }
    catch(com.ms.com.ComException e)
    {
        // Get the HRESULT

        hRes = e.getHResult();

        // If the error code is E_PENDING, we return NOERROR

        if (hRes == E_PENDING)
            hRes = NOERROR;
    }

    return hRes;
}

public void start()
{
    if (LoadCharacter(characterPath, m_MerlinID) != NOERROR)
    {
        stop();
        return;
    }

    // Other initialization code here

        .
        .
        .

}
```

Note Depending on your release of Visual J++, you might need to enable the Microsoft Language Extensions in your compiler options for this code to compile correctly.

Then get the **IAgentCharacterEx** interface that enables you to access its methods:

```
// Get the IAgentCharacterEx interface for the loaded
// character by passing its ID to the Agent server.
```

```
m_AgentEx.GetCharacterEx(m_MerlinID[0], m_Merlin);

// Show the character

m_Merlin[0].Show(FALSE, m_RequestID);

// And speak hello

m_Merlin[0].Speak("Hello World!", "", m_RequestID);
```

Similarly, to be notified of events, you must implement either the
IAgentNotifySink or the **IAgentNotifySinkEx** interface, creating and register-
ing an object of that type:

```
...
// Declare an Agent Notify Sink so that we can get
// notification callbacks from the Agent server.

private AgentNotifySinkEx m_SinkEx = null;
private int              m_SinkID[] = {-1};

public void start()
    {
    ...
    // Create and register a notify sink

    m_SinkEx = new AgentNotifySinkEx();

    m_AgentEx.Register(m_SinkEx, m_SinkID);
    ...
    // Give our notify sink access to the character

    m_SinkEx.SetCharacter(m_Merlin[0]);
    ...
    }
```

In order to access Microsoft Agent from a Java applet, you must generate Java
classes that you install with the applet. You can use the Visual J++ Java Type
Library Wizard, for example, to generate these files. If you plan to host the applet
on a Web page, you will need to build a signed Java CAB inclusive of the generated class files that download with the page. The class files are necessary to
access the Microsoft Agent Server since it is a COM object that executes outside
of the Java sandbox. To learn more about Trust-Based Security for Java, see
http://www.microsoft.com/java/security/.

Accessing Speech Services

Although Microsoft Agent's services include support for speech input, a compatible command-and-control speech recognition engine must be installed to access
Agent's speech input services. Similarly, if you want to use Microsoft Agent's

speech services to support synthesized speech output for a character, you must install a compatible text-to-speech (TTS) speech engine for your character. Because Microsoft Agent's speech services are based on the Microsoft Speech API (SAPI), you can use any engines that compatibly support the required speech interfaces. Further information on the availability and use of speech recognition and text-to-speech engines is at the Microsoft Agent Downloads for Developers page.

To enable speech input support in your application, define a **Command** object and set its **Voice** property. Microsoft Agent will automatically load speech services, so that when the user presses the Listening key or you call **Listen**, the speech recognition engine will be loaded. By default the character's language ID will determine which engine is loaded. Agent attempts to load the first engine that SAPI returns as matching this language. Use **IAgentCharacterEx::SetSRModeID** if you want to load a specific engine.

To enable text-to-speech output, use the **Speak** method. Microsoft Agent will automatically attempt to load an engine that matches the character's language ID. If the character's definition includes a specific TTS engine mode ID and that engine is available and matches the character's language ID, Agent loads that engine for the character. If not, Agent loads the first TTS engine that SAPI returns as matching the character's language setting. You can also use **IAgentCharacterEx::SetTTSModeID** to load a specific engine.

Typically, Microsoft Agent loads a speech recognition engine when the Listening mode is initiated and loads a text-to-speech engine when **Speak** is first called. However, if you want to preload the speech engine, you can do this by querying the properties related to the speech interfaces. For example, calling **IAgentCharacterEx::GetSRModeID** or **IAgentCharacterEx::GetTTSModeID** will attempt to load that type of engine.

Reference

This reference contains the following section

- Interfaces
- Events

Interfaces

Microsoft Agent defines interfaces that allow applications to access its services, enabling an application to control the animation of a character, support user input events, and specify output.

All the Microsoft Agent interfaces are defined in header (.h) files.

IAgent

IAgent defines an interface that allows applications to load characters, receive events, and check the current state of the Microsoft Agent Server. These functions are also available from **IAgentEx**.

The **GetSuspended** method included in previous versions is obsolete and returns **False** for backward compatibility.

Methods in Vtable Order

IAgent Methods	Description
Load	Loads a character's data file.
Unload	Unloads a character's data file.
Register	Registers a notification sink for the client.
Unregister	Unregisters a client's notification sink.
GetCharacter	Returns the IAgentCharacter interface for a loaded character.

IAgent::GetCharacter

```
HRESULT GetCharacter(
   long dwCharID  // character ID
);
```

Retrieves the **IAgentCharacter** for a loaded character.

- Returns S_OK to indicate the operation was successful.

DwCharID   The character's ID.

IAgent::Load

```
HRESULT Load(
   VARIANT vLoadKey,  // data provider
   long * pdwCharID,  // address of a variable for character ID
   long * pdwReqID    // address of a variable for request ID
);
```

Loads a character into the **Characters** collection.

- Returns S_OK to indicate the operation was successful.

vLoadKey   A variant data type that must be one of the following:

  filespec   The local file location of the specified character's definition file.

  URL   The HTTP address for the character's definition file.

pdwCharID   Address of a variable that receives the character's ID.

pdwReqID   Address of a variable that receives the **Load** request ID.

You can load characters from the Microsoft Agent subdirectory by specifying a relative path (one that does not include a colon or leading slash character). This prefixes the path with Agent's characters directory (located in the localized %windows%\msagent directory). You can also use a relative address to specify your own directory in Agent's Chars directory.

You cannot load the same character (a character having the same GUID) more than once from a single connection. Similarly, you cannot load the default character and other characters at the same time from a single connection, because the default character could be the same as the other character. However, you can create another connection (using CoCreateInstance) and load the same character.

Microsoft Agent's data provider supports loading character data stored as a single structured file (.ACS) with character data and animation data together, or as separate character data (.ACF) and animation (.ACA) files. Generally, use the single structured .ACS file to load a character that is stored on a local disk drive or network and accessed using conventional file protocol (such as UNC pathnames). Use the separate .ACF and .ACA files when you want to load the animation files individually from a remote site where they are accessed using HTTP protocol.

For .ACS files, using the **Load** method provides access to a character's animations; once loaded, you can use the **Play** method to animate the character. For .ACF files, you also use the **Prepare** method to load animation data. The **Load** method does not support downloading .ACS files from an HTTP site.

Loading a character does not automatically display the character. Use the **Show** method first to make the character visible.

IAgent::Register

```
HRESULT Register(
    IUnknown * punkNotifySink    // IUnknown address for client
                                 // notification sink
    long * pdwSinkID             // address of the notification sink ID
);
```

Registers a notification sink for the client application.

- Returns S_OK to indicate the operation was successful.

IUnknown   Address of **IUnknown** for your notification sink interface.

pdwSinkID   Address of notification sink ID (used to unregister the notification sink).

You need to register your notification sink (also known as a notify sink or event sink) to receive events from the Microsoft Agent server.

See also IAgent::Unregister

IAgent::UnLoad

```
HRESULT UnLoad(
    long * dwCharID   //character ID
);
```

Unloads the character data for the specified character from the **Characters** collection.

- Returns S_OK to indicate the operation was successful.

dwCharID   The character's ID.

Use this method when you no longer need a character, to free up memory used to store information about the character. If you access the character again, use the **Load** method.

See also **IAgent::Load**

IAgent::Unregister

```
HRESULT Unregister(
    long dwSinkID   //notification sink ID
);
```

Unloads the character data for the specified character from the **Characters** collection.

- Returns S_OK to indicate the operation was successful.

dwSinkID   The notification sink ID.

Use this method when you no longer need Microsoft Agent services, such as when your application shuts down.

See also **IAgent::Register**

IAgentEx

IAgentEx derives from the **IAgent** interface. It includes all the **IAgent** methods as well as provides access to additional functions.

Methods in Vtable Order.

IAgentEx Methods	Description
ShowDefaultCharacterProperties	Displays the default character properties.
GetVersion	Returns the version number for Microsoft Agent (server).

IAgentEx::ShowDefaultCharacterProperties

```
HRESULT ShowDefaultCharacterProperties(
    short x,          // x-coordinate of window
    short y,          // y-coordinate of window
    long bUseDefault  // default position flag
);
```

Displays default character properties window.

- Returns S_OK to indicate the operation was successful.

x   The x-coordinate of the window in pixels, relative to the screen origin (upper left).

y   The y-coordinate of the window in pixels, relative to the screen origin (upper left).

bUseDefault   Default position flag. If this parameter is **True**, Microsoft Agent displays the property sheet window for the default character at the last location it appeared.

Note For Windows NT 5.0, it may be necessary to call the new **AllowSetForegroundWindow** API to ensure that this window becomes the foreground window. For more information about setting the foreground window under Windows 2000, see the Win32 documentation.

See also **IAgentNotifySinkEx::DefaultCharacterChange**

IAgentEx::GetVersion

```
HRESULT GetVersion(
    short * psMajor,  // address of major version
    short * psMinor   // address of minor version
);
```

Retrieves the version number of Microsoft Agent server.

- Returns S_OK to indicate the operation was successful.

psMajor   Address of a variable that receives the major version.

psMinor   Address of a variable that receives the minor version.

IAgentCharacter

IAgentCharacter defines an interface that allows applications to query character properties and play animations. These functions are also available from **IAgentCharacterEx**. You can use some method return request IDs to track their status in the character's queue and to synchronize your code with the character's current animation state.

Methods in Vtable Order

IAgentCharacter Methods	Description
GetVisible	Returns whether the character (frame) is currently visible.
SetPosition	Sets the position of the character frame.
GetPosition	Returns the position of the character frame.
SetSize	Sets the size of the character frame.
GetSize	Returns the size of the character frame.
GetName	Returns the name of the character.
GetDescription	Returns the description for the character.
GetTTSSpeed	Returns the current TTS output speed setting for the character.
GetTTSPitch	Returns the current TTS pitch setting for the character.
Activate	Sets whether a client is active or a character is topmost.
SetIdleOn	Sets the server's idle processing.
GetIdleOn	Returns the setting of the server's idle processing.
Prepare	Retrieves animation data for the character.
Play	Plays a specified animation.
Stop	Stops an animation for a character.
StopAll	Stops all animations for a character.
Wait	Holds the character's animation queue.
Interrupt	Interrupts a character's animation.
Show	Displays the character and plays the character's Showing state animation.
Hide	Plays the character's Hiding state animation and hides the character's frame.
Speak	Plays spoken output for the character.
MoveTo	Moves the character frame to the specified location.
GestureAt	Plays a gesturing animation based on the specified location.
GetMoveCause	Retrieves the cause of the character's last move.
GetVisibilityCause	Retrieves the cause of the last change to the character's visibility state.
HasOtherClients	Retrieves whether the character has other current clients.
SetSoundEffectsOn	Determines whether a character animation's sound effects play.
GetSoundEffectsOn	Retrieves whether a character's sound effects setting is enabled.
SetName	Sets the character's name.
SetDescription	Sets the character's description.
GetExtraData	Retrieves additional data stored with the character.

IAgentCharacter::Activate

```
HRESULT Activate(
    short sState, // topmost character or client setting
);
```

Sets whether a client is active or a character is topmost.

- Returns S_OK to indicate the operation was successful.
- Returns S_FALSE to indicate the operation was not successful.

sState	You can specify the following values for this parameter:
0	Set as not the active client.
1	Set as the active client.
2	Make the topmost character.

When multiple characters are visible, only one of the characters receives speech input at a time. Similarly, when multiple client applications share the same character, only one of the clients receives mouse input (for example, Microsoft Agent control click or drag events) at a time. The character set to receive mouse and speech input is the topmost character and the client that receives input is the character's active client. (The topmost character's window also appears at the top of the character window's z-order.) Typically, the user determines which character is topmost by explicitly selecting it. However, topmost activation also changes when a character is shown or hidden (the character becomes or is no longer topmost, respectively.)

You can also use this method to explicitly manage when your client receives input directed to the character, such as when your application itself becomes active. For example, setting **State** to 2 makes the character topmost, and your client receives all mouse and speech input events generated from user interaction with the character. Therefore, it also makes your client the input-active client of the character. However, you can also set the active client for a character without making the character topmost, by setting **State** to 1. This enables your client to receive input directed to that character when the character becomes topmost. Similarly, you can set your client to not be the active client (to not receive input) when the character becomes topmost, by setting **State** to 0. You can determine if a character has other current clients using **IAgentCharacter::HasOtherClients**.

Avoid calling this method directly after a **Show** method. **Show** automatically sets the input-active client. When the character is hidden, the **Activate** call may fail, if it gets processed before the **Show** method completes.

Attempting to call this method with the **State** parameter set to 2 (when the specified character is hidden) will fail. Similarly, if you set **State** to 0, and your application is the only client, this call fails. A character must always have a topmost client.

Note Calling this method with **State** set to 1 does not typically generate an **Agent-NotifySink::ActivateInputState** event unless there are no other characters loaded or your application is already input-active.

See also **IAgentCharacter::HasOtherClients**

IAgentCharacter::GestureAt

```
HRESULT GestureAt(
    short x,          // x-coordinate of specified location
    short y,          // y-coordinate of specified location
    long * pdwReqID   // address of a request ID
);
```

Plays the associated **Gesturing** state animation based on the specified location.

- Returns S_OK to indicate the operation was successful. When the function returns, *pdwReqID* contains the ID of the request.

x   The x-coordinate of the specified location in pixels, relative to the screen origin (upper left).

y   The y-coordinate of the specified location in pixels, relative to the screen origin (upper left).

pdwReqID   Address of a variable that receives the **GestureAt** request ID.

The server automatically determines and plays the appropriate gesturing animation based on the character's current position and the specified location. When using the HTTP protocol to access character and animation data, use the **Prepare** method to ensure that the animations are available before calling this method.

IAgentCharacter::GetDescription

```
HRESULT GetDescription(
    BSTR * pbszDescription    // address of buffer for
                              // character description
);
```

Retrieves the description of the character.

- Returns S_OK to indicate the operation was successful.

pbszDescription   The address of a BSTR that receives the value of the description for the character. A character's description is defined when it is compiled with the Microsoft Agent Character Editor. The description setting is optional and may not be supplied for all characters.

IAgentCharacter::GetExtraData

```
HRESULT GetExtraData(
    BSTR * pbszExtraData    // address of buffer for
                            // additional character data
);
```

Retrieves additional data stored as part of the character.

- Returns S_OK to indicate the operation was successful.

pbszExtraData   The address of a BSTR that receives the value of the additional data for the character. A character's additional data is defined when it is compiled with the Microsoft Agent Character Editor. A character developer can supply this string by editing the .ACD file for a character. The setting is optional and may not be supplied for all characters, nor can the data be defined or changed at run time. In addition, the meaning of the data supplied is defined by the character developer.

IAgentCharacter::GetIdleOn

```
HRESULT GetIdleOn(
    long * pbOn  // address of idle processing flag
);
```

Indicates the automatic idle processing state for a character.

- Returns S_OK to indicate the operation was successful.

pbOn   Address of a variable that receives **True** if the Microsoft Agent server automatically plays **Idling** state animations for a character and **False** if not.

See also IAgentCharacter::SetIdleOn

IAgentCharacter::GetMoveCause

```
HRESULT GetMoveCause(
    long * pdwCause  // address of variable for cause of character move
);
```

Retrieves the cause of the character's last move.

- Returns S_OK to indicate the operation was successful.

pdwCause   Address of a variable that receives the cause of the character's last move and will be one of the following:

const unsigned short NeverMoved = 0;	Character has not been moved.
const unsigned short UserMoved = 1;	User dragged the character.
const unsigned short ProgramMoved = 2;	Your application moved the character.

const unsigned short OtherProgramMoved = 3;	Another application moved the character.
const unsigned short SystemMoved = 4	The server moved the character to keep it onscreen after a screen resolution change.

See also IAgentNotifySink::Move

IAgentCharacter::GetName

```
HRESULT GetName(
   BSTR * pbszName    // address of buffer for character name
);
```

Retrieves the name of the character.

- Returns S_OK to indicate the operation was successful.

pbszName   The address of a BSTR that receives the value of the name for the character.

A character's default name is defined when it is compiled with the Microsoft Agent Character Editor. A character's name may vary based on the character's language ID. Characters can be compiled with different names for different languages.

You can also set the character's name using **IAgentCharacter:SetName**; however, this changes the name for all current clients of the character.

See also IAgentCharacter::SetName

IAgentCharacter::GetPosition

```
HRESULT GetPosition(
   long * plLeft,  // address of variable for left edge of character
   long * plTop    // address of variable for top edge of character
);
```

Retrieves the character's animation frame position.

- Returns S_OK to indicate the operation was successful.

plLeft   Address of a variable that receives the screen coordinate of the character animation frame's left edge in pixels, relative to the screen origin (upper left).

plTop   Address of a variable that receives the screen coordinate of the character animation frame's top edge in pixels, relative to the screen origin (upper left).

Even though the character appears in an irregularly shaped region window, the location of the character is based on its rectangular animation frame.

See also **IAgentCharacter::SetPositionIAgentCharacter::GetSize**

IAgentCharacter::GetSize

```
HRESULT GetSize(
    long * plWidth,   // address of variable for character width
    long * plHeight   // address of variable for character height
);
```

Retrieves the size of the character's animation frame.

- Returns S_OK to indicate the operation was successful.

plWidth   Address of a variable that receives the width of the character animation frame in pixels, relative to the screen origin (upper left).

plHeight   Address of a variable that receives the height of the character animation frame in pixels, relative to the screen origin (upper left).

Even though the character appears in an irregularly shaped region window, the location of the character is based on its rectangular animation frame.

See also **IAgentCharacter::SetSize**

IAgentCharacter::GetSoundEffectsOn

```
HRESULT GetSoundEffectsOn(
    long * pbOn   // address of variable for sound effects setting
);
```

Retrieves whether the character's sound effects setting is enabled.

- Returns S_OK to indicate the operation was successful.

pbOn   Address of a variable that receives **True** if the character's sound effects setting is enabled, **False** if disabled.

The characters sound effects setting determines whether sound effects compiled as a part of the character are played when you play an associated animation. The setting is subject to the user's global sound effects setting in **IAgentAudioOutputProperties::GetUsingSoundEffects**.

See also **IAgentCharacter::SetSoundEffectsOn**,
IAgentAudioOutputProperties::GetUsingSoundEffects

IAgentCharacter::GetTTSPitch

```
HRESULT GetTTSPitch(
    long * pdwPitch    // address of variable for character TTS pitch
);
```

Retrieves the character's TTS output pitch setting.

- Returns S_OK to indicate the operation was successful.

pdwPitch   Address of a variable that receives the character's current TTS pitch setting in Hertz.

Although your application cannot write this value, you can include pitch tags in your output text that will temporarily increase the pitch for a particular utterance. This method applies only to characters configured for TTS output. If the speech synthesis (TTS) engine is not enabled (or installed) or the character does not support TTS output, this method returns zero (0).

IAgentCharacter::GetTTSSpeed

```
HRESULT GetTTSSpeed(
    long * pdwSpeed    // address of variable for character
                       // TTS output speed
);
```

Retrieves the character's TTS output speed setting.

- Returns S_OK to indicate the operation was successful.

pdwSpeed   Address of a variable that receives the output speed of the character in words per minute.

Although your application cannot write this value, you can include speed tags in your output text that will temporarily speed up the output for a particular utterance.

This property returns the current speaking output speed setting for the character. For characters using TTS output, the property returns the actual TTS output for the character. If TTS is not enabled or the character does not support TTS output, the setting reflects the user setting for output speed.

IAgentCharacter::GetVisibilityCause

```
HRESULT GetVisibilityCause(
    long * pdwCause    // address of variable for cause
                       // of character visible state
);
```

Retrieves the cause of the character's visible state.

- Returns S_OK to indicate the operation was successful.

pdwCause	Address of a variable that receives the cause of the character's last visibility state change and will be one of the following:	
	const unsigned short NeverShown = 0;	Character has not been shown.
	const unsigned short UserHid = 1;	User hid the character with the character's taskbar icon pop-up menu or us ing speech input.
	const unsigned short UserShowed = 2;	User showed the character.
	const unsigned short ProgramHid = 3;	Your application hid the character.
	const unsigned short ProgramShowed = 4;	Your application showed the char- acter.
	const unsigned short OtherProgramHid = 5;	Another applica- tion hid the char- acter.
	const unsigned short OtherProgramShowed = 6;	Another applica- tion showed the character.
	const unsigned short UserHidViaCharacterMenu = 7	User hid the character with the character's pop-up menu.
	const unsigned short UserHidViaTaskbarIcon = UserHid	User hid the character with the character's taskbar icon pop- up menu or us ing speech input.

See also IAgentNotifySink::VisibleState

IAgentCharacter::GetVisible

```
HRESULT GetVisible(
    long * pbVisible  // address of variable for character
                      // Visible setting
);
```

Determines whether the character's animation frame is currently visible.

- Returns S_OK to indicate the operation was successful.

pbVisible   Address of a variable that receives **True** if the character's frame is visible and **False** if hidden.

You can use this method to determine whether the character's frame is currently visible. To make a character visible, use the **Show** method. To hide a character, use the **Hide** method.

IAgentCharacter::HasOtherClients

```
HRESULT HasOtherClients(
    long * plNumOtherClients  // address of variable for number
);                           // of clients for character
```

Retrieves whether a character has other clients.

- Returns S_OK to indicate the operation was successful.

plNumOtherClients Address of a variable that receives the number of other connected clients for the character (total number of clients minus your client).

IAgentCharacter::Hide

```
HRESULT Hide(
    long bFast,      // play Hiding state animation flag
    long * pdwReqID  // address of request ID
);
```

Hides the character.

- Returns S_OK to indicate the operation was successful. When the function returns, *pdwReqID* contains the ID of the request.

bFast   **Hiding** state animation flag. If this parameter is **True**, the **Hiding** animation does not play before the character frame is hidden; if **False**, the animation plays.

pdwReqID   Address of a variable that receives the **Hide** request ID.

The server queues the animation associated with the **Hide** method in the character's queue. This allows you to use it to hide the character after a sequence of other animations. You can play the action immediately by using the **Stop** method before calling the **Hide** method.

When using the HTTP protocol to access character and animation data, use the **Prepare** method to ensure the availability of the **Hiding** state animation before calling this method.

Hiding a character can also result in triggering the **AgentNotifySink::Activate-InputState** event of another visible character.

Hidden characters cannot access the audio channel. The server will pass back a failure status in the **RequestComplete** event if you generate an animation request and the character is hidden.

See also **IAgentCharacter::Show**

IAgentCharacter::Interrupt

```
HRESULT Interrupt(
    long dwReqID,    // request ID to interrupt
    long * pdwReqID  // address of request ID
);
```

Interrupts the specified animation (request) of another character.

- Returns S_OK to indicate the operation was successful. When the function returns, *pdwReqID* contains the ID of the request.

dwReqID   An ID of the request to interrupt.

pdwReqID   Address of a variable that receives the **Interrupt** request ID.

If you load multiple characters, you can use this method to sync up animation between characters. For example, if another character is in a looping animation, this method will stop the looping animation and start the next animation in the character's queue.

Interrupt halts the existing animation, but does not flush the character's animation queue. It starts the next animation in the character's queue. To halt and flush a character's queue, use the **Stop** method.

You cannot use this method to have a character interrupt itself because the Microsoft Agent server queues the **Interrupt** method in the character's animation queue. Therefore, you can only use **Interrupt** to halt the animation of another character you have loaded.

IAgentCharacter::MoveTo

```
HRESULT MoveTo(
    short x,         // x-coordinate of new location
    short y,         // y-coordinate of new location
    long lSpeed,     // speed to move the character
    long * pdwReqID  // address of request ID
);
```

Plays the associated **Moving** state animation and moves the character frame to the specified location.

- Returns S_OK to indicate the operation was successful. When the function returns, this variable contains the ID of the request.

x	The x-coordinate of the new position in pixels, relative to the screen origin (upper left). The location of a character is based on the upper left corner of its animation frame.
y	The y-coordinate of the new position in pixels, relative to the screen origin (upper left). The location of a character is based on the upper left corner of its animation frame.
lSpeed	A parameter specifying in milliseconds how quickly the character's frame moves. The recommended value is 1000. Specifying zero (0) moves the frame without playing an animation.
pdwReqID	Address of a variable that receives the **MoveTo** request ID.

When using the HTTP protocol to access character and animation data, use the **Prepare** method to ensure the availability of the **Moving** state animations before calling this method. Even if the animation is not loaded, the server still moves the frame.

See also **IAgentCharacter::SetPosition**

IAgentCharacter::Play

```
HRESULT Play(
    BSTR bszAnimation,   // name of an animation
    long * pdwReqID      // address of request ID
);
```

Plays the specified animation.

- Returns S_OK to indicate the operation was successful. When the function returns, *pdwReqID* contains the ID of the request.

bszAnimation	The name of an animation.
pdwReqID	Address of a variable that receives the **IAgentCharacter::Play** request ID.

An animation's name is defined when the character is compiled with the Microsoft Agent Character Editor. Before playing the specified animation, the server attempts to play the **Return** animation for the previous animation (if one has been assigned).

When a character's animation data is stored on the user's local machine, you can use the **IAgentCharacter::Play** method and specify the name of the animation. When using the HTTP protocol to access animation data, use the **Prepare** method to ensure the availability of the animation before calling this method.

See also **IAgentCharacter::Prepare**

IAgentCharacter::Prepare

```
HRESULT Prepare(
    long dwType,      // type of animation data to load
    BSTR bszName,     // name of the animation
    long bQueue,      // queue the request
    long * pdwReqID   // address of request ID
);
```

Retrieves animation data for a character.

- Returns S_OK to indicate the operation was successful. When the function returns, *pdwReqID* contains the ID of the request.

dwType   A value that indicates the animation data type to load that must be one of the following:

const unsigned short PREPARE_ANIMATION = 0;	A character's animation data.
const unsigned short PREPARE_STATE = 1;	A character's state data.
const unsigned short PREPARE_WAVE = 2	A character's sound file (.WAV or .LWV) for spoken output.

bszName   The name of the animation or state.

The animation name is based on that defined for the character when it was saved using the Microsoft Agent Character Editor.

For states, the value can be one of the following:

"Gesturing"	To retrieve all **Gesturing** state animations.
"GesturingDown"	To retrieve **GesturingDown** animations.
"GesturingLeft"	To retrieve **GesturingLeft** animations.
"GesturingRight"	To retrieve **GesturingRight** animations.
"GesturingUp"	To retrieve **GesturingUp** animations.
"Hiding"	To retrieve the **Hiding** state animations.
"Hearing"	To retrieve the **Hearing** state animations.
"Idling"	To retrieve all **Idling** state animations.
"IdlingLevel1"	To retrieve all **IdlingLevel1** animations.
"IdlingLevel2"	To retrieve all **IdlingLevel2** animations.
"IdlingLevel3"	To retrieve all **IdlingLevel3** animations.
"Listening"	To retrieve the **Listening** state animations.
"Moving"	To retrieve all **Moving** state animations.
"MovingDown"	To retrieve all **Moving** animations.
"MovingLeft"	To retrieve all **MovingLeft** animations.
"MovingRight"	To retrieve all **MovingRight** animations.
"MovingUp"	To retrieve all **MovingUp** animations.
"Showing"	To retrieve the **Showing** state animations.
"Speaking"	To retrieve the **Speaking** state animations.

For .WAV files, set *bszName* to the URL or file specification for the .WAV file. If the specification is not complete, it is interpreted as being relative to the specification used in the **Load** method.

bQueue	A Boolean specifying whether the server queues the **Prepare** request. **True** queues the request and causes any animation request that follows it to wait until the animation data it specifies is loaded. **False** retrieves the animation data asynchronously.
pdwReqID	Address of a variable that receives the **Prepare** request ID.

If you load a character using the HTTP protocol (an .ACF file), you must use the **Prepare** method to retrieve animation data before you can play the animation. You cannot use this method if you loaded the character using the UNC protocol (an .ACS file). You also cannot retrieve HTTP data for a character using **Prepare** if you loaded that character using the UNC protocol (.ACS character file).

Animation or sound data retrieved with the **Prepare** method is stored in the browser's cache. Subsequent calls will check the cache, and if the animation data is already there, the control loads the data directly from the cache. Once loaded, the animation or sound data can be played with the **Play** or **Speak** methods.

You can specify multiple animations and states by separating them with commas. However, you cannot mix types in the same **Prepare** statement.

IAgentCharacter::SetDescription

```
HRESULT SetDescription(
    BSTR bszDescription    // character description
);
```

Sets the description of the character.

- Returns S_OK to indicate the operation was successful.

bszDescription	A BSTR that sets the description for the character. A character's default description is defined when it is compiled with the Microsoft Agent Character Editor. The description setting is optional and may not be supplied for all characters. You can change the character's description using **IAgentCharacter::SetDescription**; however, this value is not persistent (stored permanently). The character's description reverts to its default setting whenever the character is first loaded by a client.

See also IAgentCharacter::GetDescription

IAgentCharacter::SetIdleOn

```
HRESULT SetIdleOn(
    long bOn  // idle processing flag
);
```

Sets automatic idle processing for a character.

- Returns S_OK to indicate the operation was successful.

bOn   Idle processing flag. If this parameter is **True**, the Microsoft Agent
                         automatically plays **Idling** state animations.

The server automatically sets a time out after the last animation played for a
character. When this timer's interval is complete, the server begins the **Idling**
states for a character, playing its associated **Idling** animations at regular intervals. If you want to manage the **Idling** state animations yourself, set the property
to **False**. This property applies only to your client application's use of the character; the setting does not affect other clients of the character or other characters of
your client application.

See also IAgentCharacter::GetIdleOn

IAgentCharacter::SetName

```
HRESULT SetName(
    BSTR bszName    // character name
);
```

Sets the name of the character.

- Returns S_OK to indicate the operation was successful.

bszName   A BSTR that sets the character's name. A character's default name
                         is defined when it is compiled with the Microsoft Agent Character
                         Editor. You can change it using **IAgentCharacter::SetName**; how-
                         ever, this changes the character name for all current clients of the
                         character. This property is not persistent (stored permanently). The
                         character's name reverts to its default name whenever the character
                         is first loaded by a client.

The character's name may also depend on its language ID. Characters can be
compiled with different names for different languages.

The server uses the character's name setting in parts of the Microsoft Agent's interface, such as the Voice Commands Window title when the character is input-
active and in the Microsoft Agent taskbar pop-up menu.

See also IAgentCharacter::GetName

IAgentCharacter::SetPosition

```
HRESULT SetPosition(
    long lLeft,   // screen coordinate of the left edge of character
    long lTop     // screen coordinate of the top edge of character
);
```

Sets the position of the character's animation frame.

- Returns S_OK to indicate the operation was successful.

lLeft   Screen coordinate of the character animation frame's left edge in
                            pixels, relative to the screen origin (upper left).

lTop   Screen coordinate of the character animation frame's top edge in
                            pixels, relative to the screen origin (upper left).

This property's setting applies to all clients of the character. Even though the
character appears in an irregularly shaped region window, the location of the
character is based on its rectangular animation frame.

Note Unlike the **MoveTo** method, this function is not queued.

See also IAgentCharacter::GetPosition

IAgentCharacter::SetSize

```
HRESULT SetSize(
   long * lWidth,  // width of the character frame
   long * lHeight  // height of the character frame
);
```

Sets the size of the character's animation frame.

- Returns S_OK to indicate the operation was successful.

lWidth   The width of the character's animation frame in pixels.

lHeight   The height of the character's animation frame in pixels.

Changing the character's frame size scales the character to the size set with this
method. This property's setting applies to all clients of the character.

Even though the character appears in an irregularly shaped region window, the
location of the character is based on its rectangular animation frame.

See also IAgentCharacter::GetSize

IAgentCharacter::SetSoundEffectsOn

```
HRESULT SetSoundEffectsOn(
   long bOn  // character sound effects setting
);
```

Determines whether the character's sound effects are played.

- Returns S_OK to indicate the operation was successful.

bOn   Sound effects setting. If this parameter is **True**, the sound effects
                         for animations are played when the animation plays; if **False**, sound
                         effects are not played.

This setting determines whether sound effects compiled as a part of the character
are played when you play an associated animation. This property's setting applies to all clients of the character. The setting is also subject to the user's global
sound effects setting in
IAgentAudioOutputProperties::GetUsingSoundEffects.

**See also IAgentCharacter::GetSoundEffectsOn, IAgentAudioOutput-
Properties::GetUsingSoundEffects**

IAgentCharacter::Show

```
HRESULT Show(
    long bFast,       // play Showing state animation flag
    long * pdwReqID   // address of request ID
);
```

Displays a character.

- Returns S_OK to indicate the operation was successful. When the function
  returns, *pdwReqID* contains the ID of the request.

bFast   Showing state animation flag. If this parameter is **True**, the **Show-
                         ing** state animation plays after making the character visible; if **False**,
                         the animation does not play.

pdwReqID   Address of a variable that receives the **Show** request ID.

Avoid setting the bFast parameter to **True** without playing an animation beforehand, otherwise, the character frame may be displayed, but have no image to display. In particular, note that that if you call **MoveTo** when the character is not
visible, it does not play any animation. Therefore, if you call the **Show** method
with bFast set to **True**, no image will be displayed. Similarly, if you call **Hide**
then **Show** with bFast set to **True**, there will be no visible image.

When using the HTTP protocol to access character and animation data, use the
Prepare method to ensure the availability of the **Showing** state animation before
calling this method.

See also IAgentCharacter::Hide

IAgentCharacter::Speak

```
HRESULT Speak(
    BSTR bszText,     // text to speak
    BSTR bszURL,      // URL of a file to speak
```

```
    long * pdwReqID  // address of a request ID
);
```

Speaks the supplied text or audio file.

■ Returns S_OK to indicate the operation was successful.

bszText

The text the character is to speak.

bszURL

The URL (or file specification) of a sound file to use for spoken output. This can be a standard sound file (.WAV) or linguistically enhanced sound file (.LWV).

pdwReqID

Address of a variable that receives the **Speak** request ID.

To use this method with a character configured to speak using a text-to-speech (TTS) engine; simply provide the bszText parameter. You can include vertical bar characters (|) in the bszText parameter to designate alternative strings, so that each time the server processes the method, it randomly chooses a different string. Support of TTS output is defined when the character is compiled using the Microsoft Agent Character Editor.

If you want to use sound file output for the character, specify the location for the file in the bszURL parameter. When using the HTTP protocol to download a sound file, use the **Prepare** method to ensure the availability of the file before using this method. You can use the bszText parameter to specify the words that appear in the character's word balloon. If you specify a linguistically enhanced sound file (.LWV) for the bszURL parameter and do not specify text, the bszText parameter uses the text stored in the file.

The **Speak** method uses the last animation played to determine which speaking animation to play. For example, if you precede the **Speak** command with a **IAgentCharacter::Play** "GestureRight", the server will play **GestureRight** and then the **GestureRight** speaking animation. If the last animation played has no speaking animation, then Microsoft Agent plays the animation assigned to the character's **Speaking** state.

If you call **Speak** and the audio channel is busy, the character's audio output will not be heard, but the text will display in the word balloon. The word balloon's **Enabled** property must also be **True** for the text to display.

Note Set the character's language ID (using **IAgentCharacterEx::Set-LanguageID** before using the **Speak** method to ensure appropriate text display within the word balloon.

See also IAgentCharacter::Play, IAgentBalloon::GetEnabled, IAgent-Character::Prepare

IAgentCharacter::Stop

```
HRESULT Stop(
   long dwReqID  // request ID
);
```

Stops the specified animation (request) and removes it from the character's animation queue.

- Returns S_OK to indicate the operation was successful.

dwReqID   The ID of the request to stop.

Stop can also be used to halt any queued **Prepare** calls.

See also IAgentCharacter::Prepare, IAgentCharacter::StopAll

IAgentCharacter::StopAll

```
HRESULT StopAll(
   long lType,  // request type
);
```

Stops all animations (requests) and removes them from the character's animation queue.

lType   A bit field that indicates the types of requests to stop (and remove from the character's queue), comprised from the following:

const unsigned long **STOP_TYPE_ALL = 0xFFFFFFFF;**	Stops all animation requests, including non-queued **Prepare** requests.
const unsigned long **STOP_TYPE_PLAY = 0x00000001;**	Stops all **Play** requests.
const unsigned long **STOP_TYPE_MOVE = 0x00000002;**	Stops all **Move** requests.
const unsigned long **STOP_TYPE_SPEAK = 0x00000004;**	Stops all **Speak** requests.
const unsigned long **STOP_TYPE_PREPARE = 0x00000008;**	Stops all queued **Prepare** requests.

const unsigned long STOP_TYPE_NONQUEUED- PREPARE = 0x00000010;	Stops all non-queued **Prepare** requests.
const unsigned long STOP_TYPE_VISIBLE = 0x00000020;	Stops all **Hide** or **Show** requests.

See also IAgentCharacter::Stop

IAgentCharacter::Wait

```
HRESULT Wait(
    long dwReqID,    // request ID
    long * pdwReqID  // address of request ID
);
```

Holds the character's animation queue at the specified animation (request) until another request for another character completes.

■ Returns S_OK to indicate the operation was successful.

dwReqID   The ID of the request to wait for.

pdwReqID   Address of a variable that receives the **Wait** request ID.

Use this method only when you support multiple (simultaneous) characters and want to sequence their interaction. (For a single character, each animation request is played sequentially--after the previous request completes.) If you have two characters and want one character's animation request to wait until the other character's animation completes, set the **Wait** method to the other character's animation request ID.

IAgentCharacterEx

IAgentCharacterEx derives from the **IAgentCharacter** interface. It includes all the **IAgentCharacter** methods as well as provides access to additional functions.

Methods in Vtable Order

IAgentCharacterEx Methods	Description
ShowPopupMenu	Displays the pop-up menu for the character.
SetAutoPopupMenu	Sets whether the server automatically displays the character's pop-up menu.
GetAutoPopupMenu	Returns whether the server automatically displays the character's pop-up menu.
GetHelpFileName	Returns the Help filename for the character.
SetHelpFileName	Sets the Help filename for the character.
SetHelpModeOn	Sets Help mode on.

IAgentCharacterEx Methods	Description
GetHelpModeOn	Returns whether Help mode is on.
SetHelpContextID	Sets the HelpContextID for the character.
GetHelpContextID	Returns the HelpContextID for the character.
GetActive	Returns the active state for the character.
Listen	Sets the listening state for the character.
SetLanguageID	Sets the language ID for the character.
GetLanguageID	Returns the language ID for the character.
GetTTSModeID	Returns the TTS mode ID set for the character.
SetTTSModeID	Sets the TTS mode ID for the character.
GetSRModeID	Returns the current speech recognition engine's mode ID.
SetSRModeID	Sets the speech recognition engine.
GetGUID	Returns the character's identifier.
GetOriginalSize	Returns the original size of the character frame.
Think	Displays the specified text in the character's "thought" balloon.
GetVersion	Returns the version of the character.
GetAnimationNames	Returns the names of the animations for the character.
GetSRStatus	Returns the conditions necessary to support speech input.

IAgentCharacterEx::GetActive

```
HRESULT GetActive(
    short * psState  // address of active state setting
);
```

Retrieves whether your client application is the active client of the character and whether the character is topmost.

- Returns S_OK to indicate the operation was successful.

psState   Address of a variable that receives one of the following values for the state setting:

const unsigned short ACTIVATE_NOTACTIVE = 0;	Your client is not the active client of the character.
const unsigned short ACTIVATE_ACTIVE = 1;	Your client is the active client of the character.
const unsigned short ACTIVATE_INPUTACTIVE = 2;	Your client is input-active (active client of the topmost character).

This setting lets you know whether you are the active client of the character or whether your character is the input active character. When multiple client applications share the same character, the active client of the character receives mouse input (for example, Microsoft Agent control click or drag events). Similarly, when multiple characters are displayed, the active client of the topmost character (also known as the input-active client) receives **IAgentNotifySink::Command** events.

Use the **Activate** method to set whether your application is the active client of the character or to make your application the input active client (which also makes the character topmost).

See also **IAgentCharacter::Activate**, **IAgentNotifySinkEx::Active-ClientChange**

IAgentCharacterEx::GetAnimationNames

```
HRESULT GetAnimationNames(
    IUnknown ** punkEnum // address of IUnknown inteface
);
```

Retrieves the animation names for a character.

- Returns S_OK to indicate the operation was successful.

IUnknown   The address of the **IUnknown** interface for the character's animation collection.

This function enables you to enumerate the names of the animations for a character. Items in the collection have no properties, so individual items cannot be accessed directly. To access the collection, query punkEnum for the IEnumVARIANT interface:

```
IEnumVARIANT pEnum;
VARIANT vAnimName;
DWORD dwRetrieved;

hRes = punkEnum->QueryInterface(
        IID_IEnumVARIANT, (LPVOID *)&pEnum);

if (SUCCEEDED(hRes)) {

    while (TRUE) {

        hRes = pEnum->Next(1, &vAnimName, &dwRetrieved);

        if (hRes != NOERROR)
            break;
```

```
                          // vAnimName.bstrVal is the animation name

                          VariantClear(&vAnimName);
                      }

                  pEnum->Release();
              }

          punkEnum->Release();
```

Note For ACF characters, the collection returns all the animations that have been defined for the character, adding to the ones that have been retrieved with the **Get** method.

IAgentCharacterEx::GetAutoPopupMenu

```
HRESULT GetAutoPopupMenu(
   long * pbAutoPopupMenu   // address of auto pop-up menu
                            // display setting
);
```

Retrieves whether the server automatically displays the character's pop-up menu.

- Returns S_OK to indicate the operation was successful.

pbAutoPopupMenu Address of a variable that receives **True** if the Microsoft Agent server automatically handles displaying the character's pop-up menu and **False** if not.

When this property is set to **False**, your application must display the pop-up menu using **IAgentCharacter::ShowPopupMenu** method.

This property applies only to your client application's use of the character; the setting does not affect other clients of the character or other characters of your client application.

See also **IAgentCharacterEx::SetAutoPopupMenu, IAgentCharacterEx::ShowPopupMenu**

IAgentCharacterEx::GetGUID

```
HRESULT GetGUID(
   BSTR * pbszGUID  // address of character's ID
);
```

Retrieves the unique ID for the character.

- Returns S_OK to indicate the operation was successful.

pbszGUID   Address of a BSTR that receives the ID for the character.

The property returns a string representation of the GUID (formatted with braces and dashes) that the server uses to uniquely identify the character. A character identifier is set when it is compiled with the Microsoft Agent Character Editor. The property is read-only.

IAgentCharacterEx::GetHelpContextID

```
HRESULT GetHelpContextID(
   long * pulHelpID  // address of character's help topic ID
);
```

Retrieves the HelpContextID for the character.

- Returns S_OK to indicate the operation was successful.

pulHelpID   Address of a variable that receives the context number of the help topic for the character.

If you've created a WindowsHelp file for your application and set the character's **HelpFile** property, Microsoft Agent automatically calls Help when **HelpModeOn** is set to **True** and the user selects the character. If there is a context number in the **HelpContextID**, Agent calls Help and searches for the topic identified by the current context number. The current context number is the value of **HelpContextID** for the character.

IAgentCharacterEx::GetHelpContextID returns the HelpContextID you set for the character. It does not return the **HelpContextID** set by other clients.

Note Building a Help file requires the Microsoft Windows Help Compiler.

See also **IAgentCharacterEx::SetHelpContextID, IAgentCharacter-Ex::SetHelpModeOnIAgentCharacterEx::SetHelpFileName**

IAgentCharacterEx::GetHelpFileName

```
HRESULT GetHelpFileName(
   BSTR * pbszName  // address of Help filename
);
```

Retrieves the **HelpFileName** for a character.

- Returns S_OK to indicate the operation was successful.

pbszName   Address of a variable that receives the Help filename for the character.

If you've created a Windows Help file for your application and set the character's **HelpFile** property, Microsoft Agent automatically calls Help when **HelpModeOn** is set to **True** and the user clicks the character or selects a command from its pop-up menu. If there is a context number in the selected command's **HelpContext-ID** property, Help displays a topic corresponding to the current Help context; otherwise it displays "No Help topic associated with this item."

This property applies only to your client application's use of the character; the setting does not affect other clients of the character or other characters of your client application.

Note Building a Help file requires the Microsoft Windows Help Compiler.

See also IAgentCommandsEx::SetHelpContextID, IAgentCharacterEx::SetHelpModeOn, IAgentCharacterEx::SetHelpFileName

IAgentCharacterEx::GetHelpModeOn

```
HRESULT GetHelpModeOn(
    long * pbHelpModeOn  // address of help mode setting
);
```

Retrieves whether context-sensitive Help mode is on for the character.

- Returns S_OK to indicate the operation was successful.

pbHelpModeOn   Address of a variable that receives **True** if Help mode is on for the character and **False** if not.

When this property is set to **True**, the mouse pointer changes to the context-sensitive Help image when moved over the character or over the pop-up menu for the character. When the user clicks or drags the character or clicks an item in the character's pop-up menu, the server triggers the **IAgentNotifySinkEx::HelpComplete** event and exits Help mode.

In Help mode, the server does not send the **IAgentNotifySink::Click**, **IAgentNotifySink::DragStart**, **IAgentNotifySink::DragComplete**, and **IAgentNotifySink::Command** events, unless **GetAutoPopupMenu** property returns **True**. In that case, the server will send the **IAgentNotifySink::Click** event (does not exit Help mode), but only for the right mouse button to enable you to display the pop-up menu.

This property applies only to your client application's use of the character; the setting does not affect other clients of the character or other characters of your client application.

See also IAgentCharacterEx::SetHelpModeOn

IAgentCharacterEx::GetLanguageID

```
HRESULT GetLanguageID(
    long * plangID  // address of language ID setting
);
```

Retrieves the language ID set for the character.

- Returns S_OK to indicate the operation was successful.

plangID

Address of a variable that receives the language ID setting for the character.

A Long integer specifying the language ID for the character. The language ID (LANGID) for a character is a 16-bit value defined by Windows, consisting of a primary language ID and a secondary language ID. The following examples are values for some languages. To determine the values other languages, see the Win32 SDK documentation.

Arabic (Saudi)	0x0401	Italian	0x0410
Basque	0x042d	Japanese	0x0411
Chinese (Simplified)	0x0804	Korean	0x0412
Chinese (Traditional)	0x0404	Norwegian	0x0414
Croatian	0x041A	Polish	0x0415
Czech	0x0405	Portuguese	0x0816
Danish	0x0406	Portuguese (Brazilian)	0x0416
Dutch	0x0413	Romanian	0x0418
English (British)	0x0809	Russian	0x0419
English (US)	0x0409	Slovakian	0x041B
Finnish	0x040B	Slovenian	0x0424
French	0x040C	Spanish	0x0C0A
German	0x0407	Swedish	0x041D
Greek	0x0408	Thai	0x041E
Hebrew	0x040D	Turkish	0x041F
Hungarian	0x040E		

If you do not set this language ID for the character, the character's language ID will be the current system language ID.

This setting also determines the language for TTS output, word balloon text, the commands in the character's pop-up menu, and speech recognition engine. To determine if there is a compatible speech recognition engine available for the character's language, use **IAgentCharacterEx::GetSRModeID** or **IAgentCharacterEx::GetTTSModeID**.

This property applies only to your client application's use of the character; the setting does not affect other clients of the character or other characters of your client application.

Note If the language ID is set to a language that supports bidirectional text (such as Arabic or Hebrew), but the system running your application does not have bidirectional support installed, text will appear in the word balloon in logical rather than display order.

See also **IAgentCharacterEx:SetLanguageID, IAgentCharacter-Ex::GetSRModeIDIAgentCharacterEx::GetTTSModeID**

IAgentCharacterEx::GetOriginalSize

```
HRESULT GetOriginalSize(
    long * plWidth,   // address of variable for character width
    long * plHeight   // address of variable for character height
);
```

Retrieves the original size of the character's animation frame.

- Returns S_OK to indicate the operation was successful.

plWidth   Address of a variable that receives the original width of the character animation frame in pixels.

plHeight   Address of a variable that receives the original height of the character animation frame in pixels.

This call returns the original size of the character frame as built in the Microsoft Agent Character Editor.

See also **IAgentCharacter::GetSize**

IAgentCharacterEx::GetSRModeID

```
HRESULT GetSRModeID(
    BSTR * pbszModeID   // address of speech recognition engine ID
);
```

Retrieves the mode ID of the speech recognition engine set for the character.

- Returns S_OK to indicate the operation was successful.

pbszModeID   Address of a BSTR that receives the mode ID setting of the speech
recognition engine for the character.

This setting returns the engine set for a character's speech input. The mode ID
for a speech recognition engine is a string representation of the GUID (formatted
with braces and dashes) by the speech vendor uniquely identifying the engine.
For more information, see the Microsoft Speech SDK documentation.

If you do not set a speech recognition engine mode ID for the character, the
server returns an engine that matches the character's language setting (using
Microsoft Speech API interfaces). If there is no matching speech recognition engine available for the character, the server returns a null (empty) string.

When speech input is enabled (in the Advanced Character Options window), querying or setting this property will load the associated engine (if it is not already
loaded), and start speech services. That is, the Listening key is available, and the
Listening Tip is displayable. (The Listening key and Listening Tip are enabled
only if they are also enabled in Advanced Character Options.) However, if you
query the property when speech is disabled, the server does not start speech services and it returns a null string (empty string).

This function returns only the setting for your client application's use of the character; the setting does not reflect other clients of the character or other characters
of your client application.

This function does not fail if the **IAgentSpeechInputProperties::GetEnabled**
returns **False**.

Microsoft Agent's speech engine requirements are based on the Microsoft
Speech API. Engines supporting Microsoft Agent's SAPI requirements can be
installed and used with Agent.

See also **IAgentCharacterEx::SetSRModeID**

IAgentCharacterEx::GetSRStatus

```
HRESULT GetSRStatus(
   long * plStatus  // address of the speech input status
);
```

Retrieves the status of the condition necessary to support speech input.

- Returns S_OK to indicate the operation was successful.

plStatus   Address of a variable that receives one of the following values for the state setting:

const unsigned long LISTEN_STATUS_CANLISTEN = 0;	Conditions support speech input.
const unsigned long LISTEN_STATUS_NOAUDIO = 1;	There is no audio input device available on this system. (Note that this does not detect whether a microphone is installed; it can only detect whether the user has a properly installed input-enabled sound card with a working driver.)
const unsigned long LISTEN_STATUS_NOTTOPMOST = 2;	Another client is the active client of this character, or the current character is not topmost.
const unsigned long LISTEN_STATUS_ CANTOPENAUDIO = 3;	The audio input or output channel is currently busy, some other application is using audio.
const unsigned long LISTEN_STATUS_ COULDNT-INITIALIZESPEECH = 4;	An unspecified error occurred in the process of initializing the speech recognition subsystem. This includes the possibility that there is no speech engine available matching the character's language setting.
const unsigned long LISTEN_STATUS_ SPEECH-DISABLED = 5;	The user has disabled speech input in the Advanced Character Options window.
const unsigned long LISTEN_STATUS_ERROR = 6;	An error occurred in checking the audio status, but the cause of the error was not returned by the system.

This function enables you to query whether current conditions support speech recognition input, including the status of the audio device. If your application uses the **IAgentCharacterEx::Listen** method, you can use this function to better ensure that the call will succeed. Calling this method also loads the speech engine if it is not already loaded. However, it does not turn on Listening mode.

When speech input is enabled in the Agent property sheet (Advanced Character Options), querying the status will load the associated engine (if it is not already loaded), and start speech services. That is, the Listening key is available, and the

Listening Tip is displayable. (The Listening key and Listening Tip are enabled only if they are also enabled in Advanced Character Options.) However, if you query the property when speech is disabled, the server does not start speech services.

This function returns only the setting for your client application's use of the character; the setting does not reflect other clients of the character or other characters of your client application.

IAgentCharacterEx::GetTTSModeID

```
HRESULT GetTTSModeID(
    BSTR * pbszModeID  // address of TTS engine ID
);
```

Retrieves the mode ID of the TTS engine set for the character.

- Returns S_OK to indicate the operation was successful.

pbszModeID   Address of a BSTR that receives the mode ID setting of the TTS engine for the character.

This setting returns the TTS (text-to-speech) engine mode ID for a character's spoken output. The mode ID for a TTS engine is a string representation of the GUID (formatted with braces and dashes) defined by the speech vendor uniquely identifying the engine. For more information, see the Microsoft Speech SDK documentation. Querying this property will load the associated engine if it is not already loaded.

If you do not set a TTS engine mode ID for the character, the server attempts to return an engine that matches (using Microsoft Speech API interfaces) the character's compiled TTS setting and the character's current language setting. If these are different, then the character's language setting overrides its authored mode setting. If you have not set the character's language setting, the character's language is the user default language ID, and the server attempts the match based on that language ID.

This function does not fail if the **IAgentAudioObjectProperties::GetEnabled** returns **False**.

This property applies only to your client application's use of the character; the setting does not affect other clients of the character or other characters of your client application.

Microsoft Agent's speech engine requirements are based on the Microsoft Speech API. Engines supporting Microsoft Agent's SAPI requirements can be installed and used with Agent.

See also IAgentCharacterEx::SetTTSModeID

IAgentCharacterEx::GetVersion

```
HRESULT GetVersion(
   short * psMajor,   // address of major version
   short * psMinor    // address of minor version
);
```

Retrieves the version number of the character standard animation set.

- Returns S_OK to indicate the operation was successful.

psMajor   Address of a variable that receives the major version.

psMinor   Address of a variable that receives the minor version.

The standard animation set version number is automatically set when you build it with the Microsoft Agent Character Editor.

IAgentCharacterEx::Listen

```
HRESULT Listen(
   long bListen   // listening mode flag
);
```

Turns Listening mode (speech recognition input) on or off.

- Returns S_OK to indicate the operation was successful.

bListen   Listening mode flag. If this parameter is **True**, the Listening mode
                       is turned on; if **False**, Listening mode is turned off.

Setting this method to **True** enables the Listening mode (turns on speech recognition) for a fixed period of time. While you cannot set the value of the time-out, you can turn off Listening mode before the time-out expires. In addition, if the Listening mode is already on because you (or another client) successfully set the method to **True** before the time-out expires, the method succeeds and resets the time-out. However, if Listening mode is already on because the user is pressing the Listening key, the method succeeds, but the time-out is ignored and the Listening mode ends based on the user's interaction with the Listening key.

This method will succeed only when called by the input-active client. Therefore, the method will fail if your client is not the active client of the topmost character. The method will also fail if you attempt to set the method to **False** and the user is pressing the Listening key. It can also fail if there is no compatible speech engine available that matches the character's language ID setting or the user has disabled speech input using the Microsoft Agent property sheet. However, the method will not fail if the audio device is busy.

When you successfully set this method to **True**, the server triggers the **IAgentNotifySinkEx::ListeningState** event. The server also sends **IAgentNotifySinkEx::ListeningState** when the Listening mode time-out completes or when you set **IAgentCharacterEx::Listen** to **False**.

This method does not automatically call **IAgentCharacter::StopAll** and play a Listening state animation of the character as occurs when the user presses the Listening key. This enables you to use the **IAgentNotifySinkEx::ListeningStaate** event to determine whether you wish to stop the current animation and play your own appropriate animation. However, once a user utterance is detected, the server automatically calls **IAgentCharacter::StopAll** and plays a Hearing state animation.

See also IAgentNotifySinkEx::ListeningState, IAgentNotifySink-Ex::ListeningState, AgentSpeechInputProperties::GetEnabled

---

IAgentCharacterEx::SetAutoPopupMenu

```
HRESULT SetAutoPopupMenu(
    long bAutoPopupMenu,  // auto pop-up menu display setting
);
```

Sets whether the server automatically displays the character's pop-up menu.

- Returns S_OK to indicate the operation was successful.

bAutoPopupMenu   The automatic pop-up menu display flag. If this parameter is **True**, Microsoft Agent automatically displays the character's pop-up menu when the user right-clicks the character or character's taskbar icon.

This property applies only to your client application's use of the character; the setting does not affect other clients of the character or other characters of your client application.

By setting this property to **False**, you can create your own menu-handling behavior. To display the menu after setting this property to **False**, use the **IAgentCharacter::ShowPopupMenu** method.

See also IAgentCharacterEx::GetAutoPopupMenu, IAgentCharacter-Ex::ShowPopupMenu

---

IAgentCharacterEx::SetHelpContextID

```
HRESULT SetHelpContextID(
    long ulHelpID  // ID for help topic
);
```

Sets the **HelpContextID** for the character.

- Returns S_OK to indicate the operation was successful.

ulHelpID   The context number of the help topic for associated with a character; used to provide context-sensitive Help for the character.

If you've created a Windows Help file for your application and set this in the character's **HelpFile** property, Microsoft Agent automatically calls Help when **HelpModeOn** is set to **True** and the user selects the character. If there is a context number in the HelpContextID, Agent calls Help and searches for the topic identified by the current context number. The current context number is the value of **HelpContextID** for the character. If there is a context number in the **HelpContextID** property, Help displays a topic corresponding to the current Help context; otherwise it displays "No Help topic associated with this item."

This setting applies only when your client application is the active client of the topmost character. It does not affect other clients of the character or other characters that your client application is using.

Note Building a Help file requires the Microsoft Windows Help Compiler.

See also **IAgentCharacterEx::GetHelpContextID**, **IAgentCharacterEx::SetHelpModeOn**, **IAgentCharacterEx::SetHelpFileName**

IAgentCharacterEx::SetHelpFileName

```
HRESULT SetHelpFileName(
    BSTR bszName  // Help filename
);
```

Sets the **HelpFileName** for a character.

- Returns S_OK to indicate the operation was successful.

bszName   The Help filename for the character.

If you've created a Windows Help file for your application and set the character's **HelpFile** property, Microsoft Agent automatically calls Help when **HelpModeOn** is set to **True** and the user clicks the character or selects a command from its pop-up menu. If there is a context number in the **HelpContextID** property of the selected command, Help displays a topic corresponding to the current Help context; otherwise it displays "No Help topic associated with this item."

This property applies only to your client application's use of the character; the setting does not affect other clients of the character or other characters of your client application.

Note Building a Help file requires the Microsoft Windows Help Compiler.

See also **IAgentCommandsEx::SetHelpContextID**, **IAgentCharacterEx::SetHelpModeOn**, **IAgentCharacterEx::GetHelpFileName**

IAgentCharacterEx::SetHelpModeOn

```
HRESULT SetHelpModeOn(
   long bHelpModeOn  // help mode setting
);
```

Sets context-sensitive Help mode on for the character.

- Returns S_OK to indicate the operation was successful.

bHelpModeOn   Help mode flag. If this parameter is **True**, Microsoft Agent turns on Help mode for the character.

When you set this property to **True**, the mouse pointer changes to the context-sensitive Help image when moved over the character or over the pop-up menu for the character. When the user clicks or drags the character or clicks an item in the character's pop-up menu, the server triggers the **IAgentNotifySinkEx::HelpComplete** event and exits Help mode.

In Help mode, the server does not send the **Click, DragStart, DragComplete**, and **Command** events, unless the **GetAutoPopupMenu** property returns **True**. In that case, the server will send the **Click** event (does not exit Help mode), but only for the right mouse button so you can display the pop-up menu.

This property applies only to your client application's use of the character; the setting does not affect other clients of the character or other characters of your client application.

See also **IAgentCharacterEx::GetHelpModeOn, IAgentNotifySink-Ex::HelpComplete**

IAgentCharacterEx::SetLanguageID

```
HRESULT SetLanguageID(
   long langID  // language ID setting of character
);
```

Sets the language ID set for the character.

- Returns S_OK to indicate the operation was successful.

langID   The language ID setting for the character.

A Long integer specifying the language ID for the character. The language ID (LANGID) for a character is a 16-bit value defined by Windows, consisting of a primary language ID and a secondary language ID. You can use the following values for the specified languages. For more information, see the Win32 SDK documentation.

Arabic (Saudi)	0x0401	Italian	0x0410
Basque	0x042d	Japanese	0x0411
Chinese (Simplified)	0x0804	Korean	0x0412
Chinese (Traditional)	0x0404	Norwegian	0x0414
Croatian	0x041A	Polish	0x0415
Czech	0x0405	Portuguese	0x0816
Danish	0x0406	Portuguese (Brazilian)	0x0416
Dutch	0x0413	Romanian	0x0418
English (British)	0x0809	Russian	0x0419
English (US)	0x0409	Slovakian	0x041B
Finnish	0x040B	Slovenian	0x0424
French	0x040C	Spanish	0x0C0A
German	0x0407	Swedish	0x041D
Greek	0x0408	Thai	0x041E
Hebrew	0x040D	Turkish	0x041F
Hungarian	0x040E		

If you do not set the language ID for the character, its language ID will be the current system language ID if the corresponding Agent language DLL is installed; otherwise, the character's language will be English (US).

This property also determines the language for the word balloon text, the commands in the character's pop-up menu, and the speech recognition engine. It also determines the default language for TTS output. To determine if there is a compatible speech engine available for the character's language, use **IAgentCharacterEx::GetSRModeID** or **IAgentCharacterEx::GetTTSModeID**.

If you try to set the language ID for a character and the Agent language resources, the code page, or a display font for the language ID is not available, Agent returns an error and the character's language ID remains at its last setting. Setting this property does not return an error if there are no matching speech engines for the language.

This property applies only to your client application's use of the character; the setting does not affect other clients of the character or other characters of your client application.

Note If you set the character's language ID to a language that supports bidirectional text (such as Arabic or Hebrew), but the system running your application does not have bidirectional support installed, text will appear in the word balloon in logical rather than display order.

See also IAgentCharacterEx:GetLanguageID, IAgentCharacterEx::Get-SRModeID, IAgentCharacterEx::GetTTSModeID

IAgentCharacterEx::SetSRModeID

```
HRESULT SetSRModeID(
    BSTR bszModeID  // speech recognition engine ID
);
```

Sets the mode ID of the speech recognition engine set for the character.

- Returns S_OK to indicate the operation was successful.

bszModeID   The mode ID setting of the speech recognition engine for the character.

This setting sets the engine for a character's speech input. The mode ID for a speech recognition engine is the GUID defined by the speech vendor that uniquely identifies the engine's mode (formatted with braces and dashes). For more information, see the Microsoft Speech SDK documentation.

If you specify a mode ID that does not match the character's language setting, if the user has disabled speech recognition (in the Microsoft Agent property sheet), or the engine is not installed, this call will fail. If you do not set a speech recognition engine mode ID for the character, the server sets one that matches the character's language setting (using Microsoft Speech API interfaces).

When speech input is enabled in the Agent property sheet (Advanced Character Options), setting this property will load the associated engine (if it is not already loaded), and start speech services. That is, the Listening key is available, and the Listening Tip is displayable. (The Listening key and Listening tip are enabled only if they are also enabled in Advanced Character Options.) However, if you query the property when speech is disabled, the server does not start speech services.

This property applies to only the client of the character; the setting does not reflect the setting for other clients of the character or other characters of the client.

Microsoft Agent's speech engine requirements are based on the Microsoft Speech API. Engines supporting Microsoft Agent's SAPI requirements can be installed and used with Agent.

See also IAgentCharacterEx::GetSRModeID

IAgentCharacterEx::SetTTSModeID

```
HRESULT SetTTSModeID(
    BSTR bszModeID  // TTS engine ID
);
```

Sets the mode ID of the TTS engine set for the character.

- Returns S_OK to indicate the operation was successful.

bszModeID   The mode ID setting of the TTS engine for the character.

Note **SetTTSModeID** can fail if Speech.dll is not installed and the engine you specify does not match the character's compiled TTS mode setting.

This setting determines the preferred engine mode for a character's spoken TTS output. The mode ID for a TTS (text-to-speech) engine is the GUID defined by the speech vendor that uniquely identifies the mode of the engine (formatted with braces and dashes). For more information, see the Microsoft Speech SDK documentation.

If you set a TTS mode ID, it overrides the server attempt to match a speech engine based on the character's compiled TTS mode ID, the current system language ID, and the character's current language ID. However, if you attempt to set a mode ID when the user has disabled speech output in the Microsoft Agent property sheet or when the associated engine is not installed, this call will fail.

If you do not set a TTS engine mode ID for the character, the server sets an engine that matches the character's language setting (using Microsoft Speech API interfaces). Setting this property will load the associated engine if it is not already loaded.

This property applies to only your client application's use of the character; the setting does not affect other clients of the character or other characters of your client application.

Microsoft Agent's speech engine requirements are based on the Microsoft Speech API. Engines supporting Microsoft Agent's SAPI requirements can be installed and used with Agent.

See also **IAgentCharacterEx:GetTTSModeID**

IAgentCharacterEx::ShowPopupMenu

```
HRESULT ShowPopupMenu(
   short x,   // x-coordinate of pop-up menu
   short y    // y-coordinate of pop-up menu
);
```

Displays the pop-up menu for the character.

- Returns S_OK to indicate the operation was successful.

x	The x-coordinate of the character's pop-up menu in pixels, relative to the screen origin (upper left).
y	The y-coordinate of the character's pop-up menu in pixels, relative to the screen origin (upper left).

When you set **IAgentCharacterEx::SetAutoPopupMenu** to **False**, the server no longer automatically displays the menu when the character or its taskbar icon is right-clicked. You can use this method to display the menu.

The menu displays until the user selects a command or displays another menu. Only one pop-up menu can be displayed at a time; therefore, calls to this method will cancel (remove) the former menu.

This method should only be called when your client application is the active client of the character; otherwise it fails.

See also **IAgentCharacterEx::SetAutoPopupMenu**

IAgentCharacterEx::Think

```
HRESULT Think(
    BSTR bszText,      // text to think
    long * pdwReqID    // address of a request ID
);
```

Displays the character's thought word balloon with the specified text.

- Returns S_OK to indicate the operation was successful.

bszText	The text to appear in the character's thought balloon.
pdwReqID	Address of a variable that receives the **Think** request ID.

Like the **Speak** method, the **Think** method is a queued request that displays text in a word balloon, except that thoughts display in a special thought balloon. The thought balloon supports only the Bookmark speech control tag (**\Mrk**) and ignores any other speech control tags. Unlike **Speak**, the **Think** method does not change the character's animation state.

The **IAgentBalloon** settings also apply to the appearance style of the thought balloon. For example, the balloon's **Enabled** property must also be **True** for the text to display.

Microsoft Agent's automatic word breaking in the word balloon breaks words using white-space characters (for example, space and tab). However, it may break a word to fit the balloon as well. In languages like Japanese, Chinese, and Thai, where spaces are not used to break words, insert a Unicode zero width space character (0x200B) between characters to define logical word breaks.

Note Set the character's language ID (using **IAgentCharacterEx::Set-LanguageID** before using the **Speak** method to ensure appropriate text display within the word balloon.

See also IAgentBalloon::GetEnabled, IAgentBalloonEx::SetStyle, IAgent-Character::Speak

IAgentCommands

The Microsoft Agent server maintains a list of commands that are currently available to the user. This list includes commands that the server defines for general interaction, such as Hide and Microsoft Agent Properties, the list of available (but non-input-active) clients, and the commands defined by the current active client. The first two sets of commands are global commands; that is, they are available at any time, regardless of the input-active client. Client-defined commands are available only when that client is input-active.

Retrieve an **IAgentCommands** interface by querying the **IAgentCharacter** interface for **IAgentCommands**. Each Microsoft Agent client application can define a collection of commands called a **Commands** collection. To add a **Command** to the collection, use the **Add** or **Insert** method. Although you can specify a **Command's** properties using **IAgentCommand** methods, for optimum code performance, specify all of a **Command's** properties in the **IAgentCommands::Add** or **IAgentCommands::Insert** methods when initially setting the properties for a new **Command**. You can use the **IAgentCommand** methods to query or change the property settings.

For each **Command** in the **Commands** collection, you can determine whether the command appears on the character's pop-up menu, in the Voice Commands Window, in both, or in neither. For example, if you want a command to appear on the pop-up menu for the character, set the command's **Caption** and **Visible** properties. To display the command in the **Voice Commands Window**, set the command's **Caption** and **Voice** properties.

A user can access the individual commands in your Commands collection only when your client application is input-active and the character is visible. Therefore, you will typically want to set the **Caption**, **VoiceCaption**, and **Voice** properties for the **Commands** collection object as well as for the commands in the collection, because this places an entry for your **Commands** collection on a character's pop-up menu and in the Voice Commands Window. When the user switches to your client by choosing its **Commands** entry, the server automatically makes your client input-active, notifying your client application using the **IAgentNotifySink::ActivateInputState** and makes the **Commands** in its collection available. The server also notifies the client that is no longer input-active with the **IAgentNotifySink::ActivateInputState** event. This enables the server to present and accept only the **Commands** that apply to the current input-active client's context. It also serves to avoid **Command**-name collisions between clients.

A client can also explicitly request to make itself the input-active client using the **IAgentCharacter::Activate** method. This method also supports setting your application to not be the input-active client. You may want to use this method when sharing a character with another application, setting your application to be input-active when your application window gets focus and not input-active when it loses focus.

Similarly, you can use **IAgentCharacter::Activate** to set your application to be (or not be) the active client of the character. The active client is the client that receives input when its character is the topmost character. When this status changes, the server notifies your application with the **IAgentNotifySinkEx::ActiveClientChange** event.

When a character's pop-up menu is displayed, changes to the properties of a **Commands** collection or the commands in its collection do not appear until the user redisplays the menu. However, when open, the Voice Commands Window does display changes as they happen.

IAgentCommands defines an interface that allows applications to add, remove, set, and query properties for a **Commands** collection. These functions are also available from **IAgentCommandsEx**.

A **Commands** collection can appear as a command in both the pop-up menu and the Voice Commands Window for a character. To make the **Commands** collection appear, you must set its **Caption** property. The following table summarizes how the properties of a **Commands** collection affect its presentation.

Caption Property	Voice-Caption Property	Voice Property	Visible Property	Appears in Character's Pop-up Menu	Appears in Voice Commands Window
Yes	Yes	Yes	True	Yes, using **Caption**	Yes, using **VoiceCaption**
Yes	Yes	No[1]	True	Yes, using **Caption**	No
Yes	Yes	Yes	False	No	Yes, using **VoiceCaption**
Yes	Yes	No[1]	False	No	No
No[1]	Yes	Yes	True	No	Yes, using **VoiceCaption**
No[1]	Yes	Yes	False	No	Yes, using **VoiceCaption**
No[1]	Yes	No[1]	True	No	No

[1]If the property setting is null. In some programming languages, an empty string may not be interpreted the same as a null string.

Caption Property	Voice-Caption Property	Voice Property	Visible Property	Appears in Character's Pop-up Menu	Appears in Voice Commands Window
No[1]	Yes	No[1]	False	No	No
Yes	No[1]	Yes	True	Yes, using **Caption**	Yes, using **Caption**
Yes	No[1]	No[1]	True	Yes	No
Yes	No[1]	Yes	False	No	Yes, using **Caption**
Yes	No[1]	No[1]	False	No	No
No[1]	No[1]	Yes	True	No	No[2]
No[1]	No[1]	Yes	False	No	No[2]
No[1]	No[1]	No[1]	True	No	No
No[1]	No[1]	No[1]	False	No	No

[1]If the property setting is null. In some programming languages, an empty string may not be interpreted the same as a null string.

[2]The command is still voice-accessible.

Methods in Vtable Order

IAgentCommands Methods	Description
GetCommand	Retrieves a **Command** object from the **Commands** collection.
GetCount	Returns the value of the number of **Commands** in a **Commands** collection.
SetCaption	Sets the value of the **Caption** property for a **Commands** collection.
GetCaption	Returns the value of the **Caption** property of a **Commands** collection.
SetVoice	Sets the value of the **Voice** property for a **Commands** collection.
GetVoice	Returns the value of the **Voice** property of a **Commands** collection.
SetVisible	Sets the value of the **Visible** property for a **Commands** collection.
GetVisible	Returns the value of the **Visible** property of a **Commands** collection.
Add	Adds a **Command** object to a **Commands** collection.
Insert	Inserts a **Command** object in a **Commands** collection.
Remove	Removes a **Command** object in a **Commands** collection.
RemoveAll	Removes all **Command** objects from a **Commands** collection.

IAgentCommands::Add

```
HRESULT Add(
    BSTR bszCaption,    // Caption setting for Command
    BSTR bszVoice,      // Voice setting for Command
    long bEnabled,      // Enabled setting for Command
    long bVisible,      // Visible setting for Command
    long * pdwID        // address for variable for ID
);
```

Adds a **Command** to a **Commands** collection.

- Returns S_OK to indicate the operation was successful.

bszCaption	A BSTR that specifies the value of the **Caption** text displayed for a **Command** in a **Commands** collection.
bszVoice	A BSTR that specifies the value of the **Voice** text setting for a **Command** in a **Commands** collection.
bEnabled	A Boolean expression that specifies the **Enabled** setting for a **Command** in a **Commands** collection. If the parameter is **True**, the **Command** is enabled and can be selected; if **False**, the **Command** is disabled.
bVisible	A Boolean expression that specifies the **Visible** setting for a **Command** in a **Commands** collection. If the parameter is **True**, the **Command** will be visible in the character's pop-up menu (if the **Caption** property is also set).
pdwID	Address of a variable that receives the ID for the added **Command**.

See also **IAgentCommand::SetCaption, IAgentCommand::Set Enabled, IAgentCommand::SetVisible, IAgentCommand::SetVoice, IAgentCommands::Insert, IAgentCommands::Remove, IAgent-Commands::RemoveAll**

IAgentCommands::GetCaption

```
HRESULT GetCaption(
    BSTR * pbszCaption  // address of Caption text for
                        // Commands collection
);
```

Retrieves the **Caption** for a **Commands** collection.

- Returns S_OK to indicate the operation was successful.

pbszCaption	The address of a BSTR that receives the value of the **Caption** text setting displayed for a **Commands** collection.

See also **IAgentCommands::SetCaption, IAgentCommands::GetVisible, IAgentCommands::GetVoice**

IAgentCommands::GetCommand

```
HRESULT GetCommand(
   long dwCommandID,          // Command ID
   IUnknown ** ppunkCommand   // address of IUnknown interface
);
```

Retrieves a Command object from the Commands collection.

- Returns S_OK to indicate the operation was successful.

dwCommandID   The ID of a Command object in the **Commands** collection.

IUnknown   The address of the **IUnknown** interface for the **Command** object.

See also **IAgentCommand**

IAgentCommands::GetCount

```
HRESULT GetCount(
   long * pdwCount   // address of count of commands
);
```

Retrieves the number of **Command** objects in a **Commands** collection.

- Returns S_OK to indicate the operation was successful.

pdwCount   Address of a variable that receives the number of **Commands** in a **Commands** collection.

pdwCount includes only the number of **Commands** you define in your **Commands** collection. Server or other client entries are not included.

IAgentCommands::GetVisible

```
HRESULT GetVisible(
   long * pbVisible  // address of Visible
                     // setting for Commands collection
);
```

Retrieves the value of the **Visible** property for a **Commands** collection.

- Returns S_OK to indicate the operation was successful.

pbVisible   The address of a variable that receives the value of the **Visible** property for a **Commands** collection.

See also **IAgentCommands::SetVisible, IAgentCommands::SetCaption**

IAgentCommands::GetVoice

```
HRESULT GetVoice(
   BSTR * pbszVoice  // address of Voice setting for
```

```
                            // Commands collection
);
```

Retrieves the value of the **Voice** property for a **Commands** collection.

- Returns S_OK to indicate the operation was successful.

pbszVoice   The address of a BSTR that receives the value of the **Voice** text set-
                         ting for a **Commands** collection.

See also **IAgentCommands::SetVoice, IAgentCommands::GetCaption,
IAgentCommands::GetVisible**

IAgentCommands::Insert

```
HRESULT Insert(
    BSTR bszCaption,    // Caption setting for Command
    BSTR bszVoice,      // Voice setting for Command
    long bEnabled,      // Enabled setting for Command
    long bVisible,      // Visible setting for Command
    long dwRefID,       // reference Command for insertion
    long dBefore,       // insertion position flag
    long * pdwID        // address for variable for Command ID
);
```

Inserts a **Command** object in a **Commands** collection.

- Returns S_OK to indicate the operation was successful.

bszCaption   A BSTR that specifies the value of the **Caption** text displayed for
                        the **Command**.

bszVoice   A BSTR that specifies the value of the **Voice** text setting for a
                        Command.

bEnabled   A Boolean expression that specifies the **Enabled** setting for a **Com-
                        mand**. If the parameter is **True**, the **Command** is enabled and can
                        be selected; if **False**, the **Command** is disabled.

bVisible   A Boolean expression that specifies the **Visible** setting for a **Com-
                        mand**. If the parameter is **True**, the **Command** will be visible in
                        the character's pop-up menu (if the **Caption** property is also set).

dwRefID   The ID of a **Command** used as a reference for the relative insertion
                        of the new **Command**.

dBefore   A Boolean expression that specifies where to place the **Command**.
                        If this parameter is **True**, the new **Command** is inserted before the
                        referenced **Command**; if **False**, the new **Command** is placed after
                        the referenced **Command**.

pdwID   Address of a variable that receives the ID for the inserted **Command**.

See also **IAgentCommands::Add, IAgentCommands::Remove,
IAgentCommands::RemoveAll**

IAgentCommands::Remove

```
HRESULT Remove(
   long dwID  // Command ID
);
```

Removes the specified **Command** from a **Commands** collection.

- Returns S_OK to indicate the operation was successful.

dwID   The ID of a **Command** to remove from the **Commands** collection.

Removing a **Command** from a **Commands** collection also removes it from the pop-up menu and the Voice Commands Window when your application is input-active.

See also IAgentCommands::Add, IAgentCommands::Insert, IAgent-Commands::RemoveAll

IAgentCommands::RemoveAll

```
HRESULT Remove();
```

Removes all **Commands** from a **Commands** collection.

- Returns S_OK to indicate the operation was successful.

Removing all **Commands** from a **Commands** collection also removes them from the pop-up menu and the Voice Commands Window when your application is input-active. **RemoveAll** does not remove server or other client's entries.

See also IAgentCommands::Add, IAgentCommands::Insert, IAgent-Commands::Remove

IAgentCommands::SetCaption

```
HRESULT SetCaption(
   BSTR bszCaption  // Caption setting for Commands collection
);
```

Sets the **Caption** text displayed for a **Commands** collection.

- Returns S_OK to indicate the operation was successful.

bszCaption   A BSTR that specifies the value for the **Caption** property for a **Commands** collection.

Setting the **Caption** property for a **Commands** collection defines how it will appear on the character's pop-up menu when its **Visible** property is set to **True** and your application is not the input-active client. To specify an access key (unlined mnemonic) for your **Caption**, include an ampersand (&) character before that character.

If you define commands for a **Commands** collection that has its **Caption** set, you typically also define a **Caption** for its **Commands** collection.

See also **IAgentCommands::GetCaption, IAgentCommands::SetVisible, IAgentCommands::SetVoice**

IAgentCommands::SetVisible

```
HRESULT SetVisible(
    long bVisible  // the Visible setting for Commands collection
);
```

Sets the value of the **Visible** property for a **Commands** collection.

- Returns S_OK to indicate the operation was successful.

bVisible   A Boolean value that determines the **Visible** property of a **Commands** collection. **True** sets the **Commands** collection's **Caption** to be visible when the character's pop-up menu is displayed; **False** does not display it.

A **Commands** collection must have its **Caption** property set and its **Visible** property set to **True** to appear on the character's pop-up menu. The **Visible** property must also be set to **True** for commands in the collection to appear when your client application is input-active.

See also **IAgentCommands::GetVisible, IAgentCommand::SetCaption**

IAgentCommands::SetVoice

```
HRESULT SetVoice(
    BSTR bszVoice  // the Voice setting for Command collection
);
```

Sets the **Voice** text property for a **Command**.

- Returns S_OK to indicate the operation was successful.

bszVoice   A BSTR that specifies the value for the **Voice** text property of a **Commands** collection.

A **Commands** collection must have its **Voice** text property set to be voice-accessible. It also must have its **VoiceCaption** or **Caption** property set to appear in the Voice Commands Window and its **Visible** property set to **True** to appear on the character's pop-up menu.

The BSTR expression you supply can include square bracket characters ([ ]) to indicate optional words and vertical bar characters (|) to indicate alternative strings. Alternates must be enclosed in parentheses. For example, "(hello [there] | hi)" tells the speech engine to accept "hello," "hello there," or "hi" for the command. Remember to include appropriate spaces between words you include in brackets or parentheses as well as other text. Remember to include appropriate spaces between the text that's in brackets or parentheses and the text that's not in brackets or parentheses.

You can use the star (*) operator to specify zero or more instances of the words included in the group or the plus (+) operator to specify one or more instances. For example, the following results in a grammar that supports "try this", "please try this", and "please please try this", with unlimited iterations of "please":

```
"please* try this"
```

The following grammar format excludes "try this" because the + operator defines at least one instance of "please":

```
"please+ try this"
```

The repetition operators follow normal rules of precedence and apply to the immediately preceding text item. For example, the following grammar results in "New York" and "New York York", but not "New York New York":

```
"New York+"
```

Therefore, you typically want to use these operators with the grouping characters. For example, the following grammar includes both "New York" and "New York New York":

```
"(New York)+"
```

Repetition operators are useful when you want to compose a grammar that includes a repeated sequence such as a phone number or specification of a list of items:

```
"call (one|two|three|four|five|six|seven|eight|nine|zero|oh)*"
"I'd like (cheese|pepperoni|pineapple|canadian bacon|mushrooms|and)+"
```

Although the operators can also be used with square brackets (an optional grouping character), doing so may reduce the efficiency of Agent's processing of the grammar.

You can also use an ellipsis (...) to support *word spotting*, that is, telling the speech recognition engine to ignore words spoken in this position in the phrase (sometimes called *garbage* words). When you use ellipses, the speech engine recognizes only specific words in the string regardless of when spoken with adjacent words or phrases. For example, if you set this property to "[...] check mail [...]" the speech recognition engine will match phrases like "please check mail" or "check mail please" to this command. Ellipses can be used anywhere within a string. However, be careful using this technique as voice settings with ellipses may increase the potential of unwanted matches.

When defining the words and grammar for your command, include at least one word that is required; that is, avoid supplying only optional words. In addition, make sure that the word includes only pronounceable words and letters. For numbers, it is better to spell out the word rather than use an ambiguous representation. For example, "345" is not a good grammar form. Similarly, instead of "IEEE", use "I triple E". Also, omit any punctuation or symbols. For example, instead of "the #1 $10 pizza!", use "the number one ten dollar pizza". Including non-pronounceable characters or symbols for one command may cause the speech engine to fail to compile the grammar for all your commands. Finally, make your voice parameter as distinct as reasonably possible from other voice commands you define. The greater the similarity between the voice grammar for commands, the more likely the speech engine will make a recognition error. You can also use the confidence scores to better distinguish between two commands that may have similar or similar-sounding voice grammar.

You can include in your grammar words in the form of "*text\pronunciation*", where "text" is the text displayed and "pronunciation" is text that clarifies the pronunciation. For example, the grammar, "1st\first", would be recognized when the user says "first," but the **Command** event will return the text, "1st\first". You can also use IPA (International Phonetic Alphabet) to specify a pronunciation by beginning the pronunciation with a pound-sign character ("#"), then the text representing the IPA pronunciation.

For Japanese speech recognition engines, you can define grammar in the form "*kana\kanji,*" reducing the alternative pronunciations and increasing the accuracy. (The ordering is reversed for backward compatibility.) This is particularly important for the pronunciation of proper names in Kanji. However, you can just pass in "kanji," without the Kana, in which case the engine should listen for all acceptable pronunciations for the Kanji. You can also pass in just Kana.

Except for errors using the grouping or repetition formatting characters, Microsoft Agent will not report errors in your grammar, unless the engine itself reports the error. If you pass text in your grammar that the engine fails to compile, but the engine does not handle and return as an error, Agent cannot report the error. Therefore, the client application must be careful defining the grammar for the **Voice** property.

Note The grammar features available may depend on the speech recognition engine. You may want to check with the engine's vendor to determine what grammar options are supported. Use the SRModeID to use a specific engine.

Note The operation of this property depends on the state of Microsoft Agent server's speech recognition state. For example, if speech recognition is disabled or not installed, this function has no immediate effect. If speech recognition is enabled during a session, however, the command will become accessible when its client application is input-active.

See also IAgentCommands::GetVoice, IAgentCommands::SetCaption, IAgentCommands::SetVisible

IAgentCommandsEx

IAgentCommandsEx defines an interface that extends the **IAgentCommands** interface.

Methods in Vtable Order

IAgentCommandsEx Methods	Description
SetDefaultID	Sets the default command for the character's pop-up menu.
GetDefaultID	Returns the default command for the character's pop-up menu.
SetHelpContextID	Sets the context-sensitive help topic ID for a **Commands** object
GetHelpContextID	Returns the context-sensitive help topic ID for a **Command** object.
SetFontName	Sets the font to use in the character's pop-up menu.
GetFontName	Returns the font used in the character's pop-up menu.
SetFontSize	Sets the font size to use in the character's pop-up menu.
GetFontSize	Returns the font size used in the character's pop-up menu.
SetVoiceCaption	Sets the voice caption for the character's **Commands** object.
GetVoiceCaption	Returns the voice caption for the character's **Commands** object.

IAgentCommandsEx Methods	Description
AddEx	Adds a **Command** object to a **Commands** collection.
InsertEx	Inserts a **Command** object in a **Commands** collection.
SetGlobalVoiceCommandsEnabled	Enables the voice grammar for Agent's global commands.
GetGlobalVoiceCommandsEnabled	Returns whether the voice grammar for Agent's global commands is enabled.

IAgentCommandsEx::AddEx

```
HRESULT AddEx(
   BSTR bszCaption,        // Caption setting for Command
   BSTR bszVoice,          // Voice setting for Command
   BSTR bszVoiceCaption,   // VoiceCaption setting for Command
   long bEnabled,          // Enabled setting for Command
   long bVisible,          // Visible setting for Command
   long ulHelpID,          // HelpContextID setting for Command
   long * pdwID            // address for variable for ID
);
```

Adds a **Command** to a **Commands** collection.

- Returns S_OK to indicate the operation was successful.

bszCaption	A BSTR that specifies the value of the **Caption** text displayed for a **Command** in a **Commands** collection.
bszVoice	A BSTR that specifies the value of the **Voice** text setting for a **Command** in a **Commands** collection.
bszVoiceCaption	A BSTR that specifies the value of the **VoiceCaption** text displayed for a **Command** in a **Commands** collection.
bEnabled	A Boolean expression that specifies the **Enabled** setting for a **Command** in a **Commands** collection. If the parameter is **True**, the **Command** is enabled and can be selected; if **False**, the **Command** is disabled.
bVisible	A Boolean expression that specifies the **Visible** setting for a **Command** in a **Commands** collection. If the parameter is **True**, the **Command** will be visible in the character's pop-up menu (if the **Caption** property is also set).
ulHelpID	The context number of the help topic associated with the **Command** object; used to provide context-sensitive Help for the command.
pdwID	Address of a variable that receives the ID for the added **Command**.

IAgentCommandsEx::AddEx extends **IAgentCommands::Add** by including the HelpContextID property. You can also set the property using **IAgentCommandsEx::SetHelpContextID**

See also IAgentCommands::Add, IAgentCommandsEx::SetHelp-
ContextID, IAgentCommand::SetCaption, IAgentCommand::SetEnabled,
IAgentCommand::SetVisible, IAgentCommand::SetVoice, IAgent-
Commands::Insert, IAgentCommandsEx::InsertEx, IAgent-
Commands::Remove, IAgentCommands::RemoveAll

IAgentCommandsEx::GetDefaultID

```
HRESULT GetDefaultID(
    long * pdwID   // address of default command's ID
);
```

Retrieves the ID of the default command in a **Commands** collection.

■ Returns S_OK to indicate the operation was successful.

pdwID   Address of a variable that receives the ID of the **Command** set as
                    the default.

This property returns the current default **Command** object in your **Commands**
collection. The default command is bold in the character's pop-up menu. However, setting the default command does not change command handling or double-
click events.

This property applies only to your client application's use of the character; the
setting does not affect other clients of the character or other characters of your
client application.

See also IAgentCommandsEx::SetDefaultID

IAgentCommandsEx::GetFontName

```
HRESULT GetFontName(
    BSTR * pbszFontName   // address of variable for font displayed
);                        // in character's pop-up menu
```

Retrieves the value for the font displayed in the character's pop-up menu.

■ Returns S_OK to indicate the operation was successful.

pbszFontName   The address of a BSTR that receives the font name displayed in the
                    character's pop-up menu.

The font name returned corresponds to the font used to display text in the
character's pop-up menu when your client application is input-active. The default
value for the font setting is based on the menu font setting for the character's language ID setting, or if not set, the user default language ID setting.

This property applies only to your client application's use of the character; the setting does not affect other clients of the character or other characters of your client application.

See also IAgentCommandsEx::SetFontName, IAgentCommands-Ex::SetFontSize

IAgentCommandsEx::GetFontSize

```
HRESULT GetFontSize(
    long * plFontSize  // address of variable for font size
);                     // for font displayed in character's pop-up menu
```

Retrieves the value for the size of the font displayed in the character's pop-up menu.

- Returns S_OK to indicate the operation was successful.

plFontSize   The address of a value that receives the size of the font.

The point size of the font returned corresponds to the size defined to display text in the character's pop-up menu when your client is input-active. The default value for the font setting is based on the menu font setting for the character's language ID setting, or if not set, the user default language setting.

This property applies only to your client application's use of the character; the setting does not affect other clients of the character or other characters of your client application.

See also IAgentCommandsEx::SetFontSize, IAgentCommandsEx::SetFontName

IAgentCommandsEx::GetGlobalVoiceCommandsEnabled

```
HRESULT GetGlobalVoiceCommandsEnabled(
    long * pbEnabled  // address of the global voice command setting
);
```

Retrieves whether the voice grammar for Agent's global commands is enabled.

- Returns S_OK to indicate the operation was successful.

pbEnabled   The address that receives **True** if the voice grammar for Agent's global commands is enabled, **False** if disabled.

Microsoft Agent automatically adds voice parameters (grammar) for opening and closing the Voice Commands Window and for showing and hiding the character. When this method returns **False**, any voice parameters for these commands as well as the voice parameters for the **Caption** of other clients' **Commands** objects are not included in the grammar. This enables you to eliminate these from your client's current active grammar. However, this setting does not reflect the inclusion of these commands in the character's pop-up menu.

See also **IAgentCommandsEx::SetGlobalVoiceCommandsEnabled**

IAgentCommandsEx::GetHelpContextID

```
HRESULT GetHelpContextID(
    long * pulHelpID  // address of Commands object help topic ID
);
```

Retrieves the **HelpContextID** for a **Commands** object.

- Returns S_OK to indicate the operation was successful.

pulHelpID   Address of a variable that receives the context number of the help topic for the **Commands** object.

If you've created a Windows Help file for your application and set the character's **HelpFile** property, Microsoft Agent automatically calls Help when **HelpModeOn** is set to **True** and the user selects your **Commands** object. If there is a context number in the **HelpContextID**, Agent calls Help and searches for the topic identified by the current context number. The current context number is the value of **HelpContextID** for the **Commands** object.

This property applies only to your client application's use of the character; the setting does not affect other clients of the character or other characters of your client application.

Note Building a Help file requires the Microsoft Windows Help Compiler.

See also **IAgentCommandsEx::SetHelpContextID**,
IAgentCharacterEx::SetHelpModeOn,
IAgentCharacterEx::SetHelpFileName

IAgentCommandsEx::GetVoiceCaption

```
HRESULT GetVoiceCaption(
    BSTR * pbszVoiceCaption  // address of command's voice caption
);
```

Retrieves the **VoiceCaption** for a **Commands** object.

- Returns S_OK to indicate the operation was successful.

pbszVoiceCaption   The address of a BSTR that receives the value of the **Caption** text displayed for a **Command**.

The text returned is that set for your **Commands** object and appears in the Voice Commands window when your client application is input-active.

This property applies only to your client application's use of the character; the setting does not affect other clients of the character or other characters of your client application.

See also **IAgentCommandsEx::SetVoiceCaption**

IAgentCommandsEx::InsertEx

```
HRESULT InsertEx(
    BSTR bszCaption,        // Caption setting for Command
    BSTR bszVoice,          // Voice setting for Command
    BSTR bszVoiceCaption,   // VoiceCaption setting for Command
    long bEnabled,          // Enabled setting for Command
    long bVisible,          // Visible setting for Command
    long ulHelpID,          // HelpContextID setting for Command
    long dwRefID,           // reference Command for insertion
    long dBefore,           // insertion position flag
    long * pdwID            // address for variable for Command ID
);
```

Inserts a **Command** object in a **Commands** collection.

- Returns S_OK to indicate the operation was successful.

bszCaption	A BSTR that specifies the value of the **Caption** text displayed for the **Command**.
bszVoice	A BSTR that specifies the value of the **Voice** text setting for a **Command**.
bszVoiceCaption	A BSTR that specifies the value of the **VoiceCaption** text displayed for a **Command** in a **Commands** collection.
bEnabled	A Boolean expression that specifies the **Enabled** setting for a **Command**. If the parameter is **True**, the **Command** is enabled and can be selected; if **False**, the **Command** is disabled.
bVisible	A Boolean expression that specifies the **Visible** setting for a **Command**. If the parameter is **True**, the **Command** will be visible in the character's pop-up menu (if the **Caption** property is also set).
ulHelpID	The context number of the help topic associated with the **Command** object; used to provide context-sensitive Help for the command.
dwRefID	The ID of a **Command** used as a reference for the relative insertion of the new **Command**.
dBefore	A Boolean expression that specifies where to place the **Command**. If this parameter is **True**, the new **Command** is inserted before the referenced **Command**; if **False**, the new **Command** is placed after the referenced **Command**.
pdwID	Address of a variable that receives the ID for the inserted **Command**.

IAgentCommandsEx::InsertEx extends **IAgentCommands::Insert** by including the HelpContextID property. You can also set the property using **IAgentCommandsEx::SetHelpContextID**

See also **IAgentCommandsEx::AddEx, IAgentCommands-Ex::SetHelpContextID, IAgentCommands::Add, IAgentCommands::Remove, IAgentCommands::RemoveAll**

IAgentCommandsEx::SetDefaultID

```
HRESULT SetDefaultID(
    long dwID,  // default command's ID
);
```

Sets the ID of the default command in a **Commands** collection.

- Returns S_OK to indicate the operation was successful.

dwID   The ID for the **Command** to be set as the default.

This property sets the default **Command** object set in your **Commands** collection. The default command is bold in the character's pop-up menu. However, setting the default command does not actually change command handling or double-click events.

This property applies only to your client application's use of the character; the setting does not affect other clients of the character or other characters of your client application.

See also **IAgentCommandsEx::GetDefaultID**

IAgentCommandsEx::SetFontName

```
HRESULT SetFontName(
    BSTR bszFontName  // font to be displayed in character's pop-up menu
);
```

Sets the font displayed in the character's pop-up menu.

- Returns S_OK to indicate the operation was successful.

bszFontName   A BSTR that sets the font displayed in the character's pop-up menu.

This property determines the font used to display text in the character's pop-up menu. The default value for the font setting is based on the menu font setting for the character's language ID setting—or if that's not set—the user default language ID setting.

This property applies only to your client application's use of the character; the setting does not affect other clients of the character or other characters of your client application.

See also IAgentCommandsEx::GetFontName, IAgentCommands-Ex::GetFontSize, IAgentCommandsEx::SetFontSize

IAgentCommandsEx::SetFontSize

```
HRESULT SetFontSize(
    long lFontSize  // font size displayed in character's pop-up menu
);
```

Sets the size of the font displayed in the character's pop-up menu.

- Returns S_OK to indicate the operation was successful.

lFontSize   The size of the font.

This property determines the point size of the font used to display text in the character's pop-up menu when your client application is input-active. The default value for the font setting is based on the menu font setting for the character's language ID setting -- or if that's not set -- the user default language setting. If not input-active, your client application's **Commands Caption** text appears in the point size specified for the input-active client.

This property applies only to your client application's use of the character; the setting does not affect other clients of the character or other characters of your client application.

See also IAgentCommandsEx::GetFontSize, IAgentCommands-Ex::GetFontName, IAgentCommandsEx::SetFontName

IAgentCommandsEx::SetGlobalVoiceCommandsEnabled

```
HRESULT SetGlobalVoiceCommandsEnabled(
    long bEnable  // Enabled setting for Agent's global voice commands
);
```

Sets the **Enabled** property for the voice grammar of Microsoft Agent's global commands.

- Returns S_OK to indicate the operation was successful.

bEnable   A Boolean value that sets whether the voice grammar of Agent's global commands is enabled. **True** enables the voice grammar; **False** disables it.

Microsoft Agent automatically adds voice parameters (grammar) for opening and closing the Voice Commands Window and for showing and hiding the character. When set to **False**, Agent disables any voice parameters for these commands as well as the voice parameters for the **Caption** of other client's **Commands** objects. This enables you to eliminate these from your client's current active grammar. However, because this potentially blocks voice access to other clients, reset this property to **True** after processing the user's voice input.

Disabling the property does not affect the character's pop-up menu. The global commands added by the server will still appear. You cannot remove them from the pop-up menu.

See also **IAgentCommandsEx::GetGlobalVoiceCommandsEnabled**

IAgentCommandsEx::SetHelpContextID

```
HRESULT SetHelpContextID(
    long ulHelpID  // ID for help topic
);
```

Sets the **HelpContextID** for a **Command** object.

- Returns S_OK to indicate the operation was successful.

ulHelpID   The context number of the help topic associated with the **Command** object; used to provide context-sensitive Help for the command.

If you've created a Windows Help file for your application and set this in the character's **HelpFile** property. Agent automatically calls Help when **HelpModeOn** is set to **True** and the user selects the command. If there is a context number in the **HelpContextID**, Agent calls Help and searches for the topic identified by the current context number. The current context number is the value of **HelpContextID** for the command. If there is a context number in the selected command's **HelpContextID** property, Help displays a topic corresponding to the current Help context; otherwise it displays "No Help topic associated with this item."

This property applies only to your client application's use of the character; the setting does not affect other clients of the character or other characters of your client application.

Note Building a Help file requires the Microsoft Windows Help Compiler.

See also **IAgentCommandsEx::GetHelpContextID, IAgentCharacterEx::SetHelpModeOn, IAgentCharacterEx::SetHelpFileName**

IAgentCommandsEx::SetVoiceCaption

```
HRESULT SetVoiceCaption(
   BSTR bszVoiceCaption  // voice caption text
);
```

Sets the **VoiceCaption** text displayed for the **Commands** object.

- Returns S_OK to indicate the operation was successful.

bszVoiceCaption   A BSTR that specifies the text for the **VoiceCaption** property for a **Command**.

If you define a **Command** object in a **Commands** collection and set its **Voice** property, you will typically also set its **VoiceCaption** property. This text will appear in the Voice Commands Window when your client application is input-active and the character is visible. If this property is not set, the setting for the **Caption** property determines the text displayed. When neither the **VoiceCaption** or **Caption** property is set, the command does not appear in the Voice Commands Window.

See also **IAgentCommandsEx::GetVoiceCaption**

IAgentCommand

A **Command** object is an item in a **Commands** collection. The server provides the user access to your commands your client application becomes input active. To retrieve a **Command**, call **IAgentCommands::GetCommand**.

IAgentCommand defines an interface that allows applications to set and query properties for **Command** objects that can appear in a character's pop-up menu and in the Voice Commands Window. These functions are also available from **IAgentCommandEx**. A **Command** object is an item in a **Commands** collection. The server provides the user access to your commands when your client application becomes input active.

A **Command** may appear in either or both the character's pop-up menu and the Voice Commands Window. To appear in the pop-up menu, it must have a **Caption** and have the **Visible** property set to **True**. The **Visible** property for its **Commands** collection object must also be set to **True** for the command to appear in the pop-up menu when your client application is input-active. To appear in the Voice Commands Window, a **Command** must have its **VoiceCaption** and **Voice** properties set. (For backward compatibility, if there is no **VoiceCaption**, the **Caption** setting is used.)

A character's pop-up menu entries do not change while the menu is displayed. If you add or remove Commands or change their properties while the character's popup menu is displayed, the menu displays those changes when redisplayed. However, the Voice Commands Window does display changes as you make them.

The following table summarizes how the properties of a command affect its presentation.

Caption Property	Voice-Caption Property	Voice Property	Visible Property	Appears in Character's Pop-up Menu	Appears in Voice Commands Window
Yes	Yes	Yes	True	Yes, using **Caption**	Yes, using **VoiceCaption**
Yes	Yes	No[1]	True	Yes, using **Caption**	No
Yes	Yes	Yes	False	No	Yes, using **VoiceCaption**
Yes	Yes	No[1]	False	No	No
No[1]	Yes	Yes	True	No	Yes, using **VoiceCaption**
No[1]	Yes	Yes	False	No	Yes, using **VoiceCaption**
No[1]	Yes	No[1]	True	No	No
No[1]	Yes	No[1]	False	No	No
Yes	No[1]	Yes	True	Yes, using **Caption**	Yes, using **Caption**
Yes	No[1]	No[1]	True	Yes	No
Yes	No[1]	Yes	False	No	Yes, using **Caption**
Yes	No[1]	No[1]	False	No	No
No[1]	No[1]	Yes	True	No	No[2]
No[1]	No[1]	Yes	False	No	No[2]
No[1]	No[1]	No[1]	True	No	No
No[1]	No[1]	No[1]	False	No	No

[1]If the property setting is null. In some programming languages, an empty string may not be interpreted as the same as a null string.
[2]The command is still voice-accessible.

Generally, if you define a **Command** with a **Voice** setting, you also define **Caption** and **Voice** settings for its associated **Commands** collection. If the **Commands** collection for a set of commands has no **Voice** or no **Caption** setting and is currently input-active, but the **Commands** have **Caption** and **Voice** settings, the **Commands** appear in the Voice Commands Window tree view under "(undefined command)" when your client application becomes input-active.

When the server receives input that matches one of the **Command** objects you defined for your **Commands** collection, it sends a **IAgentNotifySink::Command** event, and passes back the ID of the command as an attribute of the **IAgentUserInput** object. You can then use conditional statements to match and process the command.

Methods in Vtable Order

IAgentCommand Methods	Description
SetCaption	Sets the value for the **Caption** for a **Command** object.
GetCaption	Returns the value of the **Caption** property of a **Command** object.
SetVoice	Sets the value for the **Voice** text for a **Command** object.

IAgentCommand Methods	Description
GetVoice	Returns the value of the **Caption** property of a **Command** object.
SetEnabled	Sets the value of the **Enabled** property for a **Command** object.
GetEnabled	Returns the value of the **Enabled** property of a **Command** object.
SetVisible	Sets the value of the **Visible** property for a **Command** object.
GetVisible	Returns the value of the **Visible** property of a **Command** object.
SetConfidenceThreshold	Sets the value of the **Confidence** property for a **Command** object.
GetConfidenceThreshold	Returns the value of the **Confidence** property of a **Command** object.
SetConfidenceText	Sets the value of the **ConfidenceText** property for a **Command** object.
GetConfidenceText	Returns the value of the **ConfidenceText** property of a **Command** object.
GetID	Returns the ID of a **Command** object.

IAgentCommand::GetCaption

```
HRESULT GetCaption(
    BSTR * pbszCaption  // address of Caption for Command
);
```

Retrieves the **Caption** for a **Command**.

■ Returns S_OK to indicate the operation was successful.

pbszCaption   The address of a BSTR that receives the value of the **Caption** text displayed for a **Command**.

See also **IAgentCommand::SetCaption**, **IAgentCommand::SetEnabled**, **IAgentCommand::SetVisible**, **IAgentCommand::SetVoice**, **IAgent-Commands::Add**, **IAgentCommands::Insert**

IAgentCommand::GetConfidenceText

```
HRESULT GetConfidenceText(
    BSTR * pbszTipText  // address of ConfidenceText
                        // setting for Command
);
```

Retrieves the Listening Tip text previously set for a **Command**.

■ Returns S_OK to indicate the operation was successful.

pbszTipText   The address of a BSTR that receives the value of the Listening Tip text for a **Command**.

See also **IAgentCommand::SetConfidenceThreshold**, **IAgentCommand::,** **IAgentCommand::SetConfidenceText**, **IAgentUserInput::GetItem-Confidence**

IAgentCommand::GetConfidenceThreshold

```
HRESULT GetConfidenceThreshold(
    long * plConfidenceThreshold  // address of ConfidenceThreshold
);                                // setting for Command
```

Retrieves the value of the **ConfidenceThreshold** property for a **Command**.

- Returns S_OK to indicate the operation was successful.

plConfidenceThreshold   The address of a variable that receives the value of the **ConfidenceThreshold** property for a Command.

See also IAgentCommand::SetConfidenceThreshold, IAgentCommand::SetConfidenceText, IAgentUserInput::GetItemConfidence

---

IAgentCommand::GetEnabled

```
HRESULT GetEnabled(
    long * pbEnabled  // address of Enabled setting for Command
);
```

Retrieves the value of the **Enabled** property for a **Command**.

- Returns S_OK to indicate the operation was successful.

pbEnabled   The address of a variable that receives **True** if the **Command** is enabled, or **False** if it is disabled. A disabled **Command** cannot be selected.

See also IAgentCommand::SetCaption, IAgentCommand::SetVisible, IAgentCommand::SetVoice, IAgentCommands::Add, IAgent-Commands::Insert

---

IAgentCommand::GetID

```
HRESULT GetID(
    long * pdwID  // address of ID for Command
);
```

Retrieves the ID for a Command.

- Returns S_OK to indicate the operation was successful.

pdwID   The address of a variable that receives the ID of a **Command**.

See also IAgentCommands::Add, IAgentCommands::Insert, IAgentCommands::Remove

IAgentCommand::GetVisible

```
HRESULT GetVisible(
    long * pbVisible  // address of Visible setting for Command
);
```

Retrieves the value of the **Visible** property for a **Command**.

- Returns S_OK to indicate the operation was successful.

pbVisible   The address of a variable that receives the **Visible** property for a **Command**.

See also **IAgentCommand::SetVisible, IAgentCommand::SetCaption, IAgentCommands::Add, IAgentCommands::Insert**

IAgentCommand::GetVoice

```
HRESULT GetVoice(
    BSTR * pbszVoice  // address of Voice setting for Command
);
```

Retrieves the value of the **Voice** text property for a **Command**.

- Returns S_OK to indicate the operation was successful.

pbszVoice   The address of a BSTR that receives the **Voice** text property for a **Command**.

A **Command** with its **Voice** property set and its **Enabled** property set to **True** will be voice-accessible. If its **Caption** property is also set it appears in the Voice Commands Window. If its **Visible** property is set to **True**, it appears in the character's pop-up menu.

See also **IAgentCommand::SetVoice, IAgentCommands::Add, IAgentCommands::Insert**

IAgentCommand::SetCaption

```
HRESULT SetCaption(
    BSTR bszCaption  // Caption setting for Command
);
```

Sets the **Caption** text displayed for a **Command**.

- Returns S_OK to indicate the operation was successful.

bszCaption   A BSTR that specifies the text for the **Caption** property for a **Command**.

Setting the **Caption** property for a **Command** defines how it will appear on the character's pop-up menu when its **Visible** property is set to **True** and your application is not the input-active client. To specify an access key (unlined mnemonic) for your **Caption**, include an ampersand (&) character before that character. To make it selectable, its **Enabled** property must be set to **True**.

See also IAgentCommand::GetCaption, IAgentCommand::SetEnabled, IAgentCommand::SetVisible, IAgentCommand::SetVoice, IAgentCommands::Add, IAgentCommands::Insert

IAgentCommand::SetConfidenceThreshold

```
HRESULT SetConfidenceThreshold(
    long lConfidence  // Confidence setting for Command
);
```

Sets the value of the **Confidence** property for a **Command**.

- Returns S_OK to indicate the operation was successful.

lConfidence   The value for the **Confidence** property of a **Command**.

If the confidence value returned of the best match returned in the **Command** event does not exceed the value set for the **ConfidenceThreshold** property, the text supplied in **SetConfidenceText** is displayed in the Listening Tip.

See also IAgentCommand::GetConfidenceThreshold, IAgentCommand::SetConfidenceText, IAgentUserInput::GetItemConfidence

IAgentCommand::SetConfidenceText

```
HRESULT SetConfidenceText(
    BSTR bszTipText  // ConfidenceText setting for Command
);
```

Sets the value of the Listening Tip text for a **Command**.

- Returns S_OK to indicate the operation was successful.

bszTipText   A BSTR that specifies the text for the **ConfidenceText** property of a **Command**.

If the confidence value returned of the best match returned in the **Command** event does not exceed the value set for the **ConfidenceThreshold** property, the text supplied in bszTipText is displayed in the Listening Tip.

See also IAgentCommand::SetConfidenceThreshold, IAgentCommand::, IAgentCommand::GetConfidenceText, IAgentUserInput::GetItemConfidence

IAgentCommand::SetEnabled

```
HRESULT SetEnabled(
    long bEnabled  // Enabled setting for Command
);
```

Sets the **Enabled** property for a **Command**.

- Returns S_OK to indicate the operation was successful.

bEnabled   A Boolean value that sets the value of the **Enabled** setting of a **Command**. **True** enables the **Command**; **False** disables it. A disabled **Command** cannot be selected.

A **Command** must have its **Enabled** property set to **True** to be selectable. It also must have its **Caption** property set and its **Visible** property set to **True** to appear in the character's pop-up menu. To make the **Command** appear in the **Voice Commands Window**, you must set its **Voice** property.

See also IAgentCommand::GetCaption, IAgentCommand::SetVoice, IAgentCommands::Add, IAgentCommands::Insert

IAgentCommand::SetVisible

```
HRESULT SetVisible(
    long bVisible  // Visible setting for Command
);
```

Sets the value of the **Visible** property for a **Command**.

- Returns S_OK to indicate the operation was successful.

bVisible   A Boolean value that determines the **Visible** property of a **Command**. **True** shows the **Command**; **False** hides it.

A **Command** must have its **Visible** property set to **True** and its **Caption** property set to appear in the character's pop-up menu.

See also IAgentCommand::GetVisible, IAgentCommand::SetCaption, IAgentCommands::Add, IAgentCommands::

IAgentCommand::SetVoice

```
HRESULT SetVoice(
    BSTR bszVoice  // voice text setting for Command
);
```

Sets the **Voice** property for a **Command**.

- Returns S_OK to indicate the operation was successful.

bszVoice   A BSTR that specifies the text for the **Voice** property of a **Command**.

A **Command** must have its **Voice** property and **Enabled** property set to be voice-accessible. It also must have its **VoiceCaption** property set to appear in the Voice Commands Window. (For backward compatibility, if there is no **VoiceCaption**, the **Caption** setting is used.)

The BSTR expression you supply can include square bracket characters ([ ]) to indicate optional words and vertical bar characters (|) to indicate alternative strings. Alternates must be enclosed in parentheses. For example, "(hello [there] | hi)" tells the speech engine to accept "hello," "hello there," or "hi" for the command. Remember to include appropriate spaces between the text that's in brackets or parentheses and the text that's not in brackets or parentheses.

You can use the star (*) operator to specify zero or more instances of the words included in the group or the plus (+) operator to specify one or more instances. For example, the following results in a grammar that supports "try this", "please try this", and "please please try this", with unlimited iterations of "please":

```
"please* try this"
```

The following grammar format excludes "try this" because the + operator defines at least one instance of "please":

```
"please+ try this"
```

The repetition operators follow normal rules of precedence and apply to the immediately preceding text item. For example, the following grammar results in "New York" and "New York York", but not "New York New York":

```
"New York+"
```

Therefore, you will typically want to use these operators with the grouping characters. For example, the following grammar includes both "New York" and "New York New York":

```
"(New York)+"
```

Repetition operators are useful when you want to compose a grammar that includes a repeated sequence such as a phone number or specification of a list of items:

```
"call (one|two|three|four|five|six|seven|eight|nine|zero|oh)*"
"I'd like (cheese|pepperoni|pineapple|canadian bacon|mushrooms|and)+"
```

Although the operators can also be used with the square brackets (an optional grouping character), doing so may reduce the efficiency of Agent's processing of the grammar.

You can also use an ellipsis (…) to support *word spotting*, that is, telling the speech recognition engine to ignore words spoken in this position in the phrase (sometimes called *garbage* words). Therefore, the speech engine recognizes only specific words in the string regardless of when spoken with adjacent words or phrases. For example, if you set this property to "[…] check mail […]" the speech recognition engine will match phrases like "please check mail" or "check mail please" to this command. Ellipses can be used anywhere within a string. However, be careful using this technique, because voice settings with ellipses may increase the potential of unwanted matches.

When defining the words and grammar for your command, always make sure that you include at least one word that is required; that is, avoid supplying only optional words. In addition, make sure that the word includes only pronounce-able words and letters. For numbers, it is better to spell out the word rather than using the numeric representation. Also, omit any punctuation or symbols. For example, instead of "the #1 $10 pizza!", use "the number one ten dollar pizza". Including non-pronounceable characters or symbols for one command may cause the speech engine to fail to compile the grammar for all your commands. Finally, make your voice parameter as distinct as reasonably possible from other voice commands you define. The greater the similarity between the voice grammar for commands, the more likely the speech engine will make a recognition error. You can also use the confidence scores to better distinguish between two commands that may have similar or similar-sounding voice grammar.

Setting the **Voice** property for a **Command** automatically enables Agent's speech services, making the Listening key and Listening Tip available. However, it does not load the speech recognition engine.

Note The grammar features available may depend on the speech recognition engine. You may want to check with the engine's vendor to determine what grammar options are supported. Use **IAgentCharacterEx::SRModeID** to specify an engine.

See also IAgentCommand::GetVoice, IAgentCommand::SetCaption, IAgentCommand::SetEnabled, IAgentCommands::Add, IAgent-Commands::Insert

---

IAgentCommandEx

IAgentCommandEx is derived from the **IAgentCommand** interface. It includes all the **IAgentCommand** methods and provides access to additional functions.

Methods in Vtable Order

IAgentCommandEx Methods	Description
SetHelpContextID	Sets the context-sensitive help topic ID for a **Command** object.
GetHelpContextID	Returns the context-sensitive help topic ID for a **Command** object.
SetVoiceCaption	Sets the voice caption for a **Command** object.
GetVoiceCaption	Returns the voice caption for a **Command** object.

IAgentCommandEx::GetHelpContextID

```
HRESULT GetHelpContextID(
    long * pulID   // address of command's help topic ID
);
```

Retrieves the **HelpContextID** for a **Command** object.

■   Returns S_OK to indicate the operation was successful.

pulID   Address of a variable that receives the context number of the help topic associated with the **Command** object.

If you've created a Windows Help file for your application and set your character's **HelpFile** property to this file, Microsoft Agent automatically calls Help when **HelpModeOn** is set to **True** and the user selects the command. If there is a context number in the **HelpContextID**, Agent calls Help and searches for the topic identified by the current context number. The current context number is the value of **HelpContextID** for the command.

Note Building a Help file requires the Microsoft Windows Help Compiler.

See also **IAgentCommandEx::SetHelpContextID, IAgentCharacterEx::SetHelpModeOn, IAgentCharacterEx::SetHelpFileName**

IAgentCommandEx::GetVoiceCaption

```
HRESULT GetVoiceCaption(
    BSTR * pbszVoiceCaption   // address of command's voice caption text
);
```

Retrieves the **VoiceCaption** for a **Command**.

■   Returns S_OK to indicate the operation was successful.

pbszVoiceCaption   The address of a BSTR that receives the value of the **Caption** text displayed for a **Command**.

The **VoiceCaption** is the text that appears for a **Command** object in the Voice Commands Window when your client application is input-active.

See also IAgentCommandEx::SetVoiceCaption,
IAgentCommand::SetEnabled, IAgentCommand::SetVisible,
IAgentCommand::SetVoice, IAgentCommandsEx::AddEx,
IAgentCommandsEx::InsertEx, IAgentCommands::Add,
IAgentCommands::Insert

IAgentCommandEx::SetHelpContextID

```
HRESULT SetHelpContextID(
   long ulID  //  ID for help topic
);
```

Sets the **HelpContextID** for a **Command** object.

■   Returns S_OK to indicate the operation was successful.

ulID   The context number of the help topic associated with the **Command** object; used to provide context-sensitive Help for the command.

If you've created a Windows Help file for your application and set this in the character's **HelpFile** property. Microsoft Agent automatically calls Help when **HelpModeOn** is set to **True** and the user selects the command. If there is a context number in the **HelpContextID**, Agent calls Help and searches for the topic identified by the current context number. The current context number is the value of **HelpContextID** for the command.

Note Building a Help file requires the Microsoft Windows Help Compiler.

See also IAgentCommandEx::GetHelpContextID,
IAgentCharacterEx::SetHelpModeOn,
IAgentCharacterEx::SetHelpFileName

IAgentCommandEx::SetVoiceCaption

```
HRESULT SetVoiceCaption(
   BSTR bszVoiceCaption  //  voice caption text
);
```

Sets the **VoiceCaption** text displayed for a **Command**.

■   Returns S_OK to indicate the operation was successful.

bszVoiceCaption   A BSTR that specifies the text for the **VoiceCaption** property for a
Command.

If you define a **Command** object in a **Commands** collection and set its **Voice**
property, you will typically also set its **VoiceCaption** property. This text will appear in the Voice Commands Window when your client application is input active. If this property is not set, the setting for the **Caption** property determines
the text displayed. When neither the **VoiceCaption** or **Caption** property is set,
the command does not appear in the Voice Commands Window.

See also **IAgentCommand::GetCaption, IAgentCommand::SetEnabled,
IAgentCommand::SetVisible, IAgentCommand::SetVoice, IAgent-
CommandsEx::AddEx, IAgentCommandsEx::InsertEx, IAgentCommands::Add,
IAgentCommands::Insert**

IAgentUserInput

When the server notifies the input-active client with
IAgentNotifySink::**Command** it returns information through the **UserInput** object. **IAgentUserInput** defines an interface that allows applications to query
these values.

Methods in Vtable Order

IAgentUserInput Methods	Description
GetCount	Returns the number of command alternatives re-turned in a **Command** event.
GetItemId	Returns the ID for a specific **Command** alternative.
GetItemConfidence	Returns the value of the **Confidence** property for a specific **Command** alternative.
GetItemText	Returns the value of **Voice** text for a specific **Command** alternative.
GetAllItemData	Returns the data for all **Command** alternatives.

IAgentUserInput::GetAllItemData

```
HRESULT GetAllItemData(
    VARIANT * pdwItemIndices,   // address of variable for
                                // alternative IDs
    VARIANT * plConfidences,    // address of variable for
                                // confidence scores
    VARIANT * pbszText          // address of variable for voice text
);
```

Retrieves the data for all **Command** alternatives passed to an
IAgentNotifySink::Command callback.

■ Returns S_OK to indicate the operation was successful.

pdwItemIndices	Address of a variable that receives the IDs of **Commands** passed to the **IAgentNotifySink::Command** callback.
plConfidences	Address of a variable that receives the confidence scores for **Command** alternatives passed to the **IAgentNotifySink::Command** callback.
pbszText	Address of a variable that receives the voice text for **Command** alternatives passed to the **IAgentNotifySink::Command** callback.

If speech input triggers **IAgentNotifySink::Command**, the server returns the best match, the second-best match, and the third-best match, if these are provided by the speech engine. It provides the relative confidence scores, in the range of -100 to 100, and actual text "heard" by the speech engine. If the best match was a server-supplied command, the server sends a NULL ID, but still sends a confidence score and the **Voice** text.

If speech input was not the source for the event; for example, if the user selected the command from the character's pop-up menu, the Microsoft Agent server returns the ID of the **Command** selected, with a confidence score of 100 and voice text as NULL. The other alternatives return as NULL with confidence scores of zero (0) and voice text as NULL.

Note Not all speech recognition engines may return all the values for all the parameters of this event. Check with your engine vendor to determine whether the engine supports the Microsoft Speech API interface for returning alternatives and confidence scores.

See also **IAgentUserInput::GetItemConfidence, IAgentUserInput::GetItemText, IAgentUserInput::GetItemID**

IAgentUserInput::GetCount

```
HRESULT GetCount(
    long * pdwCount   // address of a variable for
                      // number of alternatives
);
```

Retrieves the number of **Command** alternatives passed to an **IAgentNotifySink::Command** callback.

■ Returns S_OK to indicate the operation was successful.

pdwCount	Address of a variable that receives the count of **Commands** alternatives identified by the server.

If voice input was not the source for the command, for example, if the user selected the command from the character's pop-up menu, **GetCount** returns 1. If

GetCount returns zero (0), the speech recognition engine detected spoken input but determined that there was no matching command.

IAgentUserInput::GetItemConfidence

```
HRESULT GetItemConfidence(
    long dwItemIndex,     // index of Command alternative
    long * plConfidence   // address of confidence value for Command
);
```

Retrieves the confidence value for a **Command** passed to an **IAgentNotifySink::Command** callback.

- Returns S_OK to indicate the operation was successful.

dwItemIndex   The index of a **Command** alternative passed to the **IAgentNotifySink::Command** callback.

plConfidence   Address of a variable that receives the confidence score for a **Command** alternative passed to the **IAgentNotifySink::Command** callback.

If voice input was not the source for the command, for example, if the user selected the command from the character's pop-up menu, the Microsoft Agent server returns the confidence value of the best match as 100 and the confidence values for all other alternatives as zero (0).

See also IAgentUserInput::GetItemID, IAgentUserInput::GetAll-ItemData, IAgentUserInput::GetItemText

IAgentUserInput::GetItemID

```
HRESULT GetItemID(
    long dwItemIndex,      // index of Command alternative
    long * pdwCommandID    // address of a variable for
                           // number of alternatives
);
```

Retrieves the identifier of a **Command** alternative passed to an **IAgentNotifySink::Command** callback.

- Returns S_OK to indicate the operation was successful.

dwItemIndex   The index of the **Command** alternative passed to the **IAgentNotifySink::Command** callback.

pdwCommandID   Address of a variable that receives the ID of a **Command**.

If voice input triggers the **IAgentNotifySink::Command** callback, the server returns the IDs for any matching **Commands** defined by your application.

See also IAgentUserInput::GetItemConfidence, IAgentUser-Input::GetItemText, IAgentUserInput::GetAllItemData

IAgentUserInput::GetItemText

```
HRESULT GetItemText(
    Long dwItemIndex,   // index of Command alternative
    BSTR * pbszText     // address of voice text for Command
);
```

Retrieves the voice text for a **Command** alternative passed to the
IAgentNotifySink::Command callback.

- Returns S_OK to indicate the operation was successful.

dwItemIndex	The index of a **Command** alternative passed to the **IAgentNotifySink::Command** callback.
pbszText	Address of a BSTR that receives the value of the voice text for the **Command**.

If voice input was not the source for the command, for example, if the user selected the command from the character's pop-up menu, the server returns NULL
for the **Command**'s voice text.

See also **IAgentUserInput::GetItemConfidence**, **IAgentUserInput::Get-
ItemID**, **IAgentUserInput::GetAllItemData**

IAgentBalloon

IAgentBalloon defines an interface that allows applications to query properties
for the Microsoft Agent word balloon. These functions are also available from
IAgentBalloonEx.

Initial defaults for a character's word balloon are set in the Microsoft Agent
Character Editor, but once the application is running, the user may override the
Enabled and **Font** properties. If a user changes the balloon's properties, the
change affects all characters. The **IAgentBalloon** object's properties also apply
to text output through the **Think** method.

Methods in Vtable Order

IAgentBalloon Methods	Description
GetEnabled	Returns whether the word balloon is enabled.
GetNumLines	Returns the number of lines displayed in the word balloon.
GetNumCharsPerLine	Returns the average number of characters per line displayed in the word balloon.
GetFontName	Returns the name of the font displayed in the word balloon.
GetFontSize	Returns the size of the font displayed in the word balloon.
GetFontBold	Returns whether the font displayed in the word balloon is bold.
GetFontItalic	Returns whether the font displayed in the word balloon is italic.

IAgentBalloon Methods	Description
GetFontStrkethru	Returns whether the font displayed in the word balloon is displayed as strikethrough.
GetFontUnderline	Returns whether the font displayed in the word balloon is underlined.
GetForeColor	Returns the foreground color displayed in the word balloon.
GetBackColor	Returns the background color displayed in the word balloon.
GetBorderColor	Returns the border color displayed in the word balloon.
SetVisible	Sets the word balloon to be visible.
GetVisible	Returns the visibility setting for the word balloon.
SetFontName	Sets the font used in the word balloon.
SetFontSize	Sets the font size used in the word balloon.
SetFontCharSet	Sets the character set used in the word balloon.
GetFontCharSet	Returns the character set used in the word balloon.

IAgentBalloon::GetBackColor

```
HRESULT GetBackColor(
    long * plBGColor  // address of variable for background color
);                    // displayed in word balloon
```

Retrieves the value for the background color displayed in a word balloon.

- Returns S_OK to indicate the operation was successful.

plBGColor   The address of a variable that receives the color setting for the balloon background.

The background color used in a character word balloon is defined in the Microsoft Agent Character Editor. It cannot be changed by an application. However, the user can change the background color of the word balloons for all characters through the Microsoft Agent property sheet.

See also IAgentBalloon::GetForeColor

IAgentBalloon::GetBorderColor

```
HRESULT GetBorderColor (
  long * plBorderColor // address of variable for border color
);                     // displayed for word balloon
```

Retrieves the value for the border color displayed for a word balloon.

- Returns S_OK to indicate the operation was successful.

plBorderColor   The address of a variable that receives the color setting for the balloon border.

The border color for a character word balloon is defined in the Microsoft Agent Character Editor. It cannot be changed by an application. However, the user can change the border color of the word balloons for all characters through the Microsoft Agent property sheet.

See also **IAgentBalloon::GetBackColor, IAgentBalloon::GetForeColor**

IAgentBalloon::GetEnabled

```
HRESULT GetEnabled(
  long * pbEnabled   // address of variable for Enabled setting
);                   // for word balloon
```

Retrieves the value of the **Enabled** property for a word balloon.

- Returns S_OK to indicate the operation was successful.

pbEnabled   The address of a variable that receives **True** when the word balloon is enabled and **False** when it is disabled.

The Microsoft Agent server automatically displays the word balloon for spoken output, unless it is disabled. The word balloon can be disabled for a character in the Microsoft Agent Character Editor, or (by the user) for all characters in the Microsoft Agent property sheet. If the user disables the word balloon, the client cannot restore it.

IAgentBalloon::GetFontBold

```
HRESULT GetFontBold(
   long * pbFontBold   // address of variable for bold setting for
);                     // font displayed in word balloon
```

Indicates whether the font used in a word balloon is bold.

- Returns S_OK to indicate the operation was successful.

pbFontBold   The address of a value that receives **True** if the font is bold and **False** if not bold.

The font style used in a character word balloon is defined in the Microsoft Agent Character Editor. It cannot be changed by an application. However, the user can override the font settings for all characters through the Microsoft Agent property sheet.

IAgentBalloon::GetFontCharSet

```
HRESULT GetFontCharSet(
   short * psFontCharSet  // character set displayed in word balloon
);
```

Indicates the character set of the font displayed in a word balloon.

- Returns S_OK to indicate the operation was successful.

psFontCharSet   The address of a value that receives the font's character set. The following are some common settings for value:

0	Standard Windows characters (ANSI).
1	Default character set.
2	The symbol character set.
128	Double-byte character set (DBCS) unique to the Japanese version of Windows.
129	Double-byte character set (DBCS) unique to the Korean version of Windows.
134	Double-byte character set (DBCS) unique to the Simplified Chinese version of Windows.
136	Double-byte character set (DBCS) unique to the Traditional Chinese version of Windows.
255	Extended characters usually displayed by MS-DOS applications.

For other character set values, consult the Microsoft Win32 documentation.

The default character set used in a character's word balloon is defined in the Microsoft Agent Character Editor. You can change it using **IAgentBalloon::SetFontCharSet**. However, the user can override the character set setting for all characters using the Microsoft Agent property sheet.

See also IAgentBalloon::SetFontCharSet

IAgentBalloon::GetFontItalic

```
HRESULT GetFontItalic(
    long * pbFontItalic  // address of variable for italic setting for
);                       // font displayed in word balloon
```

Indicates whether the font used in a word balloon is italic.

- Returns S_OK to indicate the operation was successful.

pbFontItalic   The address of a value that receives **True** if the font is italic and **False** if not italic.

The font style used in a character's word balloon is defined in the Microsoft Agent Character Editor. It cannot be changed by an application. However, the user can override the font settings for all characters through the Microsoft Agent property sheet.

IAgentBalloon::GetFontName

```
HRESULT GetFontName(
    BSTR * pbszFontName   // address of variable for font displayed
);                        // in word balloon
```

Retrieves the value for the font displayed in a word balloon.

- Returns S_OK to indicate the operation was successful.

pbszFontName   The address of a BSTR that receives the font name displayed in a
                    word balloon.

The default font used in a character word balloon is defined in the Microsoft
Agent Character Editor. You can change it with **IAgentBalloon::SetFontName**.
The user can override the font setting for all characters using the Microsoft Agent
property sheet.

IAgentBalloon::GetFontSize

```
HRESULT GetFontSize(
    long * plFontSize   // address of variable for font size
);                      // for font displayed in word balloon
```

Retrieves the value for the size of the font displayed in a word balloon.

- Returns S_OK to indicate the operation was successful.

plFontSize   The address of a value that receives the size of the font.

The default font size used in a character word balloon is defined in the Microsoft
Agent Character Editor. You can change it with **IAgentBalloon::SetFontSize**.
However, the user can override the font size settings for all characters using the
Microsoft Agent property sheet.

IAgentBalloon::GetFontStrikethru

```
HRESULT GetFontStrikethru(
    long * pbFontStrikethru  // address of variable for
                             // strikethrough setting for font
                             // displayed in word balloon
);
```

Indicates whether the font used in a word balloon has the strikethrough style set.

- Returns S_OK to indicate the operation was successful.

pbFontStrikethru   The address of a value that receives **True** if the font strikethrough
                        style is set and **False** if not.

The font style used in a character word balloon is defined in the Microsoft
Agent Character Editor. It cannot be changed by an application. However, the
user can override the font settings for all characters using the Microsoft Agent
property sheet.

IAgentBalloon::GetFontUnderline

```
HRESULT GetFontUnderline(
    long * pbFontUnderline   // address of variable for underline setting
);                          // for font displayed in word balloon
```

Indicates whether the font used in a word balloon has the underline style set.

- Returns S_OK to indicate the operation was successful.

pbFontUnderline   The address of a value that receives **True** if the font underline style is set and **False** if not.

The font style used in a character word balloon is defined in the Microsoft Agent Character Editor. It cannot be changed by an application. However, the user can override the font settings for all characters using the Microsoft Agent property sheet.

IAgentBalloon::GetForeColor

```
HRESULT GetForeColor(
    long * plFGColor // address of variable for foreground
);                  // color displayed in word balloon
```

Retrieves the value for the foreground color displayed in a word balloon.

- Returns S_OK to indicate the operation was successful.

plFGColor   The address of a variable that receives the color setting for the balloon foreground.

The foreground color used in a character word balloon is defined in the Microsoft Agent Character Editor. It cannot be changed by an application. However, the user can override the foreground color of the word balloons for all characters through the Microsoft Agent property sheet.

See also IAgentBalloon::GetBackColor

IAgentBalloon::GetNumCharsPerLine

```
HRESULT GetNumCharsPerLine(
    long * plCharsPerLine   // address of variable for characters
);                         // per line displayed in word balloon
```

Retrieves the value for the average number of characters per line displayed in a word balloon.

- Returns S_OK to indicate the operation was successful.

pbCharsPerLine   The address of a variable that receives the number of characters per line.

The Microsoft Agent server automatically scrolls the lines displayed for spoken output in the word balloon. The average number of characters per line for a character's word balloon is defined in the Microsoft Agent Character Editor. It cannot be changed by an application.

See also IAgentBalloon::GetNumLines

IAgentBalloon::GetNumLines

```
HRESULT GetNumLines(
   long * pcLines  // address of variable for number of lines
);               // displayed in word balloon
```

Retrieves the value of the number of lines displayed in a word balloon.

- Returns S_OK to indicate the operation was successful.

pcLines   The address of a variable that receives the number of lines displayed.

The Microsoft Agent server automatically scrolls the lines displayed for spoken output in the word balloon. The number of lines for a character word balloon is defined in the Microsoft Agent Character Editor. It cannot be changed by an application.

See also IAgentBalloon::GetNumCharsPerLine

IAgentBalloon::GetVisible

```
HRESULT GetVisible(
   long * pbVisible  // address of variable for word balloon
);                 // Visible setting
```

Determines whether the word balloon is visible or hidden.

- Returns S_OK to indicate the operation was successful.

pbVisible   Address of a variable that receives **True** if the word balloon is visible and **False** if hidden.

See also IAgentBalloon::SetVisible

IAgentBalloon::SetFontCharSet

```
HRESULT SetFontCharSet(
   short sFontCharSet  // character set displayed in word balloon
);
```

Sets the character set of the font displayed in the word balloon.

- Returns S_OK to indicate the operation was successful.

sFontCharSet   The character set of the font. The following are some common settings for value:

    0   Standard Windows characters (ANSI).

    1   Default character set.

    2   The symbol character set.

    128   Double-byte character set (DBCS) unique to the Japanese version of Windows.

    129   Double-byte character set (DBCS) unique to the Korean version of Windows.

    134   Double-byte character set (DBCS) unique to the Simplified Chinese version of Windows.

    136   Double-byte character set (DBCS) unique to the Traditional Chinese version of Windows.

    255   Extended characters usually displayed by MS-DOS applications.

For other character set values, consult the Microsoft Win32 documentation.

The default character set used in a character's word balloon is defined in the Microsoft Agent Character Editor. You can change it with **IAgentBalloon::SetFontCharSet**. However, the user can override the character set setting for all characters using the Microsoft Agent property sheet. This property applies only to your client application's use of the character; the setting does not affect other clients of the character or other characters of your client application.

See also **IAgentBalloon::GetFontCharSet**

IAgentBalloon::SetFontName

```
HRESULT SetFontName(
   BSTR bszFontName  // font displayed in word balloon
);
```

Sets the font displayed in the word balloon.

- Returns S_OK to indicate the operation was successful.

bszFontName   A BSTR that sets the font displayed in the word balloon.

The default font used in a character's word balloon is defined in the Microsoft Agent Character Editor. You can change it with **IAgentBalloon::SetFontName**. However, the user can override the font setting for all characters using the Microsoft Agent property sheet.

See also IAgentBalloon::GetVisible

IAgentBalloon::SetFontSize

```
HRESULT SetFontSize(
    long lFontSize  // font size displayed in word balloon
);
```

Sets the size of the font displayed in the word balloon.

- Returns S_OK to indicate the operation was successful.

lFontSize   The size of the font.

The default font size used in a character's word balloon is defined in the Microsoft Agent Character Editor. You can change it with **IAgentBalloon::SetFontSize**. However, the user can override the font size setting for all characters using the Microsoft Agent property sheet.

See also IAgentBalloon::GetFontSize

IAgentBalloon::SetVisible

```
HRESULT SetVisible(
    long bVisible  // word balloon Visible setting
);
```

Sets the **Visible** property for the word balloon.

- Returns S_OK to indicate the operation was successful.

bVisible   Visible property setting. A value of **True** displays the word balloon; a value of **False** hides it.

See also IAgentBalloon::GetVisible

IAgentBalloonEx

IAgentBalloonEx is derived from the **IAgentBalloon** interface. It includes all the **IAgentBalloon** methods and provides access to additional functions.

Methods in Vtable Order

IAgentBalloonEx Methods	Description
GetStyle	Returns the word balloon's output style.
SetStyle	Sets the word balloon's output style.
SetNumLines	Sets the number lines output in the word balloon.
SetNumCharsPerLine	Sets the number of characters per line output in the word balloon.

IAgentBalloonEx::GetStyle

```
HRESULT GetStyle(
    long * plStyle,  // address of style settings
);
```

Retrieves the character's word balloon style settings.

- Returns S_OK to indicate the operation was successful.

plStyle   Style settings for the word balloon, which can be a combination of any of the following values:

const unsigned short **BALLOON_STYLE_BALLOONON = 0x00000001;**	The balloon is supported for output.
const unsigned short **BALLOON_STYLE _SIZETOTEXT = 0x0000002;**	The balloon height is sized to accommodate the text output.
const unsigned short **BALLOON_STYLE _AUTOHIDE = 0x00000004;**	The balloon is automatically hidden.
const unsigned short **BALLOON_STYLE _AUTOPACE = 0x00000008;**	The text output is paced based on the output rate.

When the **BalloonOn** style bit is set, the word balloon appears when the **Speak** or **Think** method is used, unless the user overrides its display through the Microsoft Agent property sheet. When not set, no balloon appears.

When the **SizeToText** style bit is set, the word balloon automatically sizes the height of the balloon to the current size of the text specified in the **Speak** or **Think** method. When not set, the balloon's height is based on the balloon's number of lines property setting. This style bit is set to 1 and an attempt to use **IAgentBalloonEx::SetNumLines** will result in an error.

When the **AutoHide** style bit is set, the word balloon automatically hides after a short time-out. When not set, the balloon displays until a new **Speak** or **Think** call, the character is hidden, or the user clicks or drags the character.

When the **AutoPace** style bit is set, the word balloon paces the output based on the current output rate, for example, one word at a time. When output exceeds the size of the balloon, the former text is automatically scrolled. When not set, all text included in a **Speak** or **Think** statement displays at once.

This property applies only to your client application's use of the character; the setting does not affect other clients of the character or other characters of your client application.

The defaults for these style bits are based on the settings when the character is compiled through the Microsoft Agent Character Editor.

See also **IAgentBalloonEx::SetStyle**

IAgentBalloonEx::SetNumCharsPerLine

```
HRESULT SetNumCharsPerLine(
   long lCharsPerLine,  // number of characters per line setting
);
```

Sets the number of characters per line that can be displayed in the character's word balloon.

- Returns S_OK to indicate the operation was successful.
- Returns E_INVALIDARG if the parameter is less than eight.

lCharsPerLine   Number of lines to display in the word balloon.

The minimum setting is 8 and the maximum is 255. If the text specified in the **Speak** or **Think** method exceeds the size of the current balloon, Agent automatically scrolls the text in the balloon.

The default setting is based on settings when the character is compiled with the Microsoft Agent Character Editor.

See also **IAgentBalloon::GetNumCharsPerLine**

IAgentBalloonEx::SetNumLines

```
HRESULT SetNumLines(
   long lLines,  // number of lines setting
);
```

Sets the number of lines of text output that can be displayed in the character's word balloon.

- Returns S_OK to indicate the operation was successful.
- Returns E_INVALIDARG if the parameter is zero.

lLines   Number of lines to display in the word balloon.

The minimum setting is 1 and maximum is 128. If the text specified in the **Speak** or **Think** method exceeds the size of the current balloon, Agent automatically scrolls the text in the balloon.

This method will fail if the **SizeToText** balloon style bit is set.

The default setting is based on settings when the character is compiled with the Microsoft Agent Character Editor.

See also **IAgentBalloon::GetNumLines, IAgentBalloonEx::GetStyle, IAgentBalloonEx::SetStyle**

IAgentBalloonEx::SetStyle

```
HRESULT SetStyle(
    long lStyle,  // style settings
);
```

Retrieves the character's word balloon style settings.

- Returns S_OK to indicate the operation was successful.

lStyle   Style settings for the word balloon, which can be a combination of any of the following values:

const unsigned short BALLOON_STYLE_BALLOONON = 0x00000001;	The balloon is supported for output.
const unsigned short BALLOON_STYLE _SIZETOTEXT = 0x0000002;	The balloon height is sized to accommodate the text output.
const unsigned short BALLOON_STYLE _AUTOHIDE = 0x00000004;	The balloon is automatically hidden.
const unsigned short BALLOON_STYLE _AUTOPACE = 0x00000008;	The text output is paced based on the output rate.

When the **BalloonOn** style bit is set, the word balloon appears when the **Speak** or **Think** method is used, unless the user overrides its display in the Microsoft Agent property sheet. When not set, no balloon appears.

When the **SizeToText** style bit is set, the word balloon automatically sizes the height of the balloon to the current size of the text specified in the **Speak** or **Think** method. When not set, the balloon's height is based on the balloon's number of lines property setting. This style bit is set to 1 and an attempt to use **IAgentBalloonEx::SetNumLines** will result in an error.

When the **AutoHide** style bit is set, the word balloon automatically hides after a short timeout. When not set, the balloon displays until a new **Speak** or **Think** call, the character is hidden, or the user clicks or drags the character.

When the **AutoPace** style bit is set, the word balloon paces the output based on the current output rate, for example, one word at a time. When output exceeds the size of the balloon, the former text is automatically scrolled. When not set, all text included in a **Speak** or **Think** statement displays at once.

The Balloon's style property can be set even if the user has disabled display of the Balloon using the Microsoft Agent property sheet.

This property applies only to your client application's use of the character; the setting does not affect other clients of the character or other characters of your client application.

The defaults for these style bits are based on their settings when the character is compiled with the Microsoft Agent Character Editor.

See also IAgentBalloonEx::GetStyle

IAgentCommandWindow

IAgentCommandWindow defines an interface that allows applications to set and query the properties of the Voice Commands Window. The Voice Commands Window is a shared resource primarily designed to enable users to view voice-enabled commands. If speech recognition is disabled, the Voice Commands Window still displays, with the text "Speech input disabled" (in the language of the character). If no speech engine is installed that matches the character's language setting, the window displays, "Speech input not available." If the input-active client has not defined voice parameters for its commands and has disabled global voice commands, the window displays, "No voice commands." You can also query the properties of the Voice Commands Window regardless of whether speech input is disabled or a compatible speech engine is installed.

Methods in Vtable Order

IAgentCommandWindow Methods	Description
SetVisible	Sets the value of the **Visible** property of the Voice Commands Window.
GetVisible	Returns the value of the **Visible** property of the Voice Commands Window.
GetPosition	Returns the position of the Voice Commands Window.
GetSize	Returns the size of the Voice Commands Window.

IAgentCommandWindow::GetPosition

```
HRESULT GetPosition(
    long * plLeft,   // address of variable for left
                     // edge of Voice Commands Window
    long * plTop     // address of variable for top
                     // edge of Voice Commands Window
);
```

Retrieves the Voice Commands Window's position.

- Returns S_OK to indicate the operation was successful.

plLeft	Address of a variable that receives the screen coordinate of the left edge of the Voice Commands Window in pixels, relative to the screen origin (upper left).
plTop	Address of a variable that receives the screen coordinate of the top edge of the Voice Commands Window in pixels, relative to the screen origin (upper left).

See also IAgentCommandWindow::GetSize

IAgentCommandWindow::GetSize

```
HRESULT GetSize(
   long * plWidth,   // address of variable for Voice
                     // Commands Window width
   long * plHeight   // address of variable for Voice
                     // Commands Window height
);
```

Retrieves the current size of the Voice Commands Window.

- Returns S_OK to indicate the operation was successful.

plWidth	Address of a variable that receives the width of the Voice Commands Window in pixels, relative to the screen origin (upper left).
plHeight	Address of a variable that receives the height of the Voice Commands Window in pixels, relative to the screen origin (upper left).

See also IAgentCommandWindow::GetPosition

IAgentCommandWindow::GetVisible

```
HRESULT GetVisible(
   long * pbVisible   // address of variable for Visible setting for
);                    // Voice Commands Window
```

Determines whether the Voice Commands Window is visible or hidden.

- Returns S_OK to indicate the operation was successful.

pbVisible	Address of a variable that receives **True** if the Voice Commands Window is visible, or **False** if hidden.

See also IAgentCommandWindow::SetVisible

IAgentCommandWindow::SetVisible

```
HRESULT SetVisible(
   long bVisible   // Voice Commands Window Visible setting
);
```

Sets the **Visible** property for the Voice Commands Window.

- Returns S_OK to indicate the operation was successful.

bVisible   **Visible** property setting. A value of·**True** displays the Voice Commands Window; **False** hides it.

The user can override this property.

See also IAgentCommandWindow::GetVisible

IAgentSpeechInputProperties

IAgentSpeechInputProperties provides access to the speech input properties maintained by the server. Most of the properties are read-only for client applications, but the user can change them in the Microsoft Agent property sheet. The Microsoft Agent server returns values only if a compatible speech engine has been installed and is enabled. Querying these properties attempts to start the speech engine.

Methods in Vtable Order

IAgentSpeechInputProperties Methods	Description
GetEnabled	Returns whether the speech recognition engine is enabled.
GetHotKey	Returns the current key assignment of the Listening key.
GetListeningTip	Returns whether the Listening Tip is enabled.

GetInstalled, **GetLCID**, **GetEngine**, and **SetEngine** methods (supported in earlier versions of Microsoft Agent) are still supported for backward compatibility. However, the methods are not stubbed and do not return useful values. Use **GetSRModeID** and **SetSRModeID** to query and set the speech recognition engine to be used with the character. Keep in mind that the engine must match the character's current language setting.

IAgentSpeechInputProperties::GetEnabled

```
HRESULT GetEnabled(
    long * pbEnabled   // address of variable for speech
);                     // recognition engine Enabled setting
```

Retrieves a value indicating whether the installed speech recognition engine is enabled.

- Returns S_OK to indicate the operation was successful.

pbEnabled   Address of a variable that receives **True** if the speech engine is currently enabled and **False** if disabled.

IAgentSpeechInputProperties::GetHotKey

```
HRESULT GetHotKey(
   BSTR * pbszHotCharKey   // address of variable for listening key
);
```

Retrieves the current keyboard assignment for the speech input Listening key.

- Returns S_OK to indicate the operation was successful.

pbszHotCharKey   Address of a BSTR that receives the current hotkey setting used to open the audio channel for speech input.

If **GetEnabled** returns **False**, querying this setting raises an error.

See also IAgentSpeechInputProperties::GetEnabled

IAgentSpeechInputProperties::GetListeningTip

```
HRESULT GetListeningTip(
   long * pbListeningTip   // address of variable for listening tip flag
);
```

Retrieves a value indicating whether the Listening Tip is enabled for display.

- Returns S_OK to indicate the operation was successful.

pbListeningTip   Address of a variable that receives **True** if the Listening Tip is enabled for display, or **False** if the Listening Tip is disabled.

If **GetEnabled** returns **False**, querying any other speech input properties returns an error.

See also IAgentSpeechInputProperties::GetEnabled

IAgentAudioOutputProperties

IAgentAudioOutputProperties provides access to audio output properties maintained by the Microsoft Agent server. These functions are also available from **IAgentAudioOutputPropertiesEx**. The properties are read-only, but the user can change them in the Microsoft Agent property sheet.

Methods in Vtable Order

IAgentAudioOutputProperties Methods	Description
GetEnabled	Returns whether audio output is enabled.
GetUsingSoundEffects	Returns whether sound-effect output is enabled.

IAgentAudioOutputProperties::GetEnabled

```
HRESULT GetEnabled(
   long * pbEnabled   // address of variable for audio
                      // output Enabled setting
);
```

Retrieves a value indicating whether character speech output is enabled.

■ Returns S_OK to indicate the operation was successful.

pbEnabled Address of a variable that receives **True** if the speech output is currently enabled and **False** if disabled.

Because this setting affects spoken output (TTS and sound file) for all characters, only the user can change this property in the Microsoft Agent property sheet.

IAgentAudioOutputProperties::GetUsingSoundEffects

```
HRESULT GetUsingSoundEffects(
   long * pbUsingSoundEffects   // address of variable sound
);                             // effects output setting
```

Retrieves a value indicating whether sound effects output is enabled.

■ Returns S_OK to indicate the operation was successful.

pbUsingSoundEffects Address of a variable that receives **True** if the sound effects output is currently enabled and **False** if disabled.

Sound effects for a character's animation are assigned in the Microsoft Agent Character Editor. Because this setting affects sound effects output for all characters, only the user can change this property in the Microsoft Agent property sheet.

IAgentAudioOutputPropertiesEx

IAgentAudioOutputPropertiesEx is derived from the **IAgentAudioOutputProperties** interface. It includes all the **IAgentAudioOutputProperties** methods and provides access to additional functions.

Methods in Vtable Order

IAgentAudioOutputPropertiesEx Methods	Description
GetStatus	Returns the status of the audio output channel.

IAgentAudioOutputPropertiesEx::GetStatus

```
HRESULT GetStatus(
   long * plStatus,   // address of audio channel status
);
```

Retrieves the status of the audio channel.

- Returns S_OK to indicate the operation was successful.

plStatus   Status of the audio output channel, which may be one of the following values:

const unsigned short **AUDIO_STATUS_AVAILABLE = 0;**	The audio output channel is available (not busy).
const unsigned short **AUDIO_STATUS_NOAUDIO = 1;**	There is no support for audio output; for example, because there is no sound card.
const unsigned short **AUDIO_STATUS_CANTOPENAUDIO = 2;**	The audio output channel can't be opened (is busy); for example, because another application is playing audio.
const unsigned short **AUDIO_STATUS_USERSPEAKING = 3;**	The audio output channel is busy because the server is processing user speech input
const unsigned short **AUDIO_STATUS_CHARACTERSPEAKING = 4;**	The audio output channel is busy because a character is currently speaking.
const unsigned short **AUDIO_STATUS_SROVERRIDEABLE = 5;**	The audio output channel is not busy, but it is waiting for user speech input.
const unsigned short **AUDIO_STATUS_ERROR = 6;**	There was some other (unknown) problem in attempting to access the audio output channel.

This setting enables your client application to query the state of the audio output channel. You can use this to determine whether to have your character speak or to try to turn on Listening mode (using **IAgentCharacterEx::Listen**).

IAgentPropertySheet

IAgentPropertySheet defines an interface that allows applications to set and query properties for the Microsoft Agent property sheet (window).

Methods in Vtable Order

IAgentPropertySheet Methods	Description
GetVisible	Returns whether the Microsoft Agent property sheet is visible.
SetVisible	Sets the **Visible** property of the Microsoft Agent property sheet.
GetPosition	Returns the position of the Microsoft Agent property sheet.
GetSize	Returns the size of the Microsoft Agent property sheet.
GetPage	Returns the current page for the Microsoft Agent property sheet.
SetPage	Sets the current page for the Microsoft Agent property sheet.

IAgentPropertySheet::GetPage

```
HRESULT GetPage(
    BSTR * pbszPage  // address of variable for current property page
);
```

Retrieves the current page of the Microsoft Agent property sheet.

- Returns S_OK to indicate the operation was successful.

pbszPage   Address of a variable that receives the current page of the property sheet (last viewed page if the window is not open). The parameter can be one of the following:

"Speech"	The Speech Input page.
"Output"	The Output page.
"Copyright"	The Copyright page.

See also **IAgentPropertySheet::SetPage**

IAgentPropertySheet::GetPosition

```
HRESULT GetPosition(
    long * plLeft,  // address of variable for left
                    // edge of property sheet
    long * plTop    // address of variable for top
                    // edge of property sheet
);
```

Retrieves the Microsoft Agent's property sheet window position.

- Returns S_OK to indicate the operation was successful.

plLeft   Address of a variable that receives the screen coordinate of the left edge of the property sheet in pixels, relative to the screen origin (upper left).

plTop   Address of a variable that receives the screen coordinate of the top edge of the property sheet in pixels, relative to the screen origin (upper left).

See also IAgentPropertySheet::GetSize

IAgentPropertySheet::GetSize

```
HRESULT GetSize(
   long * plWidth,  // address of variable for property sheet width
   long * plHeight  // address of variable for property sheet height
);
```

Retrieves the size of the Microsoft Agent property sheet window.

■ Returns S_OK to indicate the operation was successful.

plWidth	Address of a variable that receives the width of the property sheet in pixels, relative to the screen origin (upper left).
plHeight	Address of a variable that receives the height of the property sheet in pixels, relative to the screen origin (upper left).

See also IAgentPropertySheet::GetPosition

IAgentPropertySheet:: GetVisible

```
HRESULT GetVisible(
   long * pbVisible  // address of variable for property sheet
);                   // Visible setting
```

Determines whether the Microsoft Agent property sheet is visible or hidden.

■ Returns S_OK to indicate the operation was successful.

pbVisible	Address of a variable that receives **True** if the property sheet is visible and **False** if hidden.

See also IAgentPropertySheet::SetVisible

IAgentPropertySheet::SetPage

```
HRESULT SetPage(
   BSTR bszPage  // current property page
);
```

Sets the current page of the Microsoft Agent property sheet.

■ Returns S_OK to indicate the operation was successful.

bszPage	A BSTR that sets the current page of the property. The parameter can be one of the following.

"Speech"	The Speech Input page.
"Output"	The Output page.
"Copyright"	The Copyright page.

See also IAgentPropertySheet::GetPage

IAgentPropertySheet::SetVisible

```
HRESULT SetVisible(
    long bVisible  // property sheet Visible setting
);
```

Sets the **Visible** property for the Microsoft Agent property sheet.

- Returns S_OK to indicate the operation was successful.

bVisible   Visible property setting. A value of **True** displays the property
                    sheet; a value of **False** hides it.

See also IAgentPropertySheet::GetVisible

Events

IAgentNotifySink notifies clients when certain state changes occur. These functions are also available from **IAgentNotifySinkEx**.

Methods in Vtable Order

IAgentNotifySink	Description
Command	Occurs when the server processes a client-defined command.
ActivateInputState	Occurs when a character becomes or ceases to be input-active.
VisibleState	Occurs when the character's **Visible** state changes.
Click	Occurs when a character is clicked.
DblClick	Occurs when a character is double-clicked.
DragStart	Occurs when a user starts dragging a character.
DragComplete	Occurs when a user stops dragging a character.
RequestStart	Occurs when the server begins processing a **Request** object.
RequestComplete	Occurs when the server completes processing a **Request** object.
Bookmark	Occurs when the server processes a bookmark.
Idle	Occurs when the server starts or ends idle processing.
Move	Occurs when a character has been moved.
Size	Occurs when a character has been resized.
BalloonVisibleState	Occurs when the visibility state of a character's word balloon changes.

The **IAgentNotifySink::Restart** and **IAgentNotifySink::Shutdown** events, supported in earlier versions of Microsoft Agent, are now obsolete. While supported for backward compatibility, the server no longer sends these events.

IAgentNotifySink::ActivateInputState

```
HRESULT ActivateInputState(
    long dwCharID,    // character ID
    long bActivated   // input activation flag
);
```

Notifies a client application that a character's input active state changed.

- No return value.

dwCharID   Identifier of the character whose input activation state changed.

bActivated   Input active flag. This Boolean value is **True** if the character referred to by dwCharID became input active; and **False** if the character lost its input active state.

IAgentNotifySink:: BalloonVisibleState

```
HRESULT BalloonVisibleState(
    long dwCharID,    // character ID
    long bVisible     // visibility flag
);
```

Notifies a client application when the visibility state of the character's word balloon changes.

- No return value.

dwCharID   Identifier of the character whose word balloon's visibility state has changed.

bVisible   Visibility flag. This Boolean value is **True** when character's word balloon becomes visible; and **False** when it becomes hidden.

This event is sent to all clients of the character.

IAgentNotifySink::Bookmark

```
HRESULT Bookmark(
    long dwBookMarkID  // bookmark ID
);
```

Notifies a client application when its bookmark completes.

- No return value.

dwBookMarkID   Identifier of the bookmark that resulted in triggering the event.

When you include bookmark tags in a **Speak** method, you can track when they occur with this event.

See also **IAgentCharacter::Speak** and Chapter 6, "Microsoft Agent Speech Output Tags"

IAgentNotifySink::Click

```
HRESULT Click(
    long dwCharID,    // character ID
    short fwKeys,     // mouse button and modifier key state
    long x,           // x coordinate of mouse pointer
    long y            // y coordinate of mouse pointer
);
```

Notifies a client application when the user clicks a character or character's taskbar icon.

- No return value.

dwCharID   Identifier of the clicked character.

fwKeys   A parameter that indicates the mouse button and modifier key state. The parameter can return any combination of the following:

0x0001	Left Button
0x0010	Middle Button
0x0002	Right Button
0x0004	Shift Key Down
0x0008	Control Key Down
0x0020	Alt Key Down
0x1000	Event occurred on the character's taskbar icon

x   The x-coordinate of the mouse pointer in pixels, relative to the screen origin (upper left).

y   The y-coordinate of the mouse pointer in pixels, relative to the screen origin (upper left).

This event is sent to the input-active client of the character. If none of the character's clients are input-active, the server notifies the character's active client. If the character is visible, the server also makes that client input-active and sends the **IAgentNotifySink::ActivateInputState**. If the character hidden, the character is also automatically shown.

IAgentNotifySink::Command

```
HRESULT Command(
    long dwCommandID,        // Command ID of the best match
    IUnknown * punkUserInput // address of IAgentUserInput object
);
```

Notifies a client application that a **Command** was selected by the user.

- No return value.

dwCommandID   Identifier of the best match command alternative.

punkUserInput   Address of the **IUnknown** interface for the **IAgentUserInput** object.

Use **QueryInterface** to retrieve the **IAgentUserInput** interface.

The server notifies the input-active client when the user chooses a command by voice or by selecting a command from the character's pop-up menu. The event occurs even when the user selects one of the server's commands. In this case the server returns a null command ID, the confidence score, and the voice text returned by the speech engine for that entry.

See also IAgentUserInput

IAgentNotifySink::DblClick

```
HRESULT DblClick(
    long dwCharID,   // character ID
    short fwKeys,    // mouse button and modifier key state
    long x,          // x coordinate of mouse pointer
    long y           // y coordinate of mouse pointer
);
```

Notifies a client application when the user double-clicks a character.

- No return value.

dwCharID   Identifier of the double-clicked character.

fwKeys   A parameter that indicates the mouse button and modifier key state. The parameter can return any combination of the following:

0x0001	Left Button
0x0010	Middle Button
0x0002	Right Button
0x0004	Shift Key Down
0x0008	Control Key Down
0x0020	Alt Key Down
0x1000	Event occurred on the character's taskbar icon

x   The x-coordinate of the mouse pointer in pixels, relative to the screen origin (upper left).

y   The y-coordinate of the mouse pointer in pixels, relative to the screen origin (upper left).

This event is sent to the input-active client of the character. If none of the character's clients are input-active, the server notifies the character's active client. If the character is visible, the server also makes that client input-active and sends the **IAgentNotifySink::ActivateInputState**. If the character is hidden, the character is also automatically shown.

IAgentNotifySink::DragComplete

```
HRESULT DragComplete(
    long dwCharID,   // character ID
    short fwKeys,    // mouse button and modifier key state
    long x,          // x-coordinate of mouse pointer
    long y           // y-coordinate of mouse pointer
);
```

Notifies a client application when the user stops dragging a character.

- No return value.

dwCharID   Identifier of the dragged character.

fwKeys   A parameter that indicates the mouse button and modifier key state. The parameter can return any combination of the following:

0x0001	Left Button
0x0010	Middle Button
0x0002	Right Button
0x0004	Shift Key Down
0x0008	Control Key Down
0x0020	Alt Key Down

x   The x-coordinate of the mouse pointer in pixels, relative to the screen origin (upper left).

y   The y-coordinate of the mouse pointer in pixels, relative to the screen origin (upper left).

IAgentNotifySink::DragStart

```
HRESULT DragStart(
    long dwCharID,   // character ID
    short fwKeys,    // mouse button and modifier key state
    long x,          // x-coordinate of mouse pointer
    long y           // y-coordinate of mouse pointer
);
```

Notifies a client application when the user starts dragging a character.

- No return value.

dwCharID	Identifier of the dragged character.
fwKeys	A parameter that indicates the mouse button and modifier key state. The parameter can return any combination of the following:

0x0001	Left Button
0x0010	Middle Button
0x0002	Right Button
0x0004	Shift Key Down
0x0008	Control Key Down
0x0020	Alt Key Down

x	The x-coordinate of the mouse pointer in pixels, relative to the screen origin (upper left).
y	The y-coordinate of the mouse pointer in pixels, relative to the screen origin (upper left).

IAgentNotifySink::Idle

```
HRESULT Idle(
   long dwCharID,   // character ID
   long bStart      // start flag
);
```

Notifies a client application when a character's **Idling** state has changed.

- No return value.

dwCharID	Identifier of the request that started.
bStart	Start flag. This Boolean value is **True** when the character begins idling and **False** when it stops idling.

This event enables you to track when the Microsoft Agent server starts or stops idle processing for a character.

See also **IAgentCharacter::GetIdleOn**, **IAgentCharacter::SetIdleOn**

IAgentNotifySink::Move

```
HRESULT Move(
   long dwCharID,   // character ID
   long x,          // x-coordinate of new location
   long y,          // y-coordinate of new location
   long dwCause     // cause of move state
);
```

Notifies a client application when the character has been moved.

- No return value.

dwCharID	Identifier of the character that has been moved.
x	The x-coordinate of the new position in pixels, relative to the screen origin (upper left). The location of a character is based on the upper left corner of its animation frame.
y	The y-coordinate of the new position in pixels, relative to the screen origin (upper left). The location of a character is based on the upper left corner of its animation frame.
dwCause	The cause of the character move. The parameter may be one of the following:

const unsigned short NeverMoved = 0;	Character has not been moved.
const unsigned short UserMoved = 1;	User dragged the character.
const unsigned short ProgramMoved = 2;	Your application moved the character.
const unsigned short OtherProgramMoved = 3;	Another application moved the character.
const unsigned short SystemMoved = 4	The server moved the character to keep it onscreen after a screen resolution change.

This event is sent to all clients of the character.

See also **IAgentCharacter::GetMoveCause, IAgentCharacter::MoveTo**

IAgentNotifySink::RequestComplete

```
HRESULT RequestComplete(
    long dwRequestID,  // request ID
    long hrStatus      // status code
);
```

Notifies a client application when a request completes.

- No return value.

dwRequestID	Identifier of the request that started.
hrStatus	Status code. This parameter returns the status code for the request.

This event enables you to track when a queued method completes using its request ID.

See also **IAgentNotifySink::RequestStart, IAgent::Load, IAgent-Character::GestureAt, IAgentCharacter::Hide, IAgentCharacter::Interrupt, IAgentCharacter::MoveTo, IAgentCharacter::Prepare, IAgentCharacter::Play, IAgentCharacter::Show, IAgentCharacter::Speak, IAgentCharacter::Wait**

IAgentNotifySink::RequestStart

```
HRESULT RequestStart(
    long dwRequestID  // request ID
);
```

Notifies a client application when a request begins.

- No return value.

dwRequestID   Identifier of the request that started.

This event enables you to track when a queued request begins using its request ID.

See also **IAgentNotifySink::RequestComplete, IAgent::Load, IAgent-Character::GestureAt, IAgentCharacter::Hide, IAgentCharacter::Interrupt, IAgentCharacter::MoveTo, IAgentCharacter::Prepare, IAgentCharacter::Play, IAgentCharacter::Show, IAgentCharacter::Speak, IAgentCharacter::Wait**

IAgentNotifySink:: Size

```
HRESULT Size(
    long dwCharID,  // character ID
    long lWidth,    // new width
    long lHeight,   // new height
);
```

Notifies a client application when the character has been resized.

- No return value.

dwCharID   Identifier of the character that has been resized.

lWidth   The width of the character's animation frame in pixels.

lHeight   The height of the character's animation frame in pixels.

This event is sent to all clients of the character.

See also **IAgentCharacter::GetSize, IAgentCharacter::SetSize**

IAgentNotifySink::VisibleState

```
HRESULT VisibleState(
    long dwCharID,  // character ID
    long bVisible,  // visibility flag
    long dwCause,   // cause of visible state
);
```

Notifies a client application when the visibility state of the character changes.

- No return value.

dwCharID   Identifier of the character whose visibility state is changed.

bVisible   Visibility flag. This Boolean value is **True** when character becomes visible and **False** when the character becomes hidden.

dwCause   Cause of last change to the character's visibility state. The parameter may be one of the following:

const unsigned short **NeverShown = 0;**	Character has not been shown.
const unsigned short **UserHid = 1;**	User hid the character with the character's taskbar icon pop-up menu or with speech input.
const unsigned short **UserShowed = 2;**	User showed the character.
const unsigned short **ProgramHid = 3;**	Your application hid the character.
const unsigned short **ProgramShowed = 4;**	Your application showed the character.
const unsigned short **OtherProgramHid = 5;**	Another application hid the character.
const unsigned short **OtherProgramShowed = 6;**	Another application showed the character.
const unsigned short **UserHidViaCharacterMenu = 7**	User hid the character with the character's pop-up menu.
const unsigned short **UserHidViaTaskbarIcon = UserHid**	User hid the character with the character's taskbar icon pop-up menu or using speech input.

See also IAgentCharacter::GetVisibleIAgentCharacter::Get-VisibilityCause

IAgentNotifySinkEx

IAgentNotifySinkEx is derived from the **IAgentNotifySink** interface. It includes all the **IAgentNotifySink** methods and provides access to additional functions.

Methods in Vtable Order

IAgentNotifySinkEx Methods	Description
HelpComplete	Occurs when the user selects a menu or the character in Help mode.
ListeningState	Occurs when the character's listening state changes.
Suspend	Occurs when the server suspends operation.
DefaultCharacterChange	Occurs when the user changes the default character.
AgentPropertyChange	Occurs when the user changes an Agent property setting.
ActiveClientChange	Occurs when the active client of a character changes.

IAgentNotifySinkEx::ActiveClientChange

```
HRESULT ActiveClientChange(
    long dwCharID,  // character ID
    long lStatus    // active state flag
);
```

Notifies a client application if its active client is no longer the active client of a character.

- No return value.

dwCharID   Identifier of the character for which active client status changed.

lStatus   Active state change of the client, which can be a combination of any of the following values:

const unsigned short ACTIVATE_NOTACTIVE = 0;	Your client is not the active client of the character.
const unsigned short ACTIVATE_ACTIVE = 1;	Your client is the active client of the character.
const unsigned short ACTIVATE_INPUTACTIVE = 2;	Your client is input-active (active client of the topmost character).

When multiple client applications share the same character, the active client of the character receives mouse input (for example, Microsoft Agent control click or drag events). Similarly, when multiple characters are displayed, the active client of the topmost character (also known as the input-active client) receives **IAgentNotifySink::Command** events.

When the active client of a character changes, this event passes back the ID of that character and **True** if your application has become the active client of the character or **False** if it is no longer the active client of the character.

A client application may receive this event when the user selects another client application's entry in character's pop-up menu or by voice command, the client application changes its active status, or another client application quits its connection to Microsoft Agent. Agent sends this event only to the client applications that are directly affected -- those that either become the active client or stop being the active client.

You can use the **Activate** method to set whether your application is the active client of the character or to make your application the input-active client (which also makes the character topmost).

See also **IAgentCharacter::Activate, IAgentCharacterEx::GetActive, IAgentNotifySink::ActivateInputState**

IAgentNotifySinkEx::AgentPropertyChange

```
HRESULT AgentPropertyChange();
```

Notifies a client application when the user changes a Microsoft Agent property setting.

- No return value.

When the user changes a Microsoft Agent property setting in the Microsoft Agent property sheet, the server sends this event to all clients unless the server is currently suspended.

See also **IAgentNotifySinkEx::DefaultCharacterChange**

IAgentNotifySinkEx::DefaultCharacterChange

```
HRESULT DefaultCharacterChange(
   BSTR bszGUID  // character identifier
);
```

Notifies a client application when the default character changes.

- No return value.

bszGUID   The unique identifier for the character.

When the user changes the character assigned as the user's default character, the server sends this event to clients that have loaded the default character. The event returns the character's unique identifier (GUID) formatted with braces and dashes, which is defined when the character is built with the Microsoft Agent Character Editor.

When the new character appears, it assumes the same size as any already loaded instance of the character or the previous default character (in that order).

See also IAgent::Load

IAgentNotifySinkEx::HelpComplete

```
HRESULT HelpComplete(
    long dwCharID,      // character ID
    long dwCommandID,   // command ID
    long dwCause        // cause
);
```

Notifies a client application when the user selects a command or character to complete Help mode.

- No return value.

dwCharID	Identifier of the character for which Help mode completed.
dwCommandID	Identifier of the command the user selected.
dwCause	The cause for the event, which may be the following values:

const unsigned short CSHELPCAUSE_COMMAND = 1;	The user selected a command supplied by your application.
const unsigned short CSHELPCAUSE_OTHER-PROGRAM = 2;	The user selected the **Commands** object of another client.
const unsigned short CSHELPCAUSE_OPEN-COMMANDS-WINDOW = 3;	The user selected the Open Voice Commands command.
const unsigned short CSHELPCAUSE_CLOSE-COMMANDSWINDOW = 4;	The user selected the Close Voice Commands command.
const unsigned short CSHELPCAUSE_SHOW CHARACTER = 5;	The user selected the Show *CharacterName* command.
const unsigned short CSHELPCAUSE_HIDE-CHARACTER = 6;	The user selected the Hide *CharacterName* command.
const unsigned short CSHELP-CAUSE_CHARACTER = 7;	The user selected (clicked) the character.

Typically Help mode completes when the user clicks or drags the character or selects a command from the character's pop-up menu. Clicking on another character or elsewhere on the screen does not cancel Help mode. The client that set Help mode for the character can cancel Help mode by setting **IAgentCharacter::HelpModeOn** to **False**. (This does not trigger the **IAgentNotifySinkEx::HelpComplete** event.)

When the user selects a command from the character's pop-up menu in Help mode, the server removes the menu, calls Help with the command's specified **HelpContextID**, and sends this event. The context-sensitive (also known as What's This?) Help window is displayed at the pointer location. If the user selects the command by voice input, the Help window is displayed over the character. If the character is off-screen, the window is displayed on-screen nearest to the character's current position.

If the server returns **dwCommandID** as an empty string (""), it indicates that the user selected a server-supplied command.

This event is sent only to the client application that places the character into Help mode.

See also IAgentCharacterEx::SetHelpModeOn, IAgentCharacterEx::Set-HelpFileName, IAgentCharacterEx::SetHelpContextID, IAgentCommands-Ex::SetHelpContextID,

---

IAgentNotifySinkEx::ListeningState

```
HRESULT ListeningState(
   long dwCharacterID,  // character ID
   long bListening,     // listening mode state
   long dwCause         // cause
);
```

Notifies a client application when the Listening mode changes.

- No return value.

dwCharacterID   The character for which the listening state changed.

bListening   The Listening mode state. **True** indicates that Listening mode has started; **False**, that Listening mode has ended.

dwCause   The cause for the event, which may be one of the following values.

const unsigned long LSCOMPLETE_CAUSE_PROGRAM-DISABLED = 1;	Listening mode was turned off by program code.
const unsigned long LSCOMPLETE_CAUSE_PROGRAM-TIMEDOUT = 2;	Listening mode (turned on by program code) timed out.
const unsigned long LSCOMPLETE_CAUSE_USER-TIMEDOUT = 3;	Listening mode (turned on by the Listening key) timed out.
const unsigned long LSCOMPLETE_CAUSE_USER-RELEASEDKEY = 4;	Listening mode was turned off because the user released the Listening key.

const unsigned long LSCOMPLETE_CAUSE_USER-UTTERANCEENDED = 5;	Listening mode was turned off because the user finished speaking.
const unsigned long LSCOMPLETE_CAUSE_CLIENT-DEACTIVATED = 6;	Listening mode was turned off because the input active client was deactivated.
const unsigned long LSCOMPLETE_CAUSE_DEFAULT-CHARCHANGE = 7	Listening mode was turned off because the default character was changed.
const unsigned long LSCOMPLETE_CAUSE_USER-DISABLED = 8	Listening mode was turned off because the user disabled speech input.

This event is sent to all clients when the Listening mode begins after the user presses the Listening key or when its time-out ends, or when the input-active client calls the **IAgentCharacterEx::Listen** method with **True** or **False**.

The event returns values to the clients that currently have this character loaded. All other clients receive a null character (empty string).

See also **IAgentCharacterEx::Listen**

C H A P T E R   6

Microsoft Agent Speech Output Tags

The Microsoft Agent services support modifying speech output through special tags inserted in the speech text string. These tags help you change the characteristics of the output expression of the character.

Speech output tags use the following rules of syntax:

- All tags begin and end with a backslash character (\).
- The single backslash character is not enabled *within* a tag. To include a backslash character in a text parameter of a tag, use a double backslash (\\).
- Tags are case-insensitive. For example, \pit\ is the same as \PIT\.
- Tags are whitespace-dependent. For example, \Rst\ is not the same as \ Rst \.

Unless otherwise specified or modified by another tag, the speech output retains the characteristic set by the tag within the text specified in a single **Speak** method. Speech output is automatically reset through the user-defined parameters after a **Speak** method is completed.

Some tags include quoted strings. For some programming languages, such as Visual Basic Scripting Edition (VBScript) and Visual Basic, this means that you may have to use two quote marks to designate the tag's parameter or concatenate a double-quote character as part of the string. The latter is shown in this Visual Basic example:

```
Agent1.Characters("Genie").Speak "This is \map=" + chr(34) + _
   "Spoken text" + chr(34) + "=" + chr(34) + "Balloon text" _
+ chr(34) + "\."
```

For C, C++, and Java programming, precede backslashes and double quotes with a backslash. For example:

```
BSTR bszSpeak = SysAllocString(L"This is \\map=\"Spoken
text\"=\"Balloon text\"\\");

pCharacter->Speak(bszSpeak, ......);
```

For foreign languages that support double-byte character set (DBCS) characters, you can use double-byte characters to specify string parameters. However, use single-byte characters for all other parameters and characters that are used to define the tag, including the tag itself.

The following tags are supported:

Chr, **Ctx**, **Emp**, **Lst**, **Map**, **Mrk**, **Pau**, **Pit**, **Rst**, **Spd**, **Vol**

The tags are primarily designed for adjusting text-to-speech (TTS)-generated output. Only the **Mrk** and **Map** tags can be used with sound file-based spoken output.

Note Microsoft Agent does not support all the tags documented in the Microsoft Speech SDK. Parameters may also vary depending on the TTS engine selected. You can set a specific TTS engine using **TTSModeID**.

Chr Tag

Description
Sets the character of the voice.

Syntax
Chr=*string*\\

Part	Description
string	A string specifying the character of the voice.
"**Normal**"	(Default) A normal tone of voice.
"**Monotone**"	A monotone voice.
"**Whisper**"	A whispered voice.

Remarks
This tag is supported only for TTS-generated output. The range of values for the parameter may vary depending on the installed TTS engine.

Ctx Tag

Description
Sets the context of the output text.

Syntax
Ctx=*string*\\

Part	Description
string	A string specifying the context of the text that follows, which determines how symbols or abbreviations are spoken.
"Address"	Addresses and/or phone numbers.
"E-mail"	Electronic mail.
"Unknown"	(Default) Context is unknown.

Remarks

This tag is supported only for TTS-generated output. The range of values for the parameter may vary depending on the installed TTS engine.

Emp Tag

Description

Emphasizes the next word spoken. This tag must immediately precede the word.

Syntax

\Emp\

Remarks

This tag is supported only for TTS-generated output. The range of values for the parameter may vary depending on the installed TTS engine.

Lst Tag

Description

Repeats last spoken statement for the character.

Syntax

\Lst\

Remarks

This tag enables a character to repeat its last spoken statement. This tag must appear by itself in the **Speak** method; no other text or parameters can be included. When the spoken text is repeated, any other tags included in the original text are repeated, except for bookmarks. Any .WAV and .LWV files included in the text are also repeated.

Map Tag

Description

Maps spoken text to text displayed in the word balloon.

Syntax

Map="*spokentext*"="*balloontext*"\

Part	Description
spokentext	A string specifying the text for spoken output.
balloontext	A string specifying the text for word balloon output.

Remarks

This tag enables you to use different spoken text than that displayed in the word balloon.

Mrk Tag

Description

Defines a bookmark in the spoken text.

Syntax

Mrk=*number*\

Part	Description
number	A Long integer value that identifies the bookmark.

Remarks

When the server processes a bookmark, it generates a bookmark event. You must specify a number greater than zero (0) and not equal to 2147483647 or 2147483646.

See also Bookmark event

Pau Tag

Description

Pauses speech for the specified number of milliseconds.

Syntax

Pau=*number*\

Part	Description
number	The number of milliseconds to pause.

Remarks

This tag is supported only for TTS-generated output. The range of values for the parameter may vary depending on the installed TTS engine.

Pit Tag

Description

Sets the baseline pitch of the output to the specified value in hertz.

Syntax

\Pit=*number*\

Part	Description
number	The pitch in hertz.

Remarks

This tag is supported only for TTS-generated output. The range of values for the parameter may vary depending on the installed TTS engine.

Rst Tag

Description

Resets all tags to the default settings.

Syntax

\Rst\

Spd Tag

Description

Sets the baseline average talking speed of the speech output.

Syntax

\Spd=*number*\

Part	Description
number	Baseline average talking speed, in words per minute.

Remarks

This tag is supported only for TTS-generated output. The range of values for the parameter may vary depending on the installed TTS engine

Vol Tag

Description
Sets the baseline speaking volume of the speech output.

Syntax
\Vol=*number*\

Part	Description
number	Baseline speaking volume: 0 is silence and 65535 is maximum volume.

Remarks
The volume setting affects both left and right channels. You cannot set the volume of each channel separately. This tag is supported only for TTS-generated output.

CHAPTER 7

Designing Characters for Microsoft Agent

Characters

Human communication is fundamentally social. Microsoft Agent enables you to leverage this aspect of interaction using animated characters. Users will expect a character to conform to the same social, though not necessarily physical, rules they use when interacting with other people, even when they understand that the character is synthetic. To the extent that you create characters that meet their expectations, users will find your characters more believable and likable. Therefore, how you design a character can have a dramatic effect on its success.

When designing a character, first consider the profile of your target audience and what appeals to them as well as what tasks they do. Similarly, consider how well your character's design and style matches its purpose in addition to the application it supports. For example, a dog character may work well for a retrieval or security application depending on its overall appearance. Often the success is in the details. Research has shown that changing an animal character's roundness of eyes and ear shape can generate very different reactions to the character.

Also consider your character's basic personality type: dominant or submissive, emotional or reserved, sophisticated or down-to-earth; or perhaps you want to adapt its personality based on user interaction. For example, you can provide a control that enables a user to adjust whether the character volunteers more information or waits to be asked. The former would be more outgoing than the latter.

The name you supply for your character can infer a particular type of personality. For example, "Max" and "Linus" may convey very different personalities. The Microsoft Agent Character Editor enables you to set your character's name and include a short description. These attributes can be queried at run time.

In addition, decide whether you plan to use a synthetic voice (using a text-to-speech engine) or recorded voice (.WAV file). This decision may depend on the type of character you use, the languages you plan to support, and what you want the character to be able to say. For example, a synthesized voice enables your character to say almost anything. Programming what your character will say is easy and quick: You just supply the text the character will speak. However, using a computer-generated speech engine requires some extra overhead for initial installation and will be language-specific. Further, most synthesized voices sound computer-generated; they do not match the clarity and prosody of most human speech. It may be difficult to simulate a voice that matches your character, particularly if you use a character that already has an established identity or one that has a very distinctive voice. In such a case, you may want to use recorded speech files for your output. Microsoft Agent also supports lip-syncing for recorded speech output. Although audio files provide a natural voice and are easier to implement in other languages, they must be copied or downloaded to local machines. Recorded speech files also limit your character to the vocabulary contained in them. Whether you choose synthetic or recorded speech output, keep in mind that a voice carries with it additional social information about the gender, age, and personality of the speaker.

You can also decide to use the word balloon for output and the default settings for the balloon's font and color. Note, however, that the user can change the font and color attributes. In addition, you cannot assume that the word balloon's state remains constant because the user can turn the word balloon off.

Animations

A character's animations reflect its gender, age, personality, and behavior. The number and types of animations you create for a character depend on what your character does and how it responds to different situations.

Like traditional animations, digital animations involve creating a series of slightly differing images that, when displayed sequentially, provide the illusion of action. Creating high-quality animation images may require a skilled animator, but the style and presentation of the character you create also affect quality. Two-dimensional characters with simple shapes and features can sometimes be as effective as (or more effective than) highly rendered characters. It is not necessary to create a realistic image to portray an effective character. Many popular cartoon characters are not realistic in their presentation, yet they are effective because the animator understands how to convey action and emotion. At the end of this chapter you will find general information about fundamental animation design principles.

Frames

Each animation you create for a Microsoft Agent character is composed of a timed sequence of frames. Each frame in the animation is composed of one or more bitmap images. Images can be as small as you need them or as large as the frame itself.

Animation details such as eye blinking or finger movement can be included as additional images for the frame. You can overlay several images to create a composite, and vary their position in the layers. This technique enables you to reuse images in multiple frames and vary the details that change. For example, if you want to have a character wave its hand, for each frame you could use a base image with everything but the hand and overlay the base image with a different hand image. Similarly, if you want to make the character blink, you can overlay a different set of eyes over a base image for each frame. Images can also be offset from the base image. However, only the part of the image that exists within the frame's size will be displayed.

You can have as many frames in an animation as you wish; however, a typical animation averages about 14 frames so that it plays for no more than six seconds. This modest length of time ensures that your character appears responsive to user input. In addition, the greater the number of frames, the larger your animation file. For downloaded Web-based characters, keep the size of your animation file as small as possible while still providing a reasonably-sized set of frames, so that the character's animation does not appear jerky.

Image Design

You can use any graphics or animation tool to create images for animation frames, provided that you store the final images in the Windows bitmap (.BMP) format. When the images are created, use the Microsoft Agent Character Editor included on the CD (*http://www.microsoft.com/workshop/imedia/agent/ charactereditor.asp*) to assemble, sequence, and time the images, supply other character information, and compile all the information into a final character file.

Character images must be designed to a 256-color palette, preserving the 20 standard Windows system colors in their standard position in the palette (the first 10 and last 10 positions). That means your character's color palette can use the standard system colors and up to 236 other colors. When defining your palette, include any props your character uses in the animation. If your character's palette places colors in the system color positions, those character colors will be overwritten with the system colors when Microsoft Agent creates the palette.

The larger the number of colors you use in a character's color palette, the greater the possibility that part of your character's colors may get remapped for systems configured to an 8-bit (256) color setting. Consider also the palette usage of the application in which the character will be used. It's best to avoid having the character remap the colors of its host application and vice-versa. Similarly, if you plan to support multiple characters displayed at the same time, you'll probably want to maintain a consistent palette for those characters. You might consider using only the standard system colors in your character if you target users with an 8-bit color configuration. However, this still may not prevent remapping of your character's color if another application extensively redefines the color palette. On systems set to higher color resolutions, color palette remapping should not be a problem because the system manages the color palettes automatically.

Using a larger number of colors in an image can also increase the overall size of your animation file. The number of colors and frequency of variation may determine how well your character file compresses. For example, a two-dimensional character that uses only a few colors will compress better than a three-dimensional, shaded character.

You must use the same color palette for your entire character file. You cannot change the palette for different animations. If you attempt to support 8-bit color configurations, consider using the same palette for your application and any other characters you plan to support.

The 11th position in the palette is defined by default as the transparency (or alpha) color, although you can also set the color using the Microsoft Agent Character Editor. The Microsoft Agent animation services render transparent any pixels in this color, so use the color in your images only where you want transparency.

Carefully consider the shape of your character, because it can affect animation performance. To display the character, the animation services create a region window based on the overall image. Small irregular areas often require more region data and may reduce the animation performance of your character. Therefore, when possible, avoid gaps or single-pixel elements and details.

Avoid anti-aliasing the outside edge of your character. Although anti-aliasing is a good technique to reduce jagged edges, it is based on adjacent colors. Because your character may appear on top of a variety of colors, anti-aliasing the outside edge may make your character appear poorly against other backgrounds. However, you can use anti-aliasing on the inside details of your character without encountering this problem.

Frame Size

Frame size should typically be no larger than 128 x 128 pixels. Although characters can be larger or smaller in either dimension, the Microsoft Agent Character Editor uses this as its display size, and scales character images if you define a larger frame size. The 128 x 128 frame size makes reasonable tradeoffs with the space the character will occupy on the screen. Your application can scale a character at run time.

Frame Duration

You can use the Microsoft Agent Character Editor to set how long each frame of animation will display before moving to the next frame. Set the duration of each frame to at least 10 hundredths of a second (10 frames per second)—anything less might not be perceptible on some systems. You can also set the duration longer, but avoid unnatural pauses in the action.

The Microsoft Agent Character Editor also supports branching from one frame in an animation to another, based on probability percentages that you supply. For any given frame, you can define up to three different branches. Branching enables you to create animations that vary when they are played and animations that loop. However, be careful when using branching as it may create problems when trying to play one animation after another. For example, if you play a looping or branching animation, it could continue indefinitely unless you use a Stop method. If you are uncertain, avoid branching.

Frames that don't have images and are set to zero duration do not appear when included in an animation. You can use this feature to create frames that support branching without being visible. However, a frame that does not have images yet has a duration greater than zero will be displayed. Therefore, avoid including empty frames in your animation, because the user may not be able to distinguish an empty frame from when the character is hidden.

Frame Transition

When designing an animation, consider how to smoothly transition from and to the animation. For example, if you create an animation in which the character gestures right, and another in which the character gestures left, you want the character to animate smoothly from one position to the other. Although you could build this into either animation, a better solution is to define a neutral or transitional position from which the character starts and returns. Animating to the neutral position can be incorporated as part of each animation or as a separate animation. In the Microsoft Agent Character Editor, you can specify a complementary Return animation for each animation for your character. The Return animation should typically be no more than 2-4 frames so the character can quickly transition to the neutral position.

For example, using the "gesturing right, then gesturing left" scenario, you can create a GestureRight animation, starting with a frame where the character appears in a neutral position, and add frames with images that extend the character's hand to the right. Then create its Return animation: a complementary animation with images that return the character to its neutral position. You can assign this as the Return animation for the GestureRight animation. Next, create the GestureLeft animation that starts from the neutral position and extends the character's arm to the left. Finally, create a complementary Return animation for this animation as well. A Return animation typically begins with an image that follows the last image of the preceding animation.

Starting and returning to the same neutral position, either within an animation or by using a Return animation, enables you to play any animation in any order. The Microsoft Agent animation services automatically play your designated Return animation in many situations. For example, the services play the designated Return animation before playing your character's Idling state animations. It is a good idea to define and assign Return animations if your animations do not already end in the neutral position.

If you want to provide your own transitions between specific animations; for example, because you always play them in a well-defined order, you can avoid defining Return animations. However, it is still a good idea to begin and end the sequence of animations from the neutral position.

Speaking Animation

Supply mouth images for each animation during which you want the character to be able to speak, unless your character's design has no animated mouth or indication of spoken output. In general, mouth movement is very important. A character may appear less intelligent, likable, or honest if its mouth movement is not reasonably synced with its speech. Mouth images allow your character to lip-sync to spoken output. You define mouth images separately and as Windows bitmap files. They must match the same color palette as the other images in your animation.

The Microsoft Agent animation services display mouth animation frames on top of the last frame of an animation, also called the *speaking frame* of the animation. For example, when the character speaks in the GestureRight animation, the animation services overlay the mouth animation frames on the last frame of GestureRight. A character cannot speak while animating, so you only supply mouth images for only the last frame of an animation. In addition, the speaking frame must be the end frame of an animation, so a character cannot speak in a looping animation.

Typically, you would supply the mouth images in the same size as the frame (and base image), but include only the area that animates as part of the mouth movement, and render the rest of the image in the transparent color. Design the image so that it matches the image in the speaking frame when overlaid on top of it. To have it match correctly, it is likely you'll need to create a separate set of mouth images for every animation in which the character speaks.

A mouth image can include more than the mouth itself, such as the chin or other parts of the character's body while it speaks. However, if you move a hand or leg, note that it may appear to move randomly because the mouth overlay displayed will be based on the current phoneme of a spoken phrase. In addition, the server clips the mouth image to the speaking frame image's outline. Design your mouth overlay image to remain within the outline of its base speaking frame image, because the server uses the base image to create the window boundary for the character.

The Microsoft Agent Character Editor enables you to define seven basic mouth positions that correspond to common phoneme mouth shapes shown in the following table.

Mouth Animation Images

Mouth Position	Sample Image	Representation
Closed		Normal mouth closed shape.
		Also used for phonemes such as "m" as in "mom," "b" as in "bob," "f" as in "fife."
Open-wide 1		Mouth is slightly open, at full width.
		Used for phonemes such as "g" as in "gag," "l" as in "lull," "ear" as in "hear."
Open-wide 2		Mouth is partially open, at full width.
		Used for phonemes such as "n" as in "nun," "d" as in "dad," "t" as in "tot."
Open-wide 3		Mouth is open, at full width.
		Used for phonemes such as "u" as in "hut," "ea" as in "head," "ur" as in "hurt."
Open-wide 4		Mouth is completely open, at full width.
		Used for phonemes such as "a" as in "hat," "ow" as in "how."
Open-medium		Mouth is open at half width.
		Used for phonemes such as "oy" as in "ahoy," "o" as in "hot."
Open-narrow		Mouth is open at narrow width.
		Used for phonemes such as "o" as in "hoop," "o" as in "hope," "w" as in "wet."

Agent States

The Microsoft Agent animation services automatically play certain animations for you. For example, when you use **MoveTo** or **GestureAt** commands, the animation services play an appropriate animation. Similarly, after the idle time out, the services automatically play animations. To support these states, you can define appropriate animations and then assign them to the states. You can still play any animation you define directly using the **Play** method, even if you assign it to a state.

You can assign multiple animations to the same state, and the animation services will randomly choose one of your animations. This enables your character to exhibit a far more natural variety in its behavior.

Although animations that you assign to states can include branching frames, avoid looping animations (animations that branch forever). Otherwise, you will have to use the **Stop** method before you can play another animation.

It's important to define and assign at least one animation for each state that occurs for the character. If you do not supply these animations and state assignments, your character may not appear to behave appropriately to the user. However, if a state does not occur for a particular character, you need not assign an animation to that state. For example, if your host application never calls the **MoveTo** method, you can skip creating and assigning **Moving** state animations.

State	Example of Use
GesturingDown	When the GestureAt animation method is processed.
GesturingLeft	When the GestureAt animation method is processed.
GesturingRight	When the GestureAt animation method is processed.
GesturingUp	When the GestureAt animation method is processed.
Hearing	When the beginning of spoken input is detected.
Hiding	When the user or the application hides the character.
IdlingLevel1	When the character begins the Idling state.
IdlingLevel2	When the character begins the second Idling level state.
IdlingLevel3	When the character begins the final Idling level state.
Listening	When the character starts listening (the user first presses the speech input hot key).
MovingDown	When the MoveTo animation method is processed.
MovingLeft	When the MoveTo animation method is processed.
MovingRight	When the MoveTo animation method is processed.
MovingUp	When the MoveTo animation method is processed.
Showing	When the user or the application shows the character.
Speaking	When the Speak animation method is processed.

The Hearing and Listening States

The animation you assign to the Listening state plays when the user presses the push-to-talk hot key for speech input. Create and assign a short animation that makes the character look attentive. Similarly, define its Return animation to have a short duration so that the character plays its Hearing state animation when the user speaks. A Hearing state animation should also be brief, and designed to let the user know that the character is actively listening to what the user says. Head tilts or other slight gestures are appropriate. To provide natural variability, provide several Hearing state animations.

The Gesturing States

You need to create and assign Gesturing state animations only if you plan to use the GestureAt method. Gesturing state animations play when Microsoft Agent processes a call to the GestureAt method. If you define mouth overlays for your Gesturing state animations, the character can speak as it gestures.

The animation services determine the character's location and its relation to the location of the coordinates specified in the method, and play an appropriate animation. Gesturing direction is always with respect to the character; for example, GestureRight should be a gesture to the character/s right.

The Showing and Hiding States

The Showing and Hiding states play the assigned animations when the user or the host application requests to show or hide the character. These states also appropriately set the character frame's Visible state. When defining animations for these states, keep in mind that a character can appear or depart at any screen location. Because the user can show or hide any character, always support at least one animation for these states.

Animations that you assign to the Showing state typically end with a frame containing the character's neutral position image. Conversely, Hiding state animations typically begin with the neutral position. Showing and Hiding state animations can include an empty frame at the beginning or end, respectively, to provide a transition from the character's current state.

The Idling States

The Idling states are progressive. The animation services begin using the Level 1 assignments for the first idle period, and use the Level 2 animations for the second. After this, the idle cycle progresses to the Level 3 assigned animations and remains in this state until canceled, such as when a new animation request begins.

Design animations for the Idling states to communicate the state of the character, but not to distract the user. The animations should appropriately reflect the responsiveness of the character in subtle but clear ways. For example, glancing around or blinking are good animations to assign to the IdlingLevel1 state. Reading animations work well for the IdlingLevel2 state. Sleeping or listening to music with headphones are good examples of animations to assign to the IdlingLevel3 state. Animations that include many or large movements are not well suited for idle animations because they draw the user's attention. Because Idling state animations are played frequently, provide several Idling state animations, especially for the IdlingLevel1 and IdlingLevel2 states.

Note that an application can turn off the automatic idle processing for a character and manage the character's Idling state itself. The Agent Idling states are designed to help you avoid any situation where the character has no animation to play. A character image that does not change after a brief period of time is like an application displaying a wait pointer for a long time, which detracts from the sense of believability and interactivity. Maintaining the illusion does not take much: sometimes just an animated blink, visible breath, or body shift.

The Speaking State

The animation services use the Speaking state when a speaking animation cannot be found for the current animation. Assign a simple speaking animation to this state. For example, you can use a single frame consisting of the character's neutral position with mouth overlays.

The Moving States

The Moving states play when an application calls the MoveTo method. The animation services determine which animation to play based on the character's current location and the specified coordinates. Movement direction is based on the character's position. Therefore, the animation you assign to the MovingLeft animation should be based on the character's left. If you don't use the MoveTo method, you can skip creating and assigning an animation.

Moving state animations should animate the character into its moving position. The last frame of this animation is displayed as the character's frame is moved on the screen. There is no support for animating the character while its frame moves.

Standard Animation Set

While you can design a custom character to have the animations you want to use, Microsoft Agent defines a standard animation set. Characters that conform to this definition can be selected as a default character.

The following table lists the animations included in the standard animation set. Even if you are creating a custom character, you may want to use the list as a guide for designing your own characters. Characters that support the standard animation set must support at least the following animations.

Animation	Example of Use	Example Animation
Acknowledge	When the character acknowledges the user's request.	Character nods or flashes "OK" hand gesture. Note that this animation should return the character to its neutral position.
Alert [1,2]	When the character is waiting for instructions, typically played after the user turns on listening mode.	Character faces front, breathing, blinking occasionally, but clearly awaiting instruction.
Announce [1,2]	When the character has found information for the user.	Character gestures by raising eyebrows and hand or opens an envelope.
Blink	When the character finishes speaking or idle.	Character naturally blinks eyes.
Confused [1,2]	When the character doesn't understand what to do.	Character scratches head.
Congratulate [1,2]	When the character or user completes a task (a stronger form of the Acknowledge animation.)	Character performs congratulatory gesture, conveys "Yes!"
Decline [1,2]	When the character cannot do or declines the user's request.	Character shakes head, conveys "no can do."
DoMagic1 [1]	Character prepares to display something.	Character waves hands or wand.
DoMagic2 [2]	Character completes display of something.	Character completes magic gesture.
DontRecognize [1,2]	When the character didn't recognize the user's request.	Character holds hand to ear.
Explain [1,2]	When the character explains something to the user.	Character gestures as if explaining something.
GestureDown [1,2]	When the character needs to point to something below it.	Character points down.
GestureLeft [1,2]	When the character needs to point to something at its left.	Character points with left hand or morphs into an arrow pointing left.
GestureRight [1,2]	When the character needs to point to something at its right.	Character points with right hand or morphs into an arrow pointing right.
GestureUp [1,2]	When the character needs to point to something above it.	Character points up.
GetAttention [1]	When the character needs to notify the user about something important.	Character waves hands or jumps up and down.
GetAttentionContinued [1]	To emphasize the importance of the notification.	A continuation or repeat of the initial gesture.

[1] Animation requires mouth overlays and a defined speaking frame.

[2] Animation requires an assigned Return animation either based on its exit branching or an explicit Return animation.

Animation	Example of Use	Example Animation
GetAttentionReturn	When the character completes the GetAttention or GetAttentionContinued animation.	Character returns to its neutral position.
Greet [1,2]	When the user starts up the system.	Character smiles and waves.
Hearing1	When the character hears the start of a spoken utterance (actively listening).	Character leans forward and nods, or turns head showing response to speech input. Note: This animation loops to some intermediate frame that occurs after the character moves to an appropriate position.
Hearing2	When the character hears the start of a spoken utterance (actively listening).	Another variation of the type of animation used in Hearing1. Note: This animation loops to some intermediate frame that occurs after the character moves to an appropriate position.
Hide	When the user dismisses the character.	Character removes self from screen.
Idle1_1	When the character has no task and the user is not interacting with the character.	Character blinks or looks around, remaining in or returning to the neutral position.
Idle1_2	When the character has no task and the user is not interacting with the character.	Another variation of the type of animation used in Idle1_1.
Idle2_1	When the character has been idle for some time.	Character yawns or reads magazine remaining in or returning to the neutral position.
Idle2_2	When the character has been idle for some time.	Another variation of the type of animation used in Idle2_1.
Idle3_1	When the character has been idle for a long time.	Character yawns.
Idle3_2	When the character has been idle for a long time.	Character sleeps or puts on headphones to listen to music. Note: This animation loops to some intermediate frame that occurs after the character moves to an appropriate position.
LookDown	When the character needs to look down.	Character looks down.
LookLeft	When the character needs to look left.	Character looks to the left.
LookRight	When the character needs to look right.	Character looks to the right.

[1] Animation requires mouth overlays and a defined speaking frame.

[2] Animation requires an assigned Return animation either based on its exit branching or an explicit Return animation.

Animation	Example of Use	Example Animation
LookUp	When the character needs to look up.	Character looks up.
MoveDown	When the character prepares to move down.	Character transitions to a walking/flying down position.
MoveLeft	When the character prepares to move left.	Character transitions to a walking/flying left position.
MoveRight	When the character prepares to move right.	Character transitions to a walking/flying right position.
MoveUp	When the character prepares to move up.	Character transitions to a walking/flying up position.
Pleased [1,2]	When the character is pleased with the user's request or choice.	Character smiles.
Process	When the character performs some type of generic task.	Character presses buttons or uses some type of tool.
Processing	When the character is busy working on a generic task.	Character scribbles on pad of paper or uses some type of tool. Note: This animation loops to some intermediate frame that occurs after the character moves to an appropriate position.
Read [1]	When the character reads something to the user.	Character displays book or paper, reads, and looks back at user.
ReadContinued [1]	When the character reads further to the user.	Character reads again, then looks back at user.
ReadReturn	When the character completes the Read or ReadContinued animation.	Character returns to its neutral position.
Reading	When the character reads something but cannot accept input.	Character reads from a piece of paper. Note: This animation loops to some intermediate frame(s) that occurs after the character moves to an appropriate position.
RestPose [1]	When the character speaks from its neutral position	Character stands with relaxed but attentive posture.
Sad [1,2]	When the character is disappointed with the user's choice.	Character frowns or looks disappointed.
Search	When character is searches for something.	Character shuffles through file drawer or other container looking for something.

[1] Animation requires mouth overlays and a defined speaking frame.

[2] Animation requires an assigned Return animation either based on its exit branching or an explicit Return animation.

Animation	Example of Use	Example Animation
Searching	When character is searching for user-specified information.	Character shuffles through file drawer or other container looking for something. Note: This animation loops to some intermediate frame(s) that occurs after the character moves to an appropriate position.
Show	When the character starts up or returns after being summoned.	Character pops up in a puff of smoke, beams in, or walks on-screen.
StartListening [1,2]	When the character is listening.	Character puts hand to ear.
StopListening [1,2]	When the character stops listening.	Character puts hands over ears.
Suggest [1,2]	When the character has a tip or suggestion for the user.	Light bulb appears next to character.
Surprised [1,2]	When the character is surprised by the user's action or choice.	Character widens eyes, opens mouth.
Think [1,2]	When the character is thinking about something.	Character looks up and holds hand on head.
Uncertain [1,2]	When the character needs the user to confirm a request.	Character looks quizzical, conveys ("Are you sure?")
Wave [1,2]	When the user chooses to shut down the server or system.	Character waves good-bye or hello.
Write [1]	When the character is listening for instructions from the user.	Character displays paper, writes, and looks back at user.
WriteContinued [1]	When the character continues listening for instructions from the user.	Character writes on a piece of paper and looks back at user.
WriteReturn	When the character completes the Write or WriteContinued animation.	Character returns to its neutral position.
Writing	When the character writes out information for the user.	Character writes on piece of paper. Note: This animation loops.

[1] Animation requires mouth overlays and a defined speaking frame.

[2] Animation requires an assigned Return animation either based on its exit branching or an explicit Return animation.

In addition, a character must have the following state assignments.

State	Required Animations
GesturingDown	GestureDown
GesturingLeft	GestureLeft
GesturingRight	GestureRight
GesturingUp	GestureUp

State	Required Animations
Hearing	Hearing1, Hearing2
Hiding	Hide
IdlingLevel1	Blink, Idle1_1, Idle1_2
IdlingLevel2	Blink, Idle1_1, Idle1_2, Idle2_1, Idle2_2
IdlingLevel3	Idle3_1, Idle3_2
Listening	Alert
MovingDown	MoveDown
MovingLeft	MoveLeft
MovingRight	MoveRight
MovingUp	MoveUp
Showing	Show
Speaking	RestPose

Animation Principles

Effective animation design requires more than simply rendering a character. Successful animators follow a variety of principles and techniques to create "believable" characters.

Squash and Stretch

There should be a degree of distortion as an animated object moves. The amount of deformation that occurs reflects the rigidity of that object. Flattening or elongating a part of a character's body as it moves helps you convey the nature and composition of the character.

Anticipation

Anticipation sets the stage for an upcoming action. Without anticipatory actions, body movements look abrupt, rigid, and unnatural. This principle is based on how a body moves in the real world. Movement in one direction often begins with movement in the opposite direction. Legs contract before a jump. To exhale, you first inhale. Anticipatory action also has an important role in communicating the nature of both the character and the action and helps your audience prepare for the action. A key aspect of creating a believable character involves demonstrating that the character's actions stem from a purposeful intent. Anticipation helps communicate the character's motivation to the audience.

Timing

Timing defines the nature of an action. The speed that a head moves from left to right conveys whether a character is casually looking around or giving a negative response. Timing also helps convey the weight and size of an object. Larger objects tend to take longer to accelerate and decelerate than smaller ones. In addition, the pacing of a character's movements affects how it draws attention. In a normal scenario, rapid motion draws the eye, while in a frenetic environment, stationary or slow movements may have the same effect.

Staging

The background and props a character uses can also convey its mood or purpose. Staging also includes what the character wears, lighting effects, viewing angle, and the presence of other characters. These elements all contribute to reinforcing a character's personality, objectives, and actions. Effective staging involves understanding how to direct the eye to where you want to communicate.

Follow-Through and Overlapping Action

Just as a golfer's follow-through communicates the result of the swing, the transition from one action to the next is important in communicating the relationship between the actions. Actions rarely come to a sudden and complete stop. So, too, follow-through and overlapping actions allow you to establish the flow of the character's motion. You can typically implement this by varying the speed at which different parts of a body move, allowing movement beyond the primary aspect of the motion. For example, the fingers of a hand typically follow the movement of the wrist in a hand gesture. This principle also emphasizes that actions should not come to a complete stop, but smoothly blend into other actions.

Slow In-and-Out

Slow in-and-out refers to moving a character smoothly from one pose to another. The character begins and ends actions slowly. You accomplish this by the number, timing, and location of "in-between" frames. The more in-between frames you include, the slower and smoother the transition.

Arcs

Living objects in nature rarely move in a perfectly straight line. As a result, arcs or curved paths for movement provide more natural effects. Arcs also convey speed of motion. The slower the motion, the higher the arc, and the faster the motion, the flatter the arc.

Exaggeration

Good animators often exaggerate the shape, color, emotion, or actions of a character. Making aspects of the motion "larger than life" more clearly communicates the idea of the action to the audience. For example, a character's arms may stretch to the point that they appear elastic. However, exaggeration must be balanced. If used in some situations and not others, the exaggerated action may appear unrealistic and may be interpreted by the user as having a particular meaning. Similarly, if you exaggerate one aspect of an image, consider what other aspects should be exaggerated to match.

Secondary Action

Animation requires more than the mechanistic creation of in-between images from one pose to the next. A primary action is typically supported by secondary actions. Secondary actions can enhance the presentation, but should not detract from or dominate the main action. Facial expressions can often be used as secondary actions to body movement. Richness comes from adding elements that support the main idea.

Solid Drawing

Creating an animated character involves more than creating a series of images. Effective animation design considers how the character looks in different positions and from different angles. Even characters rendered as two-dimensional images become more realistic and believable if considered conceptually in three dimensions. Avoid twins: mirroring the position the face, arms, and legs on both sides of the body. This results in a wooden, unnatural presentation. Body movement is rarely symmetrical, but involves overall balancing of posture or reactions.

Appeal

Successful implementation depends on how well you understand your audience. Your character's overall image and personality should appeal to your target audience; appeal does not require photo-realism. A character's personality can be conveyed—no matter how simple its shape—by using gestures, posture, and other mannerisms. A common assignment of beginning animators is to create a variety of expressions for a flour sack or small rug. Characters with simple shapes are often more effective than complex ones. Consider, for example, that many popular characters have only three fingers and a thumb.

C H A P T E R   8

Designing Characters for Microsoft Office

This chapter provides information that can help you design and develop a Microsoft Agent character for use within Microsoft Office 2000 (Microsoft Agent characters do not work with Microsoft Office 97). This chapter assumes that you have a working knowledge of the Microsoft Agent Character Editor and know how to create Microsoft Agent Characters. More information on the Agent Character Editor and designing and developing characters is provided in Chapter 9, "Using the Microsoft Agent Character Editor." More information about creating characters for Microsoft Agent is provided in Chapter 7, "Designing Characters for Microsoft Agent.

Animation Design

Image Design

Use the Microsoft Office Palette when designing your characters to minimize any potential palette realization issues. Avoid selecting a transparency color that is similar to the colors that you use in your document.

To download the Office Palette file, see workshop/imedia/agent/images/assistpalet.bmp on the book's CD (13K).

Sounds

Microsoft Agent enables you to play sounds in your animations. We recommend you do not include sounds for your **Idle** animations. This is so there won't be a delay in the middle of the animation, if Agent has to load the system multimedia DLL.

Frame Size

Typical Office Assistants are 123 x 93 pixels. While you can create characters of other sizes, they will be scaled to 123 x 93 in the Assistant Gallery.

Frame Transition

All animations except for **Goodbye**, **Greeting**, **Show**, and **Hide** should begin and end with the RestPose animation. Microsoft Office does not play explicit **Return** animations, so you should not define them. All animations should also have Exit Branching. Exit branching enables us to "hurry up and finish" the current animation before we call the next animation. If you don't supply Exit Branching, the transition between animations may be jerky.

Character Properties

Microsoft Agent enables you to set the character's **Name, Description,** and **ExtraData** properties. Microsoft Office uses the **ExtraData** field to hold to one or more Introduction Phrases and Reminder Phrases. Microsoft Office picks from the other Introduction Phrases to put in the speech balloon in the Assistant Gallery. We use the Reminder Phrases when you receive a reminder from Outlook.

The **ExtraData** field is formatted as follows:

```
IntroPhrase1~~IntroPhrase2~~IntroPhrase3^^ReminderPhrase1~~ReminderPhrase2~~ReminderPhrase3
```

Intro Phrases are separated by a pair of tilde characters (~), followed by Reminder Phrases. These Reminder Phrases are also separated by a pair of tilde characters. The two sets of phrases are separated by two caret characters (^^). There is no limit to the number of each kind of phrase, except that there must be at least one of each.

The Office Animation Set

The following table lists the animations defined for the Microsoft Office 2000 characters. If you intend to use your character in Microsoft Office, you should support all of the animations in this table. In addition, you can add any other animations you like, but keep in mind that Microsoft Office won't call them. Animations with asterisks (*) should be 100% looping. Other animations should be brief.

Animation	Agent State	Example of When Used	Specific animation examples
Alert	None	When the character wants to alert the user	Character looks towards user
CheckingSomething*	None	Spellcheck, grammar check	Character looks something up in a reference book
Congratulate	None	Complete a wizard	Big grin, look of relief, tired but happy
EmptyTrash	None	Trash is emptied in Outlook	Character lights trash can on fire
Explain	None	When the character wants to explain something to the user	Looks briefly but attentively at user, then looks away

Animation	Agent State	Example of When Used	Specific animation examples
GestureDown	GesturingDown	Character points out something on the screen	Character looks at user and then points and looks at the screen
GestureLeft	GesturingLeft	Character points out something on the screen, such as a help topic or a piece of UI	Character looks at user and then points and looks at the screen
GestureRight	GesturingRight	"Presenting" a help topic or dialog	Character looks at user and then points and looks at the screen
GestureUp	GesturingUp	Character points out something on the screen	Character looks at user and then points and looks at the screen
GetArtsy*	None	AutoFormat	Character puts on beret, holds palette, and paints
GetAttention	None	High-priority tip	Gestures strongly to get the user's attention; for example, jumps up and down waving arms
GetTechy	None	Runs while in programming environment	Character pulls out calculator or soldering iron
GetWizardy*	None	Chart Wizard running while Character visible (action re-triggered with each new wizard panel)	Character puts on wizard hat and waves wand
Goodbye	None	Another Character is chosen	This is an elaborate disappear that begins in RestPose and ends with blank frame
Greeting	None	Character is chosen	This is an elaborate appear that begins with a blank frame, and ends in RestPose
Hearing_1*	None	Lengthy file open	Ear to the ground, listening to the computer
Hide	Hiding	Character leaves temporarily	Leaves quickly in a puff of smoke
Idle1_1	No user input	Actively listening, then curls up and goes to sleep (opportunity to show off character personality)	Blinking, looking around, waiting patiently
Idle2	No user input	Longer idle periods	Character yawns and looks sleepy
Idle3	No user input	Deep idle (when the character has been idle for a long time)	Character goes to sleep

Animation	Agent State	Example of When Used	Specific animation examples
IdleHit	None	This is a non-mapped representative sample of Idle Level 1 animations	All of the idle animations
LookDown	None	Looks down briefly	Notices a row is inserted and glances at it
LookDownLeft	None	Looks down and left briefly	Notices a row is inserted and glances at it
LookDownRight	None	Looks down and right briefly	Notices a column is inserted and glances at it
LookLeft	None	Looks left briefly	Notices a table is inserted and glances at it
LookRight	None	Looks right briefly	Notices a word is moved and glances at it
LookUp	None	Looks up briefly, as if at something going on above character on the screen	Notices toolbar button gets clicked and glances at it (Character isn't surprised as much as interested)
LookUpLeft	None	Looks left and up briefly	Notices toolbar button gets clicked and glances at it (Character isn't surprised as much as interested)
LookUpRight	None	Looks right and up briefly	Notices toolbar button gets clicked and glances at it (Character isn't surprised as much as interested)
Print	None	Printing a page of a print job	Grabs one piece of paper and sends it down to the printer
Processing*	None	General action for which we don't have specific character action	Character gets look of concentration and pulls out a hammer to hammer. Animation should have a quick entry into a loop, then a quick exit
RestPose	None	Used when the character isn't playing an animation	An image of the assistant
Save*	None	Used during a File Save operation	Character puts something into a vault
Searching*	None	Used for Find, spell check, and grammar check	Head turns and looks back at document. Animation should have a quick entry into a loop, then a quick exit
SendMail	None	Sending mail	Pulls out a letter and puts it into a mailbox

Animation	Agent State	Example of When Used	Specific animation examples
Show	Showing	Character returns from brief leave	Springs quickly on stage
Thinking*	None	Doing a complex calculation, scratches head.	Character looks upward and Animation should have a quick entry into a loop, then a quick exit
Wave	None	Accompanying alerts	Wave. Similar to Alert, but not as long or as frantic
Writing*	None	Customer changes something in Tools Options; customer typing IntelliSearch request	Pulls out pad and starts scribbling. Animation should have a quick entry into a loop, then a quick exit.

Installing Your Character

For your character to show in the Assistant Gallery, install it in the Microsoft\Office\Actors folder inside of the user's Application Data folder. The Application Data folder can be found in the Windows directory or in the User Profiles directory inside of the Windows directory. For example on Windows NT 5.0, you might install your character in C:\WinNT\Profiles\YourName\Application Data \Microsoft\Office\Actors.

CHAPTER 9

Using the Microsoft Agent Character Editor

The Microsoft Agent Character Editor enables you to compile character animations for use with Microsoft Agent. You can define animations by importing Windows bitmap images, setting their duration, and optionally including branching, sound effects, and speaking overlays. For information about designing a character's animation, see Chapter 7, "Designing Characters for Microsoft Agent."

With the Agent Character Editor you can define the character's name and description as well as output options, including text-to-speech (TTS), synthesized voice output, pop-up menu support, and the character's word balloon design.

Installing the Agent Character Editor

To install the Microsoft Agent Character Editor, open its self-extracting cabinet file. This will automatically install the appropriate files on your system. If you are downloading the Agent Character Editor from the Microsoft Web site, the downloading software gives you the option to save the file and open it or open it automatically as soon as the download completes.

If you plan to use a TTS engine for your character's output you need to install that engine before you begin creating your character. You may want to confirm the engine's vendor support for Microsoft Agent and for information on licensing provisions for use and distribution.

Starting the Agent Character Editor

To run the Agent Character Editor, choose the Agent Character Editor option from the Windows Taskbar's Start menu, or double-click the Microsoft Agent Character Editor icon on your desktop. The Editor's window will open, displaying its menus, a toolbar with frequently used commands, a tree listing the components that make up a character's definition, and a set of tabbed pages that change based on your selection in the component tree.

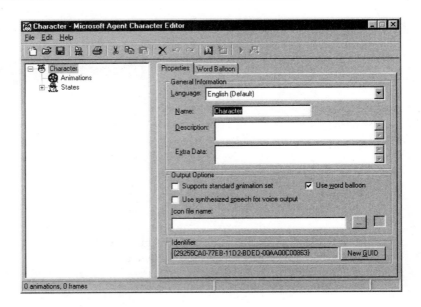

FIGURE 9-1. Microsoft Agent Character Editor window

To access fields in the window from the keyboard, you can use the TAB key and SHIFT+TAB to navigate between controls, or use the access key (ALT+*under-lined letter*) to move to a specific control. Once the Editor completes starting up, you can begin creating a new character definition or load an existing character definition.

The status bar displays information about commands or toolbar buttons when you move the pointer over them. It also displays summary information about your character animation data and status information when you build a character.

Defining a New Character

To define a new character, run the Agent Character Editor. If you have an existing character file loaded, choose the New command from the File menu. This displays a submenu of choices. If you are creating a character for your own use, choose Custom Character. If you want to create a character that can be used as an Agent default character, choose Default Character. This will pre-configure the editor with all the required animation names and animation state assignments as well as set the Supports Standard Animation Set option. Similarly, if you choose Office Assistant Character, the editor is pre-configured with the animation names and animation state assignment required for an Office Assistant character. This action selects the Character icon in the tree and displays its property pages on the right side of the window. The following sections describe how to set your character's properties and how to create animations for the character.

Setting Your Character's General Information

To begin defining a character, enter the character's name in the Name text box (32 characters maximum). Because Microsoft Agent uses the name to allow users to access the character, specify a user-friendly name. Supply a name that can be pronounced using conventional spelling, or you may disable speech input for the character. You can also specify a short optional description (256 characters) for your character in the Description text box. The server exposes what you enter in the Description text box to client applications.

You can also store your own data as part of your character using the ExtraData field. You can use this capability to include special information about your character or other data. Once compiled with the Character Editor, this information can be accessed using the ExtraData property at run time when the character is loaded.

You can set the character's name, description, and extra data information based on the character's language ID setting. To set this data for another language, select Language and enter the text. You also must have the language code pages installed on the system on which you build the character file. If you don't, the appropriate language settings will not be included in the compiled character file. You do not have to provide information in other languages. If these properties are queried at runtime using the Agent API and there are no specific settings for that language, the English (Default) settings are returned.

Setting Your Character's Output Options

If you set the Supports Standard Animation Set option, the Character Editor will check to make certain that you have included all the required animations and animation state assignments for a default character when you attempt to build the character. If something is missing, a message box will list the missing elements. For details on the standard animation set, see Chapter 7, "Designing Characters for Microsoft Agent."

For your character's spoken output, Microsoft Agent provides the choice of a synthesized, text-to-speech (TTS) voice or a voice that uses recorded sound files. If you want to use a synthesized voice, check the Use Synthesized Speech For Voice Output option. This will add a Voice page for selecting the characteristics of the voice. Choose the Voice page and use the controls on this page to select a voice, speed, and pitch of any compatible TTS engines you have installed. The range of the voice parameters you can select depends on TTS engines. If you have not yet installed a TTS engine, the Voice ID list will be empty. You must have a TTS engine installed before you define your character's voice settings in the Agent Character Editor.

If you plan to use a TTS engine for your character's output you must also install that engine on the user's system. If you select a voice based on a particular TTS engine, but the user has a different TTS engine installed, the server attempts to match the voice based on the characteristics you defined in the Agent Character Editor.

If you plan to use recorded sound files (.WAV files) for your character's spoken output, you do not need to check the Use Synthesized Speech For Voice Output option. Instead, you will need to record the spoken output audio files separately and load them from your application code.

The Use Word Balloon option enables you to determine whether you want to support a word balloon for your character. This feature can also be set at run time.

When the Use Word Balloon option is checked, you can access the Word Balloon page. The options on the Word Balloon page enable you to change the default characteristics of your word balloon. The Characters Per Line setting enables you to define the width of the balloon based on the average number of characters per line. You can set the default height based on either a fixed number of lines you want to display at once or automatically sized to the text you supply in the **Speak** method. You can also set whether the balloon automatically hides after a **Speak** method is completed and whether the balloon automatically displays or "paces" words to the character's speech output speed setting.

The Word Balloon page also enables you to set the default font for the character's word balloon and the balloon's display colors. However, be aware that users can override your word balloon font settings using the Microsoft Agent property sheet.

Setting Your Character's Identifier

Each character requires a unique identifier (GUID). The server uses the identifier to differentiate characters. When you create a new character, the Editor automatically creates a new identifier for your character. You need to change a character's identifier only if you copied the character definition file of another character or if you intentionally want to differentiate a character from a former version. To change a character's identifier, click the New GUID button and the Editor will generate a new identifier.

Creating Animations

To begin creating animations for your character, select the Animations icon in the tree. This displays the Properties page with the default settings for all animations. You can alter the frame size, the default frame duration, and color palette settings on the Properties page.

Setting Your Character's Frame Size

The animation frame height and width must remain constant throughout the entire character definition (that is, for all of that character's animations). Although you can change the frame size from its default setting (128 x 128 pixels), images displayed in the Editor will be scaled to fit default display size. If you change the default frame setting, you can display the frame's full, non-scaled size by choosing Open Frame Window from the Edit menu.

Setting Your Character's Palette

By default, the Editor uses the first bitmap image you load to set your character's default color palette, the colors that determine how the character appears, and sets the color in the 11th palette position as your transparency color. However, you can set the palette and transparency explicitly in the Palette Information group. This enables you to specify an image file to use for the palette. You can specify one of the animation image files or any graphic file. The palette file you specify must be an 8-bit (256) color file. Once loaded, you use the Change Setting button to change the transparency color.

Your character's color palette must not remap the standard system colors. The Editor will automatically reserve the system's color palette when displaying images. In addition, all your animation images must use the same color palette and transparency color. This is very important. If they do not, you may see color remapping of your images when you load them into the Editor.

While you can set the color palette for the character, on Windows systems where the Display properties are set to an 8-bit (256) color palette, the character's color will be subject to the current system palette. Because applications may change the system palette, the character may not appear with the correct color settings. Although there is no way to prevent this, you can lessen the effect by limiting the numbers of colors you use and setting the character's palette based on the palette used by the application driving the character. For example, if you are developing a character to be used with Web pages, you may want set the character's palette using the Microsoft Internet Explorer's halftone palette. You can capture the browser's palette by right-clicking on an image on a Web page and choosing the Save Picture As command and choosing Bitmap in the Save As Type option, then clicking Save. To optimize your animation image files to a specific palette file, you might want to use a product like Equilibrium DeBabelizer.

Creating a New Animation

Once you have determined your global animation settings, you can begin creating animations. To create a new animation, choose New Animation from the Edit menu or the New Animation button on the toolbar. This adds a new animation icon in the tree under the Animations icon and assigns the new icon a default name. You can rename your animation by typing in the Animation Name field. Note that animation names within a character definition must be unique. Also, avoid using characters in the name that are not valid characters for filenames.

Adding Frames

Every animation is composed of frames. To create a new frame for your animation, choose New Frame from either the Edit menu or the toolbar. This adds a new frame icon to the tree under your animation icon, and displays three tabbed pages. The General page includes controls that enable you to load and adjust an image for your frame. It also includes a display area for the frame's appearance.

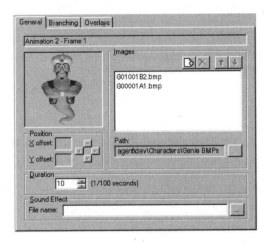

FIGURE 9-2. The Frame Image display and controls

A frame can contain one or more images. To define an image for a frame, click the Add Image File button just above the Images list box. The Select Image Files dialog box displays, which allows you to select a bitmap image file.

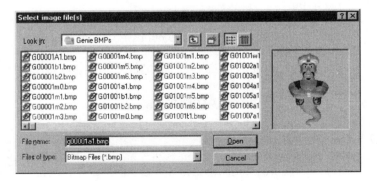

FIGURE 9-3. The Select Image Files dialog box

Select the file you want to load, choose Open, and the image appears in the frame display on the General page. The Editor accepts images stored as 1-bit (monochrome), 4-bit, or 8-bit Windows bitmap format, or as GIF format.

You can use the four arrow buttons beneath the image in the Position box to adjust the image's appearance within the frame. If the image is larger than your frame's size, only the portion of the image that appears within the frame will display. If you increase the frame size, the image may be scaled to fit within the display area of the Editor.

You can also display a frame by choosing Open Frame Window from the Edit menu. This displays the current frame in a separate window without scaling the images loaded into the frame. This window's initial size is based on your frame's height and width settings. You can resize it smaller, but not larger. The Frame Window reflects the changes you make using the controls in the Editor and also allows you to view the frame while viewing its other property pages.

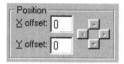

FIGURE 9-4. Image Position controls

You can compose a frame from multiple images. Each time you select the Add Image button and choose another image, the image gets added to the list and to the image display area. You can also add multiple images by selecting more than one file. Press SHIFT or CTRL while you click in the Select Image Files dialog box, and then choose Open. The Move Up and Move Down buttons above the Images list box move a selected image in the display order (z-order) for the frame. You can also move images by dragging them within the list. Selecting an image in the list and clicking the Delete button removes an image. To change an image you have loaded to another image file, you can click the filename to edit it directly or use the Ellipsis (...) button to bring up the Select Image Files dialog box and select a different file.

FIGURE 9-5. The Ellipsis button

You can use the Duration text box to set the duration for the frame; that is, how long the frame will be displayed. If a frame has no image and zero duration, the frame will not be displayed when the animation plays.

You can also specify a sound effect file to play when the frame is displayed. If you plan to load the character from a Web server, you may want to compress the sound effect file to minimize load time. You can then specify the compressed sound file in the Agent Character Editor. In addition, avoid using a sound effect with a duration longer than the duration of your animation and especially avoid a sound effect that loops, because the Microsoft Agent animation services do not send an animation complete event until the sound completes. Also avoid specifying a sound effect for any animation you assign to the **Listening** or **Hearing** states, because this interferes with speech input. Finally, while you can include more than one sound effect in an animation, avoid placing them so they overlap, because this may affect the timing of the animation. Also, keep in mind that sound effects may play at different rates based on the user's hardware.

To add frames to your animation, choose the New Frame command again and follow the same procedure. As an option, you can also load multiple images and automatically generate new frames for them. To use this feature, choose New Frames From Images from the Edit menu. The frames will be created in alphabetic order based on the image filenames. When you are finished defining all frames for your animation, you can choose the New Animation command again to begin a new animation.

There are other ways to add frames to animations and move frames within or between animations. You can select another frame (from the same or another animation) and choose Cut or Copy, then select the animation or a frame in that animation and choose Paste. You can also drag a frame from one animation to another. If you drag within an animation, the action moves the frame. If you drag to another animation, it copies the frame. Dragging to a preceding frame in the same animation inserts the frame before the frame to which you drag. Dragging to a following frame places it after the frame to which you drag. If you drag a frame using the right mouse button, releasing the button displays a pop-up menu with your transfer choices.

You can also create an animation by copying an existing animation (select the animation and choose Copy), and selecting the Animations icon or another animation icon and choosing Paste. The Editor automatically creates a new name for the animation, although you can change the name.

Branching

When you create a frame, you can also define which frame plays next. By default, the next frame played in the animation sequence is always the next frame in the z-order. However, by choosing the Branching page, you can set the probability for up to three other frames that the server may play. Enter the probability percentage and the target frame number in the appropriate fields. You can specify branching even for frames that don't have images and have their duration set to zero. This enables you to branch without first displaying a particular image.

You can use the branching feature to create animations that will loop indefinitely. However, note that when a looping animation plays, other animations in the character's queue will not play until an event—such as a user pressing the push-to-talk

key or the client application calling the **Stop** method—halts the looping animation. Therefore, carefully consider the context in which the animation will be
used before creating a looping animation.

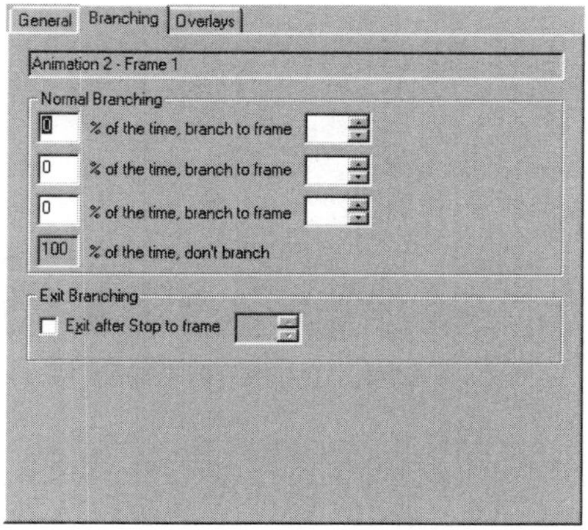

FIGURE 9-6. The Branching page

The branching page also enables you to create Exit Branching. An exit branch is
a branch to a frame that the animation will take when the animation is stopped
and before the next animation is played. Defining exit branches will enable you
to move smoothly during the transition from one animation to another. Your exit
branching must not create a circular loop, but must eventually be able to exit to
the last frame of the animation.

You do not have to provide an exit branch for each frame, however, if you don't,
the animation will follow the frame's normal branching. If the frame has no explicit
branch, then the animation automatically branches to the frame that follows it.
For example, if you branch from frame 3 to frame 1 and frame 1 has no other
branching (normal or exit branch), frame 1 will branch to frame 2. If frame 2 has
no branching, the animation will branch back to frame 3 and you have a circular
loop. Instead, you could branch from frame 3 to frame 1 and then set frame 1's
exit branch to any frame that is after frame 3 and normally proceeds to the last
frame of the animation.

Sometimes you may need to create an explicit final frame of an animation that is
not played visibly, but provides an end of the animation. For example, you need
to exit the animation, but exiting to the last frame would not be appropriate. You
can do this by creating a blank, zero duration frame as the last frame of the animation. This allows the animation to play normally through the last frame of the
animation and also enables you to provide a final exit point for your exit branching.

Previewing an Animation

You can preview your animation in the Agent Character Editor by choosing the Preview command on the Edit menu or the Preview button on the toolbar. This plays your animation, including any branches and sound effects, starting from the current selected frame. It resets to the current selected frame when the animation completes. To play your entire animation, go to the tree view, select the animation's icon or first frame of the animation, and choose the Preview command. The Editor animates your frames on the General page. To stop the preview before it ends, choose the Stop Preview command. The Preview command automatically changes to Stop Preview while the preview plays.

You can also preview your exit branching by choosing the Preview Exit Branching command on the Edit menu or on the toolbar. This enables you to test how the exit branching will appear from any specific frame.

Assigning Speaking Overlays

You can define a character so that it speaks during the last frame of its animation. On this frame, choose the Overlay page. This page enables you to load and assign mouth image files to the standard mouth positions supported by Microsoft Agent. Click the Add Image button and select the image from the dialog box. You can also select multiple images, and the Editor will load and assign the images starting with the mouth position you selected. Click the Move Up and Move Down buttons or drag an entry to change an image assignment in the list. Click the Delete button to remove an image. You can also edit the pathname of an assigned file by clicking its entry in the list and retyping its filename, or by choosing the Ellipsis (...) button to display the Select Image Files dialog box.

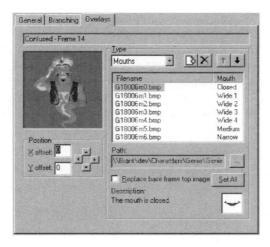

FIGURE 9-7. The Overlay page image controls

Your mouth overlays must fit within the outline of the base frame over which they will appear. If they do not, they will be clipped to the base frame.

If you want to have the character speak with its mouth outside of the base frame—for instance, when the character is to speak facing sideways—first create the base frame with the character's head (or the area that will move as the character speaks) as its top image. Then, define your mouth overlays to replace that image and set the Replace Base Frame Top Image option. You can also use the Set All button to set this option for all your mouth overlays in the frame.

Assigning a Return Animation

To create a smooth transition from one animation to the next, design your animation sequences to begin and end with a neutral image. For more information, see Chapter 7, "Designing Characters for Microsoft Agent." However, this does not mean that every animation must end at the neutral position. You can animate a character through a sequence of frames, have it speak during the last frame, and create a separate, complementary animation that returns the character to the neutral position. This complementary animation is called a Return animation.

You can define a Return animation by creating an explicit animation for this purpose. You can also create a Return animation using the exit branching you define within the animation. To assign a Return animation, select the animation in the tree, and select either the Return animation you created or Use Exit Branching from the Return Animation drop-down list on the Properties page.

Creating and assigning a Return animation has an added benefit: When the server gets a request to play another animation, it will attempt to play the Return animation for the last animation it played, if a Return animation is assigned. This ensures a smooth transition. If an animation begins and ends at the neutral position, you don't need to define a Return animation. Similarly, if you intend to handle transitions from one animation to another yourself, you may not need to assign a Return animation.

Assigning Animations to States

The Microsoft Agent animation services automatically play animations when the hosting client application uses certain methods. For example, when an application calls the **MoveTo** and **GestureAt** methods, the server automatically determines where the character is displayed and plays an appropriate animation. Similarly, Microsoft Agent automatically plays Idle animations when the user has not interacted with the character for several seconds. These conditions, when the server automatically plays animations on an application's behalf, are called *states*. However, for the server to know which animation to play, you must assign animations to these states.

To assign an animation or animations to a state, create the appropriate animation, expand the States entry in the tree view of the Editor window, and select the State icon. The list of animations you have created appear in a list box on the right side of the window. Check the animation you want to assign to this state. Note that you can assign more than one animation to the same state. This allows the server to randomly select different animations for the state. Assigning an animation to a state does not prevent an animation from playing that animation directly.

You can also assign an animation to a state by selecting the animation's entry in the tree. The Assign To State list box on the Properties page lists the states. Select the check box of the state to which you're assigning the animation.

The Editor does not support creating additional states because states only apply to situations where the server must play an animation automatically on behalf of the client application. Thus, there is no benefit in defining your own state. If need be, you can play any animation explicitly using the **Play** method.

Saving Your Character Definition

You can save your character's definition file by choosing the Save command on the File menu or the Save Character Definition button on the toolbar. If you want to save the character definition file with a new name, choose the Save As command on the File menu. The Editor saves a character's editable definition as an Agent Character Definition (.ACD) file. You can also edit this self-documenting text file format with most text editors and word processing applications.

Printing Your Character Definition

To print your character's definition, choose the Print command on the File menu or the Print button on the toolbar. To set the properties for your printed output, choose the Page Setup command and choose your settings before selecting the Print command.

Building a Character

When you are done creating your animations, the character and images must be compiled into a special format that Microsoft Agent uses to load this data. To build a character, select the Build Character command on the File menu or from the toolbar. If you have unsaved edits in your character definition file, the Editor saves the definition file before displaying the Build Character dialog box.

The Agent Character Editor will automatically propose a filename based on your character definition filename. The Build Character dialog box also includes a drop-down list so you can choose between building the character as a single storage file (.ACS) or as multiple files. If you choose the latter, the Editor builds an .ACF file that includes character's data and an .ACA file for each animation you created. If you plan to install and access a character stored on the same machine as your client application, you would typically choose the single structured file format. This format provides easy and efficient installation and access to the character. However, if the character will be accessed from a Web server using the HTTP protocol, build your character using the .ACF (individual) file format. This latter file structure allows a Web page script to load individual animation files, storing the data in the user's browser file cache. It provides more efficient access over the Web because animation data can be downloaded as needed rather than requiring the user to wait for the entire set of animations to download at one time. In addition, because the character's data is stored in the browser cache, the file space can be automatically reclaimed.

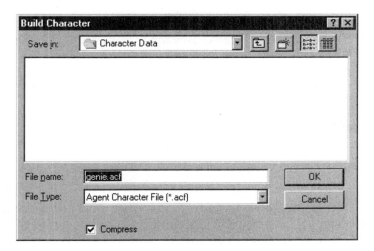

FIGURE 9-8. The Build Character dialog box

Although you can also download character data (either as a single structured file or multiple files) from a Web server and install elsewhere on a user's machine, such a method requires security provisions for downloading and installation. As a result, the Microsoft Agent API does not include support for downloadable installation of a character except to the browser's cache. However, you can still support this scenario by creating your own installation control and distribute it following appropriate security conventions. For more information, see the Microsoft Internet Client Software Development Kit at http://msdn.microsoft.com /developer/sdk/inetsdk/asetup/default.htm.

The Compress option enables you to set whether the character data is compressed. Typically, you will want to set this option to compact your character data, although building a character with the compacted data takes longer.

Once you build a character, subsequent builds will be faster if you build the character to the same directory location. The Character Editor automatically verifies and copies those files that have not changed, and recompiles any data that has been edited.

If the Editor detects any errors in the character file while building the character, it writes the information out to a log file and displays a message box. You can choose to view the log file or ignore it and read it later with a text editor. However, note that the Editor will overwrite the log file the next time you build a character file.

Editing an Existing Character

To edit an existing character, choose Open on the File menu, select the character's definition file (.ACD) in the resulting dialog box, and choose Open. The file will load into the Editor. Note that you cannot load compiled character files (.ACS, .ACF, or .ACA) with the Editor.

Because the character's definition file (.ACD) is a text file, you can also edit a character's definition by opening the file with a text editor or word processing program. However, when completing your changes, make sure to save the file in its original format before loading it into the character editor for compilation.

Command Reference

The File Menu

New

Resets the Agent Character Editor for creating a new character definition. If an existing character is loaded and has unsaved edits, the Editor displays a message to determine whether to save or discard unsaved changes.

Open

Displays the Open File dialog box, enabling you to open an existing character definition file for editing. If an existing character is loaded and has unsaved edits to a file, the Editor displays a message to determine whether to save or discard unsaved changes.

Save

Saves the character definition. If the character definition does not exist (has not been named), the Editor displays the Save As dialog box for input of the filename.

Save As

Displays the Save As dialog box, enabling you to enter a new name for the character definition file.

Print

Displays the Print dialog box, enabling you to choose a printing option and to print the character definition file.

Build Character

Displays the Build Character dialog box, which includes options for defining how to build a character's data and animation files for use with Microsoft Agent.

Page Setup

Displays the Page Setup dialog box that enables you to set the printing options for the character definition file.

Most Recently Open Files

Keeps track of the recent character definition files you opened. Choosing a file automatically opens that file for editing. If an existing character is loaded and has unsaved edits to a file, the Editor displays a message to determine whether to save or discard unsaved changes.

Exit

Quits the Agent Character Editor. If an existing character is loaded and has unsaved edits to a file, the Editor displays a message to determine whether to save or discard unsaved changes.

The Edit Menu

Undo

Removes a change made in the Editor.

Redo

Reverses an undo action in the Editor.

Cut

Removes the selected item from the Editor and places it on the Windows Clipboard.

Copy

Copies the selected item in the Editor to the Windows Clipboard.

Paste

Copies data from the current Windows Clipboard to the selected location.

Delete

Removes the selected item from the Editor.

New Animation

Creates a new animation object in the Editor.

New Frame

Creates a new frame for an animation.

New Frames from Files

Displays the Select Image Files dialog box and creates frames using the selected files.

Open Frame Window

Displays the current frame and its images in a separate window without scaling the images loaded into the frame.

Preview | Stop Preview

Plays (or stops playing) an animation, starting from its selected frame.

Preview | Stop Preview Exit Branching

Plays (or stops playing) an animation's exit branching, starting from its selected frame.

The Help Menu

Help Topics

Displays the Help Topics dialog box, enabling you to select an Editor help topic.

About Microsoft Agent Character Editor

Displays a dialog box with copyright and version information for the Editor.

Toolbar buttons

New Custom Character

Resets the Editor for creating a new Custom character definition. If an existing character is loaded and has unsaved edits to a file(s), the Editor displays a message to determine whether to save or discard unsaved changes.

Open Character Definition

Displays the Open File dialog box, enabling you to open an existing character definition file for editing. If an existing character is loaded and has unsaved edits to a file(s), the Editor displays a message to determine whether to save or discard unsaved changes.

Save Character Definition

Saves the character definition. If the character definition does not exist (has not been named), the Editor displays the Save As dialog box for input of the filename.

Build Character

Builds a Microsoft Agent character from the character definition.

Print Character Definition

Prints the current character definition file open in the Editor.

Cut

Removes the selected item in the Editor and places it on the Windows Clipboard.

Copy

Copies the selected item in the Editor to the Windows Clipboard.

Paste

Copies data from the current Windows Clipboard to the selected location.

Delete

Removes the selected item from the Editor.

Undo

Removes a change made in the Editor.

Redo

Reverses an undo action in the Editor.

New Animation

Creates a new animation object in the Editor.

New Animation Frame

Creates a new frame for an animation.

Preview

Plays an animation, starting from its selected frame.

Preview Exit Branching

Plays an animation's exit branching, starting from its selected frame.

Stop Preview

Stops playing the preview of an animation.

Add Image File

Displays the Select Image File dialog box. Selected images are added to the list.

Move Up

Moves an image up in the ordered (z-ordered) list. In a frame's images list, this moves the image up in the visual z-order.

Move Do

Moves an i   'own in the ordered (z-ordered) list. In a frame's images list, this moves   ge down in the visual z-order.

C H A P T E R   1 0

Using the Microsoft Linguistic Information Sound Editing Tool

The Microsoft Linguistic Information Sound Editing Tool enables you to generate phoneme and word-break information for enhancing Windows sound (.wav) files to support high-quality lip-syncing character animation.

You can use linguistically enhanced sound files generated with the sound editor to support lip-syncing Microsoft Agent character output. To do so, simply pass the file as a parameter to the **Speak** method.

See also Chapter 4, "Programming the Microsoft Agent Control," or Chapter 5, "Programming the Microsoft Agent Server Interface."

Installing the Sound Editor

The recommended system configuration for using the sound editor is a PC with a Pentium 166, at least 48 Megabytes of RAM, and a Windows compatible sound card. If you want to record spoken input with the tool, you will also need a compatible microphone.

To install the Microsoft Linguistic Sound Editing Tool, open its self-extracting installation file. This will automatically install the appropriate files on your system. If you download the sound editor from the Microsoft Agent Web site, you can choose to install the editor after downloading or save it to your disk to be subsequently opened and installed. The installation tool will propose to install itself in the Tools subdirectory of Microsoft Agent. We recommend that you use this location.

The Microsoft Command and Control speech recognition engine (version. 4.0) must also be installed before you can use the sound editor. This normally gets installed with the sound editor, but if it was subsequently uninstalled, you can reinstall it from the Microsoft Agent Web site at *http://www.microsoft.com/workshop/ imedia/agent/agentdl.asp* (also included on the book's CD). The sound editor can only generate linguistic information based on the language supported by the speech engine. To generate information for other languages, a compatible speech recognition engine for that language must be installed. Contact your speech engine vendor to determine whether they support the Microsoft Linguistic Sound Editing Tool.

Starting the Sound Editor

To run the Microsoft Linguistic Information Sound Editing Tool, choose it from the Start menu or double-click the sound editor's icon. The sound editor's window will open, displaying its menus, a toolbar for frequently used commands, a text box for entering the words the editor uses to process the sound file, and a display area for viewing and editing the audio and linguistic data.

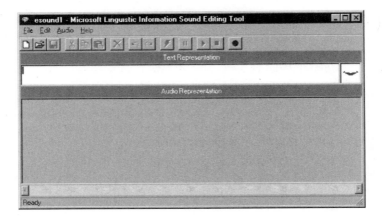

FIGURE 10-1. Microsoft Linguistic Information Sound Editing Tool Window

Once the sound editor starts up, you can begin recording a new sound file or load an existing sound file.

Creating a New Sound File

When you first start the editor, you can create a new sound file by choosing Record from the Audio menu or clicking the Record button on the sound editor's toolbar, and then speaking into the microphone attached to your system. Click the Stop button on the toolbar to stop recording. You can select the Play command from the Audio menu or the toolbar to see how Microsoft Agent processes the sound file without linguistic enhancement. To create another new file, select New from the File menu or the toolbar.

Loading an Existing Sound File

You can also load an existing Windows sound file (.wav) or linguistically enhanced sound file (.lwv) by choosing the Open command from the File menu or the toolbar. This displays the Open dialog box. Select a file and click Open to load the file into the editor.

FIGURE 10-2. The Open Dialog Box

Generating Linguistic Information

Once you have recorded a new sound file, or loaded an existing sound file, you can generate phonetic and word-break information by entering text that corresponds to your sound file in the Text Representation box. Then choose the Generate Linguistic Info command from the Edit menu or from the toolbar. The sound editor displays a progress message and begins processing your sound file. When it finishes generating linguistic information, it displays a mapping of word and phoneme labels for the sound file in boxes in the Audio Representation box. Note that the Generate Linguistic Info command remains disabled until you enter a text representation for your sound file.

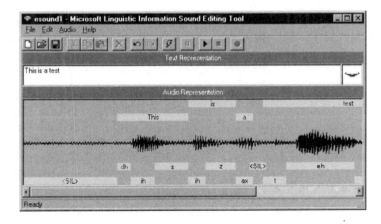

FIGURE 10-3. Word and Phoneme Labels Generated for a Sound File

If the editor doesn't produce an acceptable set of word or phoneme labels, choose the Generate Linguistic Info command again. If the editor does not generate any linguistic information, check your text representation to ensure that all the words are correctly ordered and spelled, and that you don't have any unnecessary spaces around punctuation. Then choose the Generate Linguistic Info command again. You can edit the text representation by selecting text in the Text Representation text box and using the Cut, Copy, and Paste commands on the Edit menu. If you are uncertain of the words the sound file includes, you can play the sound file by choosing Play from the Edit menu or the editor's toolbar. If the editor still fails to produce linguistic labels, try recording your sound file again. A poor quality recording, especially with excessive background noise, is likely to reduce the probability of generating reasonable linguistic information.

You can also manually create your own linguistic information by selecting part of the audio representation and choosing Insert Phoneme or Insert Word from the Edit menu. These commands are also available if you right-click within the selection.

To see how the linguistic information could be used for lip-syncing character animation with Microsoft Agent, choose the Play button on the toolbar and the editor will play your sound file, animating a sample mouth image based on the generated label information.

You can change the phoneme label display to show the IPA (International Phonetic Alphabet) assignments by choosing the Phoneme Label Display command on the Edit menu, then the IPA command. This displays the byte value for the phoneme. To change back to the descriptive names, choose the Phoneme Label Display command again, then choose Name.

Playing a Sound File

You can play standard Windows sound files or linguistically enhanced sound files by choosing the Play command from the Audio menu or the editor's toolbar. The Pause and Stop commands enable you to pause or stop playing the sound file. As you play the file, the sample mouth image animates to show how the lip-sync information could be used by a Microsoft Agent character.

You can also play a selected portion of a sound file by dragging a selection in the Audio Representation or clicking a word or phoneme label, then choosing Play. You can extend an existing selection by pressing SHIFT and clicking, or pressing SHIFT and dragging to the new location in the Audio Representation.

Editing Linguistic Information

You can edit a file's linguistic information in several ways. For example, you can adjust a word or phoneme label's boundary by moving the pointer to the edge of the box that defines the range of the label. When the pointer changes to the boundary move pointer, drag left or right. The editor automatically adjusts the adjacent word or phoneme boundary as well.

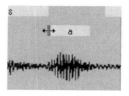

FIGURE 10-4. Adjusting a Word or Phoneme Label Boundary

Adjusting a phoneme label's boundary changes the timing of a phoneme when the audio plays. For characters developed for use with Microsoft Agent, changing the phoneme label boundary may change the timing or duration for a mouth image mapped to that phoneme. Changing the boundary of a word label changes the timing of the word's appearance in the character's word balloon.

You can also replace a phoneme assignment by selecting the phoneme label and choosing Replace Phoneme from the Edit menu, or right-clicking the phoneme label and choosing Replace Phoneme from the pop-up menu. The editor displays the Replace Phoneme dialog box and highlights the label's current phoneme assignment. You can choose a replacement phoneme by selecting one in the IPA list or by choosing another entry in the Name list. If more than one IPA translation is available for that name, choose an item in the IPA list. To enter an IPA designation for a phoneme that may not be directly included in the language, type in its hex value or multiple hex values, concatenated with a plus (+) character. Once you have selected the replacement phoneme information, choose OK, and the editor replaces the phoneme label you selected.

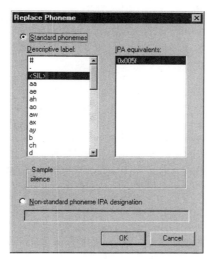

FIGURE 10-5. Replace Phoneme Dialog Box

Similarly, you can replace a word label by clicking the label's box and choosing Replace Word, or by right-clicking the label's box and choosing Replace Word from the pop-up menu. The editor displays the Replace Word dialog box. Enter the replacement word and choose OK.

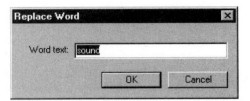

FIGURE 10-6. Replace Word Dialog Box

For characters developed for use with Microsoft Agent, replacing a phoneme label may change the mouth image displayed when the sound file plays. Replacing a word replaces the text that appears in the character's word balloon when the **Speak** method is called.

You can also insert a new phoneme label or word by making a selection in the Audio Representation and choosing Insert Phoneme or Insert Word from the Edit menu, or right-clicking within the selection and choosing the commands from the pop-up menu. These commands bring up dialog boxes similar to the Replace Phoneme and Replace Word dialog boxes, except that the editor inserts the new word or phoneme rather than replacing the existing information.

Finally, you can delete a phoneme or word by selecting its label and choosing Delete Phoneme or Delete Word. This removes its linguistic information from the file.

Saving a Sound File

When you are ready to save your sound file, choose the Save command on the File menu or on the editor's toolbar. The editor displays the Save As dialog box and proposes a name and default file type based on whether you generated linguistic information for the file. If you save the file as a sound file (.wav), the editor saves just the audio data. If you save the file information as a linguistically enhanced sound file (.lwv), the word and phoneme information are automatically included as part of a modified sound file. Once you have confirmed or edited the name, location, file type, and format, choose the Save button.

If you want to save a sound file with a new name, different location, or different format, choose the Save As command on the File menu. When the Save As dialog box appears, type in the new filename and click the Save button.

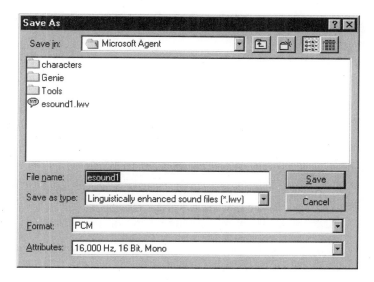

FIGURE 10-7. The Save As Dialog Box

You can also save a portion of the sound file. For example, you may want to save the file without excessive silence at its beginning or end. In the Audio Representation, select the portion of the file you want to save, and choose Save Selection As from the File menu. The command is enabled only when you have a selection in the Audio Representation.

Using the Editor with a Different Speech Engine

While the sound editor installs the Microsoft Speech Recognition Engine (4.0), it may be used with another speech engine, if that engine supports the required interfaces documented in the Speech Engine Requirements document. Before attempting to use the editor with another engine, confirm with your vendor that he or she can comply with these requirements.

To use the sound editor with another speech engine, choose the Speech Engine command on the Edit menu. This displays a dialog box showing the current engine in use. To choose another engine, display the list of engines, then click OK. If there are no other engines listed, you do not have any other compatible engines included.

Command Reference

The File Menu

New

Resets the sound editor for creating a new enhanced sound file. If an existing sound file is loaded and has unsaved edits, the sound editor displays a message to determine whether to save or discard unsaved changes.

Open

Displays the Open dialog box, enabling you to open an existing sound file. If an existing sound file is loaded and has unsaved edits, the sound editor displays a message to determine whether to save or discard unsaved changes.

Save

Saves a sound file. If the sound file does not exist (has not been named), the sound editor displays the Save As dialog box for input of the filename.

Save As

Displays the Save As dialog box, enabling you to enter a new name for the sound file.

Save Selection As

Displays the Save Selection As dialog box, enabling you to enter a name for the selected part of the sound file.

Most Recently Open Files

Keeps track of the recent character definition files you opened. Choosing a file automatically opens that file for editing. If an existing character is loaded and has unsaved edits to a file, the sound editor displays a message to determine whether to save or discard unsaved changes.

Exit

Quits the sound editor. If an existing file is loaded and has unsaved edits, the sound editor displays a message to determine whether to save or discard unsaved changes.

The Edit Menu

Undo

Removes a change made in the sound editor.

Redo

Reverses an undo action in the sound editor.

Cut

Removes the selected text and places it on the clipboard.

Copy

Copies the selected text to the clipboard.

Paste

Copies text on the clipboard to the insertion point or selection in the Text Representation text box.

Delete

Removes the selected text.

Select All

Selects the text in the Text Representation text box.

Generate Linguistic Info

Begins generating word-break and phoneme information for a sound file.

Insert Phoneme

Displays the Insert Phoneme dialog box that enables you to insert a selected phoneme label.

Replace Phoneme

Displays the Replace Phoneme dialog box that enables you to replace the selected phoneme label.

Delete Phoneme

Deletes the selected phoneme label.

Insert Word

Displays the Insert Word dialog box that enables you to insert a word label in the Audio Representation.

Replace Word

Displays the Replace Word dialog box that enables you to replace the selected word label in the Audio Representation.

Delete Word

Deletes the selected word label in the Audio Representation.

Phoneme Label Display

Changes the phoneme label display between descriptive names and IPA byte values.

Speech Engine

Enables you to change the speech engine you use to generate the word break and phoneme information.

The Audio Menu

Play

Plays the sound file or selected portion of the sound file.

Record

Records a new sound file.

Pause

Pauses the play of the sound file or selected portion of the sound file. Use Play to resume playing.

Stop

Stops recording or playing the sound file or selected portion of the sound file.

The Help Menu

Help Topics

Displays the Help Topics dialog box, enabling you to select a sound editor help topic.

About Microsoft Linguistic Sound Editing Tool

Displays a dialog box with copyright and version information for the sound editor.

Toolbar buttons

New

Resets the sound editor for creating a new sound file. If an existing sound file is loaded and has unsaved edits, the sound editor displays a message to determine whether to save or discard unsaved changes.

Open

Displays the Open File dialog box, enabling you to open an existing sound file. If an existing sound file is loaded and has unsaved edits, the sound editor displays a message to determine whether to save or discard unsaved changes.

Save

Saves the sound file. If the file does not exist (has not been named), the editor displays the Save As dialog box for input of the filename.

Cut

Removes the selected text from the editor and places it on the Windows Clipboard.

Copy

Copies the selected text in the editor to the Windows Clipboard.

Paste

Copies text from the current Windows Clipboard to the selected location in the Text Representation text box.

Delete

Removes the selected text from the sound editor.

Undo

Removes a change made in the sound editor.

Redo

Reverses an undo action in the sound editor.

Generate Linguistic Info

Generates phoneme and word labels for the sound file.

Pause

Pauses playing of the sound file.

Play

Plays the sound file or selected portion of the sound file.

Stop

Stops recording or playing the sound file or selected portion of the sound file.

Record

Starts recording a sound file.

A P P E N D I X   A

Animations for Microsoft Characters

Animations for Genie Character

Genie supports the animations listed in the table below. Refer to Chapter 5, "Programming the Microsoft Agent Server Interface" and Chapter 4, "Programming the Microsoft Agent Control" for information on how to call the character's animations.

If accessing these character animations using the HTTP protocol and the control's **Get** or server's **Prepare** method, consider how you will download them. Instead of downloading all the animations at once, you may want to retrieve the **Showing** and **Speaking** state animations first. This will enable you to display the character quickly and have it speak while bringing down other animations asynchronously. In addition, to ensure that character and animation data load successfully, use the **RequestComplete** event. If a load request fails, you can retry loading the data or display an appropriate message.

If an animation's **Return** animations is defined using Exit branches, you do not need to call it explicitly; Agent automatically plays the **Return** animation before the next animation. However, if a **Return** animation is listed, you must call the animation using the **Play** method before another animation to provide a smooth transition. If no **Return** animation is listed, the animation typically ends without needing a transitional animation.

The character file includes sound effects for some animation as noted in the following table. Sound effects play only if this option is enabled in the Microsoft Agent property sheet. You can also disable sound effects in your application.

Animation	Return Animation	Supports Speaking	Sound Effects	Assigned to State	Description
Acknowledge	None	No	No	None	Nods head
Alert	Yes, using Exit branches	Yes	No	**Listening**	Straightens and raises eyebrows
Announce	Yes, using Exit branches	Yes	No	None	Raises hand
Blink	None	No	No	**IdlingLevel1 IdlingLevel2**	Blinks eyes
Confused	Yes, using Exit branches	Yes	No	None	Scratches head
Congratulate	Yes, using Exit branches	Yes	**Yes**	None	Applauds
Congratulate_2	Yes, using Exit branches	Yes	No	None	Gives thumbs-up gesture
Decline	Yes, using Exit branches	Yes	No	None	Raises hands and shakes head
DoMagic1	None	Yes	No	None	Turns to side and raises hands
DoMagic2	Yes, using Exit branches	No	**Yes**	None	Lowers hands, clouds appear
DontRecognize	Yes, using Exit branches	Yes	No	None	Holds hand to ear
Explain	Yes, using Exit branches	Yes	No	None	Extends arms to side
GestureDown	Yes, using Exit branches	Yes	No	**Gesturing-Down**	Gestures down
GestureLeft	Yes, using Exit branches	Yes	No	**Gesturing-Left**	Gestures left
GestureRight	Yes, using Exit branches	Yes	No	**Gesturing-Right**	Gestures right
GestureUp	Yes, using Exit branches	Yes	No	**Gesturing-Up**	Gestures up
GetAttention	**GetAttention-Return**	Yes	No	None	Waves arms
GetAttention-Continued	**GetAttention-Return**	Yes	No	None	Waves arms again
GetAttention-Return	None	No	No	None	Returns to neutral position
Greet	Yes, using Exit branches	Yes	No	None	Bows

Animation	Return Animation	Supports Speaking	Sound Effects	Assigned to State	Description
Hearing_1	None	No	**No**	**Hearing**	Ears extend (*looping animation)
Hearing_2	None	No	**No**	**Hearing**	Tilts head left (*looping animation)
Hearing_3	None	No	**No**	**Hearing**	Turns head left (*looping animation)
Hearing_4	None	No	**No**	**Hearing**	Turns head right (*looping animation)
Hide	None	No	**Yes**	**Hiding**	Disappears into smoke
Idle1_1	None	No	**No**	**IdlingLevel1 IdlingLevel2**	Takes breath
Idle1_2	None	No	**No**	**IdlingLevel1 IdlingLevel2**	Glances right and blinks
Idle1_3	Yes, using Exit branches	No	**No**	**IdlingLevel1 IdlingLevel2**	Glances left and blinks
Idle1_4	None	No	**No**	**IdlingLevel1 IdlingLevel2**	Glances up to the right and blinks
Idle1_5	Yes, using Exit branches	No	**No**	**IdlingLevel1 IdlingLevel2**	Glances down and blinks
Idle1_6	None	No	**No**	**IdlingLevel1 IdlingLevel2**	Glances up and blinks
Idle2_1	None	No	**No**	**IdlingLevel2**	Wisp snakes
Idle2_2	Yes, using Exit branches	No	**No**	**IdlingLevel2**	Reveals scroll and reads
Idle2_3	Yes, using Exit branches	No	**No**	**IdlingLevel2**	Reveals scroll and writes
Idle3_1	None	No	**Yes**	**IdlingLevel3**	Yawns
Idle3_2	Yes, using Exit branches	No	**Yes**	**IdlingLevel3**	Falls asleep (*looping animation)
LookDown	**LookDown-Return**	No	**No**	None	Looks down
LookDownBlink	**LookDown-Return**	No	**No**	None	Blinks looking down
LookDown-Return	None	No	**No**	None	Returns to neutral position
LookLeft	**LookLeft-Return**	No	**No**	None	Looks left

* If you play a looping animation, you must use **Stop** to clear it before other animations in the character's queue will play.

Animation	Return Animation	Supports Speaking	Sound Effects	Assigned to State	Description
LookLeftBlink	LookLeft-Return	No	No	None	Blinks looking left
LookLeft-Return	None	No	No	None	Returns to neutral position
LookRight	LookRight-Return	No	No	None	Looks right
LookRightBlink	LookRight-Return	No	No	None	Blinks looking right
LookRight-Return	None	No	No	None	Returns to neutral position
LookUp	LookUp-Return	No	No	None	Looks up
LookUpBlink	LookUp-Return	No	No	None	Blinks looking up
LookUpReturn	None	No	No	None	Returns to neutral position
MoveDown	Yes, using Exit branches	No	Yes	Moving-Down	Flies down
MoveLeft	Yes, using Exit branches	No	Yes	MovingLeft	Flies left
MoveRight	Yes, using Exit branches	No	Yes	Moving-Right	Flies right
MoveUp	Yes, using Exit branches	No	Yes	MovingUp	Flies up
Pleased	Yes, using Exit branches	Yes	No	None	Smiles and holds hands together
Process	No	No	No	None	Spins into a cloud
Processing	Yes, using Exit branches	No	No	None	Spins into a cloud (*looping animation)
Read	ReadReturn	Yes	Yes	None	Reveals scroll, reads and looks up
Read-Continued	ReadReturn	Yes	No	None	Reads and looks up
ReadReturn	None	No	No	None	Returns to neutral position
Reading	Yes, using Exit branches	No	Yes	None	Reveal scroll and reads (*looping animation)
RestPose	None	Yes	No	Speaking	Neutral position
Sad	Yes, using Exit branches	Yes	No	None	Sad expression

* If you play a looping animation, you must use **Stop** to clear it before other animations in the character's queue will play.

Animation	Return Animation	Supports Speaking	Sound Effects	Assigned to State	Description
Search	No	No	No	None	Reveals binoculars and turns
Searching	Yes, using Exit branches	No	No	None	Reveals binoculars and turns (*looping animation)
Show	None	No	Yes	Showing	Appears out of smoke
StartListening	Yes, using Exit branches	Yes	No	None	Puts hand to ear
StopListening	Yes, using Exit branches	Yes	No	None	Puts hands over ears
Suggest	Yes, using Exit branches	Yes	No	None	Displays lightbulb
Surprised	Yes, using Exit branches	Yes	No	None	Looks surprised
Think	Yes, using Exit branches	Yes	No	None	Looks up with hand on chin
Thinking	No	No	No	None	Looks up with hand on chin (*looping animation)
Uncertain	Yes, using Exit branches	Yes	No	None	Moves one hand to chin, other to hip, and raises right eyebrow
Wave	Yes, using Exit branches	Yes	No	None	Waves
Write	WriteReturn	Yes	Yes	None	Reveals scroll, writes and looks up
Write-Continued	WriteReturn	Yes	Yes	None	Writes and looks up
WriteReturn	None	No	No	None	Returns to neutral position
Writing	Yes, using Exit branches	No	Yes	None	Reveals scroll, writes (*looping animation)

* If you play a looping animation, you must use **Stop** to clear it before other animations in the character's queue will play.

Animations for Merlin Character

Merlin supports the animations listed in the table below. Refer to Chapter 5, "Programming the Microsoft Agent Server Interface" and Chapter 4, "Programming the Microsoft Agent Control" for information on how to call the character's animations.

If accessing these character animations using the HTTP protocol and the control's **Get** or server's **Prepare** method, consider how you will download them. Instead of downloading all the animations at once, you may want to retrieve the **Showing** and **Speaking** state animations first. This will enable you to display the character quickly and have it speak while bringing down other animations asynchronously. In addition, to ensure that character and animation data load successfully, use the **RequestComplete** event. If a load request fails, you can retry loading the data or display an appropriate message.

If an animation's **Return** animation is defined using Exit branches, you do not need to call it explicitly; Agent automatically plays the **Return** animation before the next animation. However, if a **Return** animation is listed, you must call the animation using the **Play** method before another animation to provide a smooth transition. If no **Return** animation is listed, the animation typically ends without needing a transitional animation.

The character file includes sound effects for some animations as noted in the following table. Sound effects play only if this option is enabled in the Microsoft Agent property sheet. You can also disable sound effects in your application.

Animation	Return Animation	Supports Speaking	Sound Effects	Assigned to State	Description
Acknowledge	None	No	No	None	Nods head
Alert	Yes, using Exit branches	Yes	No	Listening	Straightens and raises eyebrows
Announce	Yes, using Exit branches	Yes	Yes	None	Raises trumpet and plays
Blink	None	No	No	IdlingLevel1 IdlingLevel2	Blinks eyes
Confused	Yes, using Exit branches	Yes	Yes	None	Scratches head
Congratulate	Yes, using Exit branches	Yes	Yes	None	Displays trophy
Congratulate_2	Yes, using Exit branches	Yes	Yes	None	Applauds
Decline	Yes, using Exit branches	Yes	No	None	Raises hands and shakes head
DoMagic1	None	Yes	No	None	Raises magic wand
DoMagic2	Yes, using Exit branches	No	Yes	None	Lowers wand, clouds
DontRecognize	Yes, using Exit branches	Yes	No	None	Holds hand to ear
Explain	Yes, using Exit branches	Yes	No	None	Extends arms to side

Animation	Return Animation	Supports Speaking	Sound Effects	Assigned to State	Description
GestureDown	Yes, using Exit branches	Yes	No	Gesturing-Down	Gestures down
GestureLeft	Yes, using Exit branches	Yes	No	Gesturing-Left	Gestures left
GestureRight	Yes, using Exit branches	Yes	No	Gesturing-Right	Gestures right
GestureUp	Yes, using Exit branches	Yes	No	Gesturing-Up	Gestures up
GetAttention	GetAttention-Return	Yes	Yes	None	Leans forward and knocks
GetAttention-Continued	GetAttention-Return	Yes	Yes	None	Leaning forward, knocks again
GetAttention-Return	None	No	No	None	Returns to neutral position
Greet	Yes, using Exit branches	Yes	Yes	None	Bows
Hearing_1	None	No	No	Hearing	Ears extend (*looping animation)
Hearing_2	None	No	No	Hearing	Tilts head left (*looping animation)
Hearing_3	None	No	No	Hearing	Turns head left (*looping animation)
Hearing_4	None	No	No	Hearing	Turns head right (*looping animation)
Hide	None	No	Yes	Hiding	Disappears under cap
Idle1_1	Yes, using Exit branches	No	No	IdlingLevel1 IdlingLevel2	Takes breath
Idle1_2	Yes, using Exit branches	No	No	IdlingLevel1 IdlingLevel2	Glances left and blinks
Idle1_3	Yes, using Exit branches	No	No	IdlingLevel1 IdlingLevel2	Glances right
Idle1_4	Yes, using Exit branches	No	No	IdlingLevel1 IdlingLevel2	Glances up to the right and blinks
Idle2_1	None	No	No	IdlingLevel2	Looks at wand and blinks
Idle2_2	None	No	No	IdlingLevel2	Holds hands and blinks
Idle3_1	None	No	Yes	IdlingLevel3	Yawns
Idle3_2	Yes, using Exit branches	No	Yes	IdlingLevel3	Falls asleep (*looping animation)

* If you play a looping animation, you must use **Stop** to clear it before other animations in the character's queue will play.

Animation	Return Animation	Supports Speaking	Sound Effects	Assigned to State	Description
LookDown	LookDown-Return	No	No	None	Looks down
LookDownBlink	LookDown-Return	No	No	None	Blinks looking down
LookDown-Return	None	No	No	None	Returns to neutral position
LookLeft	LookLeft-Return	No	No	None	Looks left
LookLeftBlink	LookLeft-Return	No	No	None	Blinks looking left
LookLeft-Return	None	No	No	None	Returns to neutral position
LookRight	LookRight-Return	No	No	None	Looks right
LookRightBlink	LookRight-Return	No	No	None	Blinks looking right
LookRight-Return	None	No	No	None	Returns to neutral position
LookUp	LookUp-Return	No	No	None	Looks up
LookUpBlink	LookUp-Return	No	No	None	Blinks looking up
LookUpReturn	None	No	No	None	Returns to neutral position
MoveDown	Yes, using Exit branches	No	Yes	Moving-Down	Flies down
MoveLeft	Yes, using Exit branches	No	Yes	MovingLeft	Flies left
MoveRight	Yes, using Exit branches	No	Yes	Moving-Right	Flies right
MoveUp	Yes, using Exit branches	No	Yes	MovingUp	Flies up
Pleased	Yes, using Exit branches	Yes	No	None	Smiles and holds hands together
Process	No	No	Yes	None	Stirs cauldron
Processing	Yes, using Exit branches	No	No	None	Stirs cauldron (*looping animation)
Read	ReadReturn	Yes	Yes	None	Opens book, reads and looks up

* If you play a looping animation, you must use **Stop** to clear it before other animations in the character's queue will play.

Animation	Return Animation	Supports Speaking	Sound Effects	Assigned to State	Description
Read-Continued	**ReadReturn**	Yes	**Yes**	None	Reads and looks up
ReadReturn	None	No	**Yes**	None	Returns to neutral position
Reading	Yes, using Exit branches	No	**Yes**	None	Reads (*looping animation)
RestPose	None	Yes	**No**	**Speaking**	Neutral position
Sad	Yes, using Exit branches	Yes	**No**	None	Sad expression
Search	No	No	**Yes**	None	Looks into crystal ball
Searching	Yes, using Exit branches	No	**Yes**	None	Looks into crystal ball (*looping animation)
Show	None	No	**Yes**	**Showing**	Appears out of cap
StartListening	Yes, using Exit branches	Yes	**No**	None	Puts hand to ear
StopListening	Yes, using Exit branches	Yes	**No**	None	Puts hands over ears
Suggest	Yes, using Exit branches	Yes	**Yes**	None	Displays lightbulb
Surprised	Yes, using Exit branches	Yes	**Yes**	None	Looks surprised
Think	Yes, using Exit branches	Yes	**No**	None	Looks up with hand on chin
Thinking	No	No	**No**	None	Looks up with hand on chin (*looping animation)
Uncertain	Yes, using Exit branches	Yes	**No**	None	Leans forward and raises eyebrow
Wave	Yes, using Exit branches	Yes	**No**	None	Waves
Write	**WriteReturn**	Yes	**Yes**	None	Opens book, writes and looks up
Write-Continued	**WriteReturn**	Yes	**Yes**	None	Writes and looks up
WriteReturn	None	No	**Yes**	None	Returns to neutral position
Writing	Yes, using Exit branches	No	**Yes**	None	Writes (*looping animation)

* If you play a looping animation, you must use **Stop** to clear it before other animations in the character's queue will play.

Animations for Peedy Character

Peedy supports the animations listed in the table below. Refer to Chapter 5, "Programming the Microsoft Agent Server Interface" and Chapter 4, "Programming the Microsoft Agent Control" for information on how to call the character's animations.

If accessing these character animations using the HTTP protocol and the control's **Get** or server's **Prepare** method, consider how you will download them. Instead of downloading all the animations at once, you may want to retrieve the **Showing** and **Speaking** state animations first. This enables you to display the character quickly and have it speak while bringing down other animations asynchronously. In addition, to ensure that character and animation data load successfully, use the **RequestComplete** event. If a load request fails, you can retry loading the data or display an appropriate message.

If an animation's **Return** animation is defined using Exit branches, you do not need to call it explicitly; Agent automatically plays the **Return** animation before the next animation. However, if a **Return** animation is listed, you must call the animation using the **Play** method before another animation to provide a smooth transition. If no **Return** animation is listed, the animation typically ends without needing a transitional animation.

The character file includes sound effects for some animations as noted in the following table. Sound effects play only if this option is enabled in the Microsoft Agent property sheet. You can also disable sound effects in your application.

Animation	Return Animation	Supports Speaking	Sound Effects	Assigned to State	Description
Acknowledge	None	No	No	None	Nods head
Alert	Yes, using Exit branches	Yes	No	Listening	Straightens and raises eyebrows
Announce	Yes, using Exit branches	Yes	Yes	None	Paper airplane flies in and unfolds
Blink	None	No	No	IdlingLevel1 IdlingLevel2	Blinks eyes
Confused	Yes, using Exit branches	Yes	Yes	None	Eyes spin around
Congratulate	Yes, using Exit branches	Yes	Yes	None	Displays blue ribbon
Decline	Yes, using Exit branches	Yes	No	None	Shakes head
DoMagic1	None	Yes	Yes	None	Raises magic wand
DoMagic2	Yes, using Exit branches	No	Yes	None	Lowers wand, clouds appear

Animation	Return Animation	Supports Speaking	Sound Effects	Assigned to State	Description
DontRecognize	Yes, using Exit branches	Yes	**No**	None	Shakes head and holds wing to ear
Explain	Yes, using Exit branches	Yes	**No**	None	Extends arms to side
GestureDown	Yes, using Exit branches	Yes	**No**	**Gesturing-Down**	Gestures down
GestureLeft	Yes, using Exit branches	Yes	**No**	**Gesturing-Left**	Gestures left
GestureRight	Yes, using Exit branches	Yes	**No**	**Gesturing-Right**	Gestures right
GestureUp	Yes, using Exit branches	Yes	**No**	**Gesturing-Up**	Gestures up
GetAttention	**GetAttention-Return**	Yes	**Yes**	None	Jumps up with wings outstretched
GetAttention-Continued	**GetAttention-Return**	Yes	**Yes**	None	Jumps up with wings outstretched again
GetAttention-Return	None	No	**No**	None	Returns to neutral position
Greet	Yes, using Exit branches	Yes	**Yes**	None	Bows
Hearing_1	None	No	**No**	**Hearing**	Tilts head right (*looping animation)
Hearing_2	None	No	**No**	**Hearing**	Tilts head left (*looping animation)
Hearing_3	None	No	**No**	**Hearing**	Turns head right then left (*looping animation)
Hide	None	No	**Yes**	**Hiding**	Flies away
Idle1_1	None	No	**No**	**IdlingLevel1 IdlingLevel2**	Takes breath
Idle1_2	None	No	**No**	**IdlingLevel1 IdlingLevel2**	Glances right and blinks
Idle1_3	None	No	**No**	**IdlingLevel1 IdlingLevel2**	Glances left and blinks
Idle1_4	None	No	**No**	**IdlingLevel1 IdlingLevel2**	Glances up and blinks
Idle1_5	None	No	**No**	**IdlingLevel1 IdlingLevel2**	Glances down and blinks
Idle2_1	Yes, using Exit branches	No	**No**	**IdlingLevel2**	Puts on sunglasses

* If you play a looping animation, you must use **Stop** to clear it before other animations in the character's queue will play.

Animation	Return Animation	Supports Speaking	Sound Effects	Assigned to State	Description
Idle2_2	None	No	**Yes**	**IdlingLevel2**	Eats a cracker
Idle3_1	None	No	**Yes**	**IdlingLevel3**	Yawns
Idle3_2	Yes, using Exit branches	No	**Yes**	**IdlingLevel3**	Falls asleep (*looping animation)
Idle3_3	Yes, using Exit branches	No	**No**	**IdlingLevel3**	Listens to music (*looping animation)
LookDown	**LookDown-Return**	No	**No**	None	Looks down
LookDownBlink	**LookDown-Return**	No	**Yes**	None	Blinks looking down
LookDown-Return	None	No	**No**	None	Returns to neutral position
LookDownLeft	**LookDown-LeftReturn**	No	**No**	None	Looks down left
LookDownLeft-Blink	**LookDown-LeftReturn**	No	**Yes**	None	Blinks looking down left
LookDownLeft-Return	None	No	**No**	None	Returns to neutral position
LookDownRight	**LookDown-RightReturn**	No	**No**	None	Looks down right
LookDown-RightBlink	**LookDown-RightReturn**	No	**Yes**	None	Blinks looking down right
LookDown-RightReturn	None	No	**No**	None	Returns to neutral position
LookLeft	**LookLeft-Return**	Yes	**No**	None	Looks left
LookLeftBlink	**LookLeft-Return**	Yes	**Yes**	None	Blinks looking left
LookLeft-Return	None	No	**No**	None	Returns to neutral position
LookRight	**LookRight-Return**	Yes	**No**	None	Looks right
LookRightBlink	**LookRight-Return**	Yes	**Yes**	None	Blinks looking right
LookRight-Return	None	No	**No**	None	Returns to neutral position
LookUp	**LookUp-Return**	No	**No**	None	Looks up

* If you play a looping animation, you must use **Stop** to clear it before other animations in the character's queue will play.

Animation	Return Animation	Supports Speaking	Sound Effects	Assigned to State	Description
LookUpBlink	LookUp-Return	No	Yes	None	Blinks looking up
LookUpReturn	None	No	No	None	Returns to neutral position
LookUpLeft	LookUp-LeftReturn	No	No	None	Looks up left
LookUpLeft-Blink	LookUp-LeftReturn	No	Yes	None	Blinks looking up left
LookUpLeft-Return	None	No	No	None	Returns to neutral position
LookUpRight	LookUp-RightReturn	No	No	None	Looks up right
LookUpRight-Blink	LookUp-RightReturn	No	Yes	None	Blinks looking up right
LookUpRight-Return	None	No	No	None	Returns to neutral position
MoveDown	Yes, using Exit branches	No	Yes	Moving-Down	Flies down
MoveLeft	Yes, using Exit branches	No	Yes	MovingLeft	Flies left
MoveRight	Yes, using Exit branches	No	Yes	Moving-Right	Flies right
MoveUp	Yes, using Exit branches	No	Yes	MovingUp	Flies up
Pleased	Yes, using Exit branches	Yes	No	None	Smiles
Process	None	No	Yes	None	Uses calculator
Processing	Yes, using Exit branches	No	Yes	None	Uses calculator (*looping animation)
Read	ReadReturn	Yes	Yes	None	Opens magazine, reads and looks up
Read-Continued	ReadReturn	Yes	Yes	None	Reads and looks up
ReadReturn	None	No	Yes	None	Returns to neutral position
Reading	Yes, using Exit branches	No	Yes	None	Reads (*looping animation)
RestPose	None	Yes	No	Speaking	Neutral position
Sad	Yes, using Exit branches	Yes	No	None	Sad expression

* If you play a looping animation, you must use **Stop** to clear it before other animations in the character's queue will play.

Animation	Return Animation	Supports Speaking	Sound Effects	Assigned to State	Description
Search	None	No	**Yes**	None	Reveals telescope and rotates
Searching	Yes, using Exit branches	No	**Yes**	None	Reveals telescope and rotates (*looping animation)
Show	None	No	**Yes**	**Showing**	Flies in
StartListening	Yes, using Exit branches	Yes	**No**	None	Puts wing to ear
StopListening	Yes, using Exit branches	Yes	**No**	None	Puts wings to ears
Suggest	Yes, using Exit branches	Yes	**Yes**	None	Displays lightbulb
Surprised	Yes, using Exit branches	Yes	**Yes**	None	Looks surprised
Think	Yes, using Exit branches	Yes	**No**	None	Looks up with wing on face
Thinking	None	No	**No**	None	Looks up with wing on face (*looping animation)
Uncertain	Yes, using Exit branches	Yes	**No**	None	Leans to right and shrugs
Wave	Yes, using Exit branches	Yes	**No**	None	Waves
Write	**WriteReturn**	Yes	**Yes**	None	Takes out pencil and pad, writes and looks up
Write-Continued	**WriteReturn**	Yes	**Yes**	None	Writes and looks up
WriteReturn	None	No	**No**	None	Returns to neutral position
Writing	Yes, using Exit branches	No	**Yes**	None	Takes out pencil and pad, writes (*looping animation)

* If you play a looping animation, you must use **Stop** to clear it before other animations in the character's queue will play.

Animations for Robby Character

Robby supports the animations listed in the table below. Refer to Chapter 5, "Programming the Microsoft Agent Server Interface" and Chapter 4, "Programming the Microsoft Agent Control" for information on how to call the character's animations.

If accessing these character animations using the HTTP protocol and the control's **Get** or server's **Prepare** method, consider how you will download them. Instead of downloading all the animations at once, you may want to retrieve the **Showing** and **Speaking** state animations first. This will enable you to display the character quickly and have it speak while bringing down other animations asynchronously. In addition, to ensure that character and animation data load successfully, use the **RequestComplete** event. If a load request fails, you can retry loading the data or display an appropriate message.

If an animation's **Return** animation is defined using Exit branches, you do not need to call it explicitly; Agent automatically plays the **Return** animation before the next animation. However, if a **Return** animation is listed, you must call the animation using the **Play** method before another animation to provide a smooth transition. If no **Return** animation is listed, the animation typically ends without needing a transitional animation.

The character file includes sound effects for some animations as noted in the following table. Sound effects play only if this option is enabled in the Microsoft Agent property sheet. You can also disable sound effects in your application.

Animation	Return Animation	Supports Speaking	Sound Effects	Assigned to State	Description
Acknowledge	None	No	No	None	Nods head
Alert	Yes, using Exit branches	Yes	No	**Listening**	Straightens
Announce	Yes, using Exit branches	Yes	**Yes**	None	Prints out paper and reports
Blink	None	No	No	**IdlingLevel1 IdlingLevel2**	Blinks eyes
Confused	Yes, using Exit branches	Yes	No	None	Scratches head
Congratulate	Yes, using Exit branches	Yes	No	None	Raises hands then clasps hands
Decline	Yes, using Exit branches	Yes	No	None	Raises hand and shakes head
DoMagic1	None	Yes	No	None	Removes device
DoMagic2	Yes, using Exit branches	No	**Yes**	None	Presses button and beam appears
DontRecognize	Yes, using Exit branches	Yes	No	None	Holds hand to ear
Explain	Yes, using Exit branches	Yes	No	None	Gestures with arms
GestureDown	Yes, using Exit branches	Yes	No	**Gesturing-Down**	Gestures down
GestureLeft	Yes, using Exit branches	Yes	No	**GesturingLeft**	Gestures left

Animation	Return Animation	Supports Speaking	Sound Effects	Assigned to State	Description
GestureRight	Yes, using Exit branches	Yes	No	Gesturing-Right	Gestures right
GestureUp	Yes, using Exit branches	Yes	No	Gesturing-Up	Gestures up
GetAttention	GetAttention-Return	Yes	No	None	Waves arms
GetAttention-Continued	GetAttention-Return	Yes	No	None	Waves arms again
GetAttention-Return	None	No	No	None	Returns to neutral position
Greet	Yes, using Exit branches	Yes	No	None	Holds up hand
Hearing_1	Yes, using Exit branches	No	No	Hearing	Tilts head right (*looping animation)
Hearing_2	Yes, using Exit branches	No	No	Hearing	Tilts head left (*looping animation)
Hearing_3	Yes, using Exit branches	No	No	Hearing	Cocks head left (*looping animation)
Hearing_4	Yes, using Exit branches	No	No	Hearing	Tilts head down (*looping animation)
Hide	None	No	Yes	Hiding	Disappears through door
Idle1_1	None	No	No	IdlingLevel1 IdlingLevel2	Glances right
Idle1_2	None	No	No	IdlingLevel1 IdlingLevel2	Glances up and blinks
Idle1_3	None	No	No	IdlingLevel1 IdlingLevel2	Glances down and blinks
Idle1_4	None	No	No	IdlingLevel1 IdlingLevel2	Glances left and blinks
Idle2_1	None	No	No	IdlingLevel2	Folds arms
Idle2_2	None	No	Yes	IdlingLevel2	Removes head and makes adjustment
Idle3_1	None	No	No	IdlingLevel3	Yawns
Idle3_2	None	No	Yes	IdlingLevel3	Shuts down
LookDown	LookDown-Return	No	No	None	Looks down
LookDown-Return	None	No	No	None	Returns to neutral position

* If you play a looping animation, you must use **Stop** to clear it before other animations in the character's queue will play.

Animation	Return Animation	Supports Speaking	Sound Effects	Assigned to State	Description
LookLeft	LookLeft-Return	No	No	None	Looks left
LookLeft-Return	None	No	No	None	Returns to neutral position
LookRight	LookRight-Return	No	No	None	Looks right
LookRight-Return	None	No	No	None	Returns to neutral position
LookUp	LookUp-Return	No	No	None	Looks up
LookUpReturn	None	No	No	None	Returns to neutral position
MoveDown	Yes, using Exit branches	No	Yes	Moving-Down	Flies down
MoveLeft	Yes, using Exit branches	No	Yes	MovingLeft	Flies left
MoveRight	Yes, using Exit branches	No	Yes	Moving-Right	Flies right
MoveUp	Yes, using Exit branches	No	Yes	MovingUp	Flies up
Pleased	Yes, using Exit branches	Yes	Yes	None	Smiles and straightens up
Process	No	No	Yes	None	Presses buttons, prints, reads, then tosses printout
Processing	Yes, using Exit branches	No	Yes	None	Presses buttons, prints, reads, then tosses printout
Read	ReadReturn	Yes	Yes	None	Prints, reads, and looks up
ReadContinued	ReadReturn	Yes	Yes	None	Reads and looks up
ReadReturn	None	No	Yes	None	Returns to neutral position
Reading	Yes, using Exit branches	No	Yes	None	Prints, reads, and looks up (*looping animation)
RestPose	None	Yes	No	Speaking	Neutral position
Sad	Yes, using Exit branches	Yes	No	None	Sad expression
Search	No	No	Yes	None	Reveals toolbox and removes tool
Searching	Yes, using Exit branches	No	Yes	None	Reveals toolbox and removes tools (*looping animation)

* If you play a looping animation, you must use **Stop** to clear it before other animations in the character's queue will play.

Animation	Return Animation	Supports Speaking	Sound Effects	Assigned to State	Description
Show	None	No	**Yes**	**Showing**	Appears through doorway
StartListening	Yes, using Exit branches	Yes	**No**	None	Puts hand to ear
StopListening	Yes, using Exit branches	Yes	**No**	None	Puts hands over ears
Suggest	Yes, using Exit branches	Yes	**Yes**	None	Displays light bulb
Surprised	Yes, using Exit branches	Yes	**No**	None	Looks surprised
Think	Yes, using Exit branches	Yes	**Yes**	None	Scratches head
Thinking	No	No	**Yes**	None	Scratches head (*looping animation)
Uncertain	Yes, using Exit branches	Yes	**No**	None	Shrugs
Wave	Yes, using Exit branches	Yes	**No**	None	Waves
Write	**WriteReturn**	Yes	**Yes**	None	Reveals pencil and clipboard, writes and looks up
Write-Continued	**WriteReturn**	Yes	**Yes**	None	Writes and looks up
WriteReturn	None	No	**No**	None	Returns to neutral position
Writing	Yes, using Exit branches	No	**Yes**	None	Reveals pencil and clipboard, writes (*looping animation)

* If you play a looping animation, you must use **Stop** to clear it before other animations in the character's queue will play.

APPENDIX   B

Troubleshooting Microsoft Agent

If you have difficulty running Microsoft Agent on your machine, please refer to the following list of symptoms and try the suggested steps to isolate and solve the problem. If these suggestions don't resolve the problem, let us know by sending a bug report to *http://www.microsoft.com/workshop/imedia/agent/ agentbugform.asp*.

Page Loading and Installation Problems

When I attempt to load a page scripted for Microsoft Agent, nothing happens.

This can occur if one of the following conditions exists:

- Check your browser's security options. Your browser must be set to enable the loading of ActiveX scripts and playing of ActiveX controls.

- If you are accessing pages scripted with Microsoft Agent and using Microsoft Internet Explorer, you must have version 3.02 or later (download the latest version of Internet Explorer at *http://www.microsoft.com*. In Microsoft Internet Explorer, open the View menu, choose Options, click the Security tab, and select all the Active Content check boxes.

- A Java applet on the page can also cause this error. To run Microsoft Agent on the same page as a Java applet requires version 2.0 of the Microsoft Virtual Machine (VM). For more information, see Appendix C, "Microsoft Agent Technical Notes."

When I attempt to load a page scripted for Microsoft Agent, I get the message, "Unable to initialize Microsoft Agent."

This usually occurs when you don't have Microsoft Agent or some other control that page uses installed, and choose No when you are prompted to install the control. Try refreshing the page, though the page may work only if you install all the components it requires.

When I attempt to load a page scripted for Microsoft Agent, I get a scripting error: VBScript Runtime Error, Object required."

One of the following conditions may cause the message to display:

- Your security options for Microsoft Internet Explorer must be set to enable ActiveX controls and plug-ins. Check your browser's security page. In Microsoft Internet Explorer, open the View menu, choose Options, click the Security tab, and make sure the Enable ActiveX Controls And Plug-Ins check box is checked.

- You are running on a dual-boot Windows 95 or Windows 98 /Windows NT system and you have installed Microsoft Agent on one operating system but are trying to access the page from the other operating system. Although the operating systems may share directories and files, the registry information used by Microsoft Agent is not shared, so you must install Microsoft Agent on the operating system you use to access Web pages scripted with the character.

When I attempt to install Microsoft Agent on Microsoft Windows NT, I get a message indicating that I need to be an administrator.

Because Microsoft Agent writes files to your system directory when it installs, you must have administrator (not user) privileges to install.

When I attempt to install Microsoft Agent on Windows NT 4.0, I get one of the following errors:

Process (Regsvr32 /s windows\msagent\AgentCtl.dll). Error while creating this file. Cannot find this file.

Note The directory location cited in the error message varies depending on how you installed Windows.

A required DLL MSVCRT.DLL was not found. Error creating process <c:\windows\msagent\agentsvr.exe /regserver>. Reason: One of the library files needed to run this application cannot be found.

Note The directory location cited in the error message varies depending on how you installed Windows.

Installation of Microsoft Agent requires the proper installation of Regsvr32.exe, Msvcrt.dll (the Microsoft C run-time library), and up-to-date OLE dlls. See DCOM update at *http://www.microsoft.com/com/dcom/dcom1_2/dcom1_2.asp*. The best way to ensure that all the correct system files are present is to install Microsoft Internet Explorer 4.0 or later.

When I attempt to load a page scripted for Microsoft Agent, I get the message, "The component has been digitally "signed" by its publisher, but the signature does not match the component. It is possible that this component has been damaged or tampered with? Do you want to continue?"

This may appear if you attempt to install Microsoft Agent on Microsoft Internet Explorer 3.02. You can either continue with the installation or update your browser to Internet Explorer 4.0 or later.

When I attempt to load a page scripted for Microsoft Agent using Netscape Navigator (or other Internet browsers), I get errors.

Microsoft Agent is implemented using ActiveX interfaces. You can use it only with a browser (such as Microsoft Internet Explorer) that supports embedding ActiveX objects through script on a page, and only on systems running Microsoft Windows 95, Windows 98, and Windows NT 4.0 (or later). If you are not using Microsoft Internet Explorer (*http://www.microsoft.com*), check with your browser vendor for further information on ActiveX support.

Please note that Microsoft Agent will not run in Internet Explorer 4.0 Platform Preview due to a bug in the Internet Explorer 4.0 Preview version. Install the final release version of Internet Explorer 4.0.

Output Problems

The character leaves images or trails behind when it moves.

When an Agent character animates, it requires the application windows behind the character to update themselves on a timely basis. When the character moves across the screen, it is normal to sometimes see some residual images that disappear quickly (depending on the speed of your PC and the applications you are running). If they don't, the following may be the cause:

- Your system does not meet the minimum system requirements for Agent. Check Agent's system requirements with your system (*http://www.microsoft.com/workshop/imedia/agent/sysreq.asp*).

- The application window behind the character does not process updates in a timely fashion. Try dragging the character over the desktop or a folder window, or shut down some of your applications. If you see a noticeable improvement, the problem may be unavoidable.

- You may not have the official release of the Microsoft Internet Explorer 4.0 (or later) installed. Early pre-release versions of Internet Explorer 4.0 did not handle updating the screen correctly. This would result in residual images of the character remaining on the screen. To fix the problem, install the latest official release of the Internet Explorer (*http://www.microsoft.com/ie/ download.htm*).

- There may be a problem with your system's screen drivers or hardware. Make certain you have the latest drivers for your graphic hardware. If the problem still persists, you may want to contact your PC vendor.

The character doesn't produce any audio output when it speaks.

This symptom could have several causes. Try the following to isolate the problem:

- Verify that your speakers are plugged in and your sound card is compatible with Windows. It is a good idea to test them with another sound application to confirm that audio output is working properly.

- Verify that no other application is currently using the audio output device.

- Verify that the character you are using has been configured for spoken output. (You may need to check with the Web site or application supplier.)

- Verify that your Microsoft Agent settings are enabled for spoken output using the following procedure:

  1. Open the Try Out Microsoft Agent link on the Microsoft Agent home page (*http://www.microsoft.com/workshop/imedia/agent/default.asp*). When the character appears, right-click it and select Advanced Character Options from the pop-up menu.

  2. When the property sheet appears, select the Output page.

  3. Set the Play Spoken Audio option and click OK.

- If the character uses a text-to-speech (TTS) engine to produce spoken output, verify that you have installed a compatible TTS engine. For example, when installed as an Internet Explorer 4.0 add-on component, only the core components of Microsoft Agent are installed. The core components do not include a text-to-speech engine. Without this TTS engine (a Microsoft Speech API-compatible engine), Microsoft Agent sample characters will not produce spoken output. Compatible engines can be found at the Microsoft Agent Downloads page (*http://www.microsoft.com/workshop/imedia/agent/agentdl.asp*).

- Verify that Microsoft Agent's use of MIDI is not blocking the audio channel (for more information, see the following topic).

Applications that play MIDI have no audio output when Microsoft Agent is running.

Microsoft Agent uses MIDI to play a tone when you press the Listening key. If you find that this interferes with other applications that play MIDI or interferes with speech input, you can turn off the Play Tone When You Can Speak option in the Microsoft Agent properties using the following procedure:

1. Open the Try Out Microsoft Agent link on the Microsoft Agent home page (*http://www.microsoft.com/workshop/imedia/agent/default.asp*). When the character appears in the taskbar, right-click it and choose Advanced Character Options from the pop-up menu.

2. When the property sheet displays, select the Speech Input page.

3. Uncheck the Play Tone When You Can Speak option and click OK.

I get the following message: An outgoing call cannot be made since the application is dispatching an input-synchronous call.

This message may occur under the following circumstances:

When a Web page including Microsoft Agent is closed (by right-clicking the page's taskbar entry and choosing Close from the pop-up menu), this may occur. This is due to a timing problem between Agent and the browser when they are shutting down at the same time. The error is harmless. Click OK to dismiss the message.

What occurred was the Agent-enabled Web page (or application) attempted to request a specific text-to-speech (TTS) engine. Speech.dll was not installed. Try installing the Speech control panel from *http:www.microsoft.com/sitebuilder/ workshop/imedia/agent/agentdl.asp* Downloads page.

Speech Input Problems

The character does not respond to my spoken input.

This symptom may be caused by a number of problems. Try the following to isolate the problem:

- Verify that your microphone is correctly plugged in. It is a good idea to test it with another sound input application to ensure that it works properly.

- Verify that a compatible speech engine is installed. Under Windows 95, Windows 98, and Windows NT 4.0, open the Control Panel. If you find the Speech object there, open it, and it will list the speech engines available and installed on your system. If the Speech object is not present, install it from the Microsoft Agent Downloads page (*http://www.microsoft.com/workshop/ imedia/agent/agentdl.asp*). You can install the Microsoft Command and Control speech recognition engine from the Microsoft Agent site (*http://www.micro-soft.com/workshop/imedia/agent/agentdl.asp*).

- Verify that your sound card is compatible with Microsoft Windows 95, Windows 98, or Windows NT.

  The best way to do this is to run the Sound Recorder application that comes with Windows. It can usually be found on the Start menu. Click the Start button, click Programs, click Accessories, click Multimedia, and then click

Sound Recorder. When the Sound Recorder window displays, click the Record button and talk into your microphone. The line in the window should animate in response to your voice input.

If the Sound Recorder application doesn't work on your system, contact the sound card manufacturer's technical support department for assistance. Your sound card may not be compatible with Windows or there may be a problem with the software drivers for your sound card.

- Verify that your sound input for speech input is set properly:

  1. Open the Speech input object in the Control Panel. If the Speech object is not present, install it from the Microsoft Agent Downloads page (*http:// www.microsoft.com/workshop/imedia/agent/agentdl.asp*).

  2. Select the speech input engine you have installed.

  3. Choose the Microphone Settings Wizard button. If this button appears disabled, a compatible speech engine is not installed or the speech engine you installed may not support automatic adjustment.

- Verify that the Agent-enabled application or Web page supports speech input. Not all pages (or applications) support speech input. Press and hold the Listening key. Typically this will be the Scroll Lock key unless you changed it. A pop-up window should appear under the character. The text in the tip will tell you the listening state of the character. If no tip appears, either the application or Web page does not support speech input, or you don't have a compatible speech engine installed. If the tip does appear and indicates the character is listening, speak one of the character's voice commands. If you do not know what voice commands are available, release the Listening key and right-click the character. Then choose Open Voice Commands Window from the pop-up menu. If the command does not appear, speech support is not available for the application or Web page you are using. If it does appear, press and hold the Listening key again. If the Listening tip appears under the character and indicates that the character is listening, speak one of the commands listed in the window. If the character does not respond, go to the next step.

- Verify that no other application is currently using the audio output device.

- Verify that Microsoft Agent's use of MIDI is not blocking the audio channel (see "Applications that play MIDI have no audio output when Microsoft Agent is running" in the Output Problems section).

- If you followed the steps above but still have problems with speech input, verify that your sound card and driver software is compatible with the speech engine you are using. Check with the technical support for your sound card and your speech engine manufacturer.

The MIDI tone seems to disrupts speech input.

Reduce the MIDI volume using the following steps:

1. Open the Volume Control window by right-clicking the speaker icon in the taskbar or by opening the Multimedia object in the Control Panel. Click the Volume button in the Playback section of the Audio page.

2. Decrease the MIDI volume by moving slider down.

The character does not respond to voice input, but I can hear my voice through my speakers when I talk into my microphone.

Your sound card is not set up properly for use with Microsoft Agent. Choose the Microphone Settings Wizard on the property sheet of the Speech object in the Control Panel. (See the steps for "The character does not respond to my spoken input" for information on how to access this button.)

A P P E N D I X   C

Microsoft Agent Technical Notes

General

With the release of Microsoft Agent version 2.0, will my pages built with the previous release (1.52) still work?

The 2.0 release of Microsoft Agent is compatible with the previous 1.52 release. However, note that Agent 2.0 installs to a different directory than Agent 1.5. If you are using the Agent ActiveX control and you keep both versions 1.5 and 2.0 installed, you should convert your code to use the 2.0 version to avoid any design time incompatibilities.

Can I define my own character?

Yes. You can use any animation rendering package, provided that you can produce your images in a 2-bit (monochrome), 4-bit, or 8-bit color Windows bitmap format. Then you can use the Microsoft Agent Character Editor, available for download at *http://www.microsoft.com/workshop/imedia/agent/agentdl.asp*, to assemble and compile your animations.

Will Microsoft Agent be available for platforms other than Microsoft Windows 95, Windows 98, and Windows NT?

Microsoft Agent is currently only offered for the Microsoft Windows platform.

Will Microsoft Agent be available in other languages?

Microsoft Agent includes support for the following languages in addition to English (U.S.): Arabic, French, German, Hebrew, Italian, Japanese, Korean, Spanish, simplified Chinese, and traditional Chinese. We are also considering other languages. Check the Agent Web site (*http://www.microsoft.com/workshop/imedia/agent/agentdl.asp*) for availability of current languages.

Please note that this language support is for Agent's core services; speech input and output engines are not a part of Agent core services and so we do not currently offer speech engine support for all the languages for which Agent is available. However, additional language speech engines may be available from other vendors. Check our Speech Recognition (*http://www.microsoft.com/workshop/ imedia/agent/agentdevdl.asp#sr*) and Text-To-Speech (*http://www.microsoft.com/ workshop/imedia/agent/agentdevdl.asp#tts*) pages for further information on what engines are available.

How do I uninstall Microsoft Agent?

Microsoft Agent 2.0 has been designed to be a Microsoft operating system component. As a result, once it is installed it cannot be uninstalled without reinstalling the operating system.

Licensing

Can I distribute Microsoft Agent and its characters?

Microsoft Agent can be automatically downloaded directly from the Microsoft site by including the Microsoft Agent control's CLSID in an HTML <OBJECT> tag on your Web page, which will automatically offer to download and install the control when a user without Microsoft Agent installed loads the page. Such use is covered in the Microsoft Agent End User License agreement that displays when Microsoft Agent is installed. This license does not include provisions for you to distribute Agent from your server or as a part of your application. Application developers who wish to include Microsoft Agent and any of its components as part of their application must complete a distribution license. A distribution license is required for any individual or company that wishes to distribute any Microsoft Agent component, regardless whether for profit. For more information about distribution licenses, see Appendix E, "Microsoft Agent Licensing and Distribution."

Can I use the Microsoft Agent characters?

You may use the Microsoft characters designated for download at the Microsoft Agent Web site subject to the conditions included in the End User License Agreement or the Microsoft Agent Distribution License Agreement. For further information, see Appendix E, " Microsoft Agent Licensing and Distribution." Note that such use requires that the character be used only as part of a script or application that uses Microsoft Agent. The character images alone cannot be included in packaging or promotional material.

Note that the Microsoft Agent 2.0 characters (ACS format) available from our Downloading page, automatically install to the \Chars subdirectory of Microsoft Agent's directory that is installed in the directory where Windows is installed.

You may access the ACF/ACA version of the characters from the Microsoft servers following the information included on the Microsoft Agent Character Data page (*http://www.microsoft.com/workshop/imedia/agent/characterdata.asp*). To post this latter format to your own server, you must submit a distribution license agreement and request these files. They are not made available without a valid distribution license.

How do I modify the Microsoft supplied characters?

Modification of the Microsoft-supplied characters is not supported. However, you may create and distribute your own characters.

Can I distribute the speech engines that are supplied with Microsoft Agent with my own applications?

Microsoft licenses certain speech engines for use with Microsoft Agent-enabled Web sites and applications. To see the engines that may be licensed, see Appendix E, "Microsoft Agent Licensing and Distribution."

Can I distribute the Microsoft Agent Character Editor and Microsoft Linguistic Information Sound Editing Tool?

Distribution of these tools is limited to downloading them from the Microsoft Web site or dispensing them as part of any software development kit Microsoft may provide.

Programming/Scripting Information

When I use Microsoft Visual Basic (or other development tools) for scripting Microsoft Agent, I do not see all the properties and events used in your samples. How do I access them?

Most of the events, methods, and properties supported by the Microsoft Agent control are exposed only at run time. Consult Chapter 4, "Programming the Microsoft Agent Control" for further information.

The Map tag (or some other tag) doesn't seem to work.

Some tags include quoted strings. For some programming languages, such as Visual Basic Scripting Edition (VBScript) and Visual Basic, you may have to use two quote marks to designate the tag's parameter or concatenate a double-quote character as part of the string. The latter is shown in this Visual Basic example:

```
Agent1.Characters("Genie").Speak "This is \map=" + chr(34) + "Spoken text" _
+ chr(34) + "=" + chr(34) + "Balloon text" + chr(34) + "\."
```

For C, C++, and Java programming, precede backslashes and double quotes with a backslash. For example:

```
BSTR bszSpeak = SysAllocString(L"This is \\map=\"Spoken text\"=\"Balloon text\"\\");

pCharacter->Speak(bszSpeak, ......);
```

Note that Microsoft Agent does not support all the tags specified in the Microsoft Speech API. In addition, support for some parameters may depend on the text-to-speech engine installed. For further information, see Chapter 6, "Microsoft Agent Speech Output Tags."

I seem to get RequestStart and RequestComplete events in my scripts even though I don't set any requests.

This is a problem in Visual Basic Scripting Edition (VBScript) 1.0. It has been addressed in VBScript 2.0, which can be downloaded from the VBScript Web Page: *http://microsoft.com/msdownload/vbscript/scripting.asp.*

I don't seem to get RequestStart and RequestComplete events in my script (or program).

This could be caused by one of the following problems:

- Your programming language doesn't fully support ActiveX controls. Check your documentation to ensure that it supports the ActiveX interface and events for ActiveX objects.

- On a scripted Web page, another control has failed to install or load. Check to ensure that all other controls are installed and loading properly without Microsoft Agent.

- On a scripted Web page with frames, you have the <OBJECT> tag for the Microsoft Agent control on one page, and the events scripted on another page. Events are sent only to the page that hosts the control.

I am using the Microsoft Agent control with other ActiveX controls on my Web page, and I don't seem to get any events.

Check to see if the other controls are correctly installed. If another ActiveX control fails to correctly register itself, the Microsoft Agent control may receive its events.

What programming languages can I use to program the Microsoft Agent control?

Microsoft Agent should be supportable from any language that supports the ActiveX interface. It includes code samples for Microsoft Visual Basic, VBScript, JScript, C/C++, and Java.

Can I access the parameters returned from Microsoft Agent using JScript?

Yes, but currently the only way to do this is using the <SCRIPT LANGUAGE ="JScript" FOR="*object*" EVENT="event()"> syntax. Although this syntax is supported for Microsoft Internet Explorer, other browsers do not support it, so you may want to avoid using JScript for this part of your page's script.

Can Microsoft Agent be used with speech recognition or speech synthesis (text-to-speech, or TTS) engines other than those supplied by Microsoft?

Yes, provided that the engine supports the Microsoft Speech API (SAPI) interfaces required by Microsoft Agent. Check with the engine supplier.

My page includes HTML Object tags for Microsoft Agent, the Lernout & Hauspie TruVoice TTS engine, and the Microsoft Command and Control speech recognition engine, but not all the components install.

Typically, the problem can be corrected by refreshing the page. As a general practice, it is best to specify the Microsoft Agent Control <OBJECT> tag first, then the Lernout & Hauspie TruVoice engine, then the Command and Control speech recognition engine.

After calling the MoveTo method, my character seems to freeze even though I have Return animations assigned to Moving state animations.

When you play an animation, the animation services continue to display its last frame until another animation is called. Therefore, you should play another animation after calling **MoveTo**. If you defined a **Return** animation for the **Moving** state animation, the server will play it first.

When I query the character's Pitch property, it returns a value of -1.

This occurs if the character has been compiled using a speech engine's default pitch property; that is, the pitch was not changed when the character was built.

When running under Internet Explorer 4.0 Preview 1 or 2, events don't fire after Microsoft Agent has been running, or the character leaves behind parts of its animation.

These problems are related to the Internet Explorer 4.0 Preview 1 and 2. Install the official commercial release of Internet Explorer 4.0 from *http://www.microsoft .com/ie/download/*.

When my code attempts to set the TTS mode ID for a text-to-speech engine, I get the following error: An outgoing call cannot be made since the application is dispatching an input-synchronous call.

To set the TTSModeID property, you must have Speech.dll installed. This is typically a part of the speech engine's installation code. You may also install this by installing the Speech object control panel, available from the Microsoft Agent Downloads page.

When I retry loading a character that failed to load, the call fails with a "Character already loaded" error.

The Microsoft Agent control does not unload a character object (release the reference) when its associated character file fails to load. If you want to retry loading the character, you must explicitly call **Unload** before you call **Load** the second time. If you attempt this from a Web page script, you also need to precede the **Unload** call with an On Error Resume Next statement, or the **Unload** call will also fail. (Note that JScript has no On Error Resume Next statement.)

However, you may not need to include code to immediately retry loading a character when the file fails to load. Microsoft Internet Explorer and the Microsoft Agent server component automatically attempt to retry several times, so the chances that your retry will result in a successful load are remote. A better strategy is to wait (set a timer) a few seconds before you retry.

How can I install Microsoft Agent as part of my application or from my Web server?

You can install Agent from the Microsoft Web site by including its CLSID in an HTML Object tag. However, if you want to include and install Agent from your own application installation program or from your own server, you must download the Microsoft Agent self-installing cabinet file, by downloading it from the Downloads page. When downloading, choose the browser's Save rather than Run option. Whenever this file is run, it automatically will install Microsoft Agent on the target machine. Therefore you can specify the file in your installation script.

Note that to distribute Microsoft Agent in this way requires that you submit a distribution license agreement. For further information see Appendix E, "Microsoft Agent Licensing and Distribution." Further information is included in the license agreement about installation.

Do not attempt to install Microsoft Agent by copying its various .DLLs and attempting to register it yourself. Attempting to install Agent by any other means then executing its self-installing cabinet file is not supported.

The target system must also include recent versions of MSVCRT.DLL (VC++ runtime), REGSVR32.EXE (registration tool included with Microsoft VC++), and COM. The best way to ensure that the correct versions are installed is to require that Microsoft Internet Explorer 3.02 or later is installed. However, you can also license these runtime requirements. (For the latest version of COM, access the DCOM update from the Microsoft web site.)

Microsoft Agent 2.0 will not install on Microsoft Windows NT5 since this version of the operating system already includes Agent.

Can I use the Visual Basic Setup Wizard to install Microsoft Agent?

While you can create your own installation program using Visual Basic (VB) code you can't use the Visual Basic Setup Wizard to do this. To install Agent from VB, you can use Shell command, specifying the Microsoft Agent self-installing cabinet file.

How do I install Microsoft Agent to install on Windows NT 5.0?

Microsoft Agent 2.0 does not install on Windows NT 5.0 because it is already included as a part of the operating system.

Agentsvr crashes when I call Speak with a WAV file.

This may result when the character has been using TTS for spoken output, then changes to use a WAV file. Text was not supplied in the first parameter of the Speak method.

To avoid the crash, include a space character in the first parameter of the Speak method, even if you have no text output.

A P P E N D I X   D

Microsoft Agent Error Codes

Microsoft Agent returns the following error information:

Error Number	Hex Value	Description
-2147213311	0x80042001	The specified Microsoft Agent client was not found.
-2147213310	0x80042002	The character ID is not valid. Verify that the ID has been defined and is spelled correctly.
-2147213309	0x80042003	The specified animation is not supported. Verify that the animation name is correct.
-2147213308	0x80042004	No animation exists for this state. Verify that an animation has been assigned to this state.
-2147213306	0x80042006	The command name was not found. Verify that the command name you specified is correct.
-2147213305	0x80042007	The specified command name parameter has already been defined.
-2147213304	0x80042008	The specified Microsoft Agent client was not found.
-2147213302	0x8004200A	The specified method failed because the character is hidden.
-2147213301	0x8004200B	The character is already loaded. Check for previous **Load** method calls.
-2147213300	0x8004200C	The current character's settings do not support a word balloon.
-2147213299	0x8004200D	The Voice Commands Window cannot be displayed because speech input support has not been completely defined for this character. Verify that speech input is enabled and that there is a speech recognition engine and voice commands defined for the character.
-2147213298	0x8004200E	The **Get** method was specified with an invalid Type parameter. Verify that the type you specified is supported and spelled correctly.
-2147213297	0x8004200F	The specified animation is not valid. It may be damaged or has no frames.
-2147213296	0x80042010	A character cannot be moved while it is being dragged.
-2147213295	0x80042011	The specified operation failed because it requires the character to be active.
-2147213294	0x80042012	The specified language for the character is not supported on this computer.
-2147213293	0x80042013	The specified speech engine could not be found, the speech engine does not match the specified language for the character, or speech audio output is currently disabled.

Error Number	Hex Value	Description
-2147213292	0x80042014	The specified speech engine could not be found, the speech engine does not match the specified language for the character, or speech input is currently disabled.
-2147213291	0x80042015	The specified engine mode ID does not support the current language for the character.
-2147213290	0x80042016	The specified operation failed because spoken audio output for all characters has been disabled in the Advanced Character Options.
-2147213289	0x80042017	There are no standard characters installed on this system.
-2147213288	0x80042018	The default character and other characters cannot be loaded at the same time by a single control.
-2147213055	0x80042101	The Request object was not found. The Request object no longer exists in the character's animation queue.
-2147213054	0x80042102	The specified Request object is not valid.
-2147213053	0x80042103	The **Stop** method was used incorrectly. A character cannot use the **Stop** method to interrupt another character. Try the Interrupt method.
-2147213052	0x80042104	The Interrupt method was used incorrectly. A character cannot interrupt itself.
-2147213051	0x80042105	A character cannot wait on its own requests.
-2147213050	0x80042106	The specified bookmark is invalid. Make sure the bookmark specified is not reserved by Microsoft Agent.
-2147213048	0x80042108	The specified Request object was removed from the character queue.
-2147213046	0x8004210A	The operation was interrupted because the Listening key was pressed.
-2147213045	0x8004210B	The operation was interrupted because of spoken input.
-2147213044	0x8004210C	The operation was interrupted by the application.
-2147213043	0x8004210D	The operation was interrupted because the character was hidden.
-2147213042	0x8004210E	The **Lst** speech tag cannot be used with additional text or a URL.
-2147212799	0x80042201	The Microsoft Agent Data Provider was not able to start.
-2147212798	0x80042202	The specified character data file version is not supported by the installed version of Microsoft Agent. You need to update the character.
-2147212797	0x80042203	The version of Microsoft Agent installed is older than the specified character file. Verify that you have the correct version of Microsoft Agent installed.
-2147212796	0x80042204	The specified file is not a Microsoft Agent character file. Verify the file name is correct.
-2147212795	0x80042205	The character ID is not valid. Verify that the ID has been correctly defined and is spelled correctly.
-2147212794	0x80042206	The specified file is not a valid sound (.WAV) file.
-2147212793	0x80042207	The specified sound file is not valid or does not include the correct data.

Error Number	Hex Value	Description
-2147212792	0x80042208	There was a problem in accessing the system's multimedia component.
-2147212791	0x80042209	Microsoft Agent does not support the specified URL protocol.
-2147212543	0x80042301	The audio device cannot be accessed. Verify that the sound card and drivers are correctly installed.
-2147212542	0x80042302	Microsoft Agent could not find any compatible speech recognition engines.
-2147212540	0x80042304	There is a problem in the specified Commands object definition.
-2147212539	0x80042305	The text for the Voice property of a command is either missing a right parenthesis or includes a misplaced left parenthesis.
-2147212538	0x80042306	The text for the Voice property of a command is missing a right square bracket or includes a misplaced left square bracket.
-2147212537	0x80042307	The text for the Voice property of a command is missing a left parenthesis, includes a misplaced right parenthesis, or has no text between parentheses.
-2147212536	0x80042308	The text for the Voice property of a command is missing a left square bracket, includes a misplaced right square bracket, or has no text between square brackets.
-2147212535	0x80042309	The text for the Voice property of a command is missing surrounding parentheses or square brackets for specifying alternative text.
-2147212534	0x8004230A	There was a problem in accessing the speech recognition mode. Verify that the speech engine is correctly installed.
-2147212287	0x80042401	The audio device cannot be accessed. Verify that the sound card and drivers are correctly installed.
-2147212286	0x80042402	The text-to-speech (TTS) engine cannot be started.
-2147212285	0x80042403	The text-to-speech (TTS) engine cannot be started.
-2147212284	0x80042404	The text-to-speech (TTS) engine cannot be started.
-2147212283	0x80042405	The text-to-speech (TTS) engine cannot be started.
-2147212282	0x80042406	The Microsoft Agent lip sync component failed.
-2147212281	0x80042407	The Microsoft Agent lip sync component failed.
-2147212280	0x80042408	The Microsoft Agent lip sync component failed.
-2147212030	0x80042502	Microsoft Agent was unable to start. Verify that Microsoft Agent is properly installed.
-2147024894	0x80070002	The system cannot find the file specified.*
-2147024883	0x8007000C	The data is invalid.*
-2147023436	0x800705B4	This operation returned because the timeout period expired. *
-2146697214	0x800C0002	Invalid URL.* Please verify that the specified URL exists and is correct.
-2146697212	0x800C0004	Server access failure.* The attempt to connect with the server failed. Please verify that the server is running and available.

* Errors whose descriptions include an asterisk are Windows system errors. They are provided here because they may commonly occur in Agent-enabled applications. For information on other errors not included here, see the Win32 documentation.

Error Number	Hex Value	Description
-2146697210	0x800C0006	File not found.* The file could not be found at the specified URL. Please make sure the URL is correct.
-2146697205	0x800C000B	Server connection time-out.* The connection to the server timed out. Please verify that the server is running and available.
-2146697202	0x800C000E	Server security access failure.* There was a security problem when accessing the server.

* Errors whose descriptions include an asterisk are Windows system errors. They are provided here because they may commonly occur in Agent-enabled applications. For information on other errors not included here, see the Win32 documentation.

A P P E N D I X   E

Microsoft Agent Licensing and Distribution

The following uses for Microsoft Agent Version 2.0 are currently royalty-free, subject to the end-user license agreement displayed when the Microsoft Agent installation file is run and do not require a distribution license:

- You can automatically cause Microsoft Agent to download from the Microsoft site by including the CLSID for Microsoft Agent in an HTML <OBJECT> tag on one of your site's pages, as described on the download page for developers at *http://www.microsoft.com/sitebuilder/workshop/imedia/agent/agentdevdl.asp*.

- You can automatically cause the speech engines to download from the Microsoft site by including their CLSIDs in an HTML <OBJECT> tag on one of your site's pages, as described on the download page for developers at *http://www.microsoft.com/sitebuilder/workshop/imedia/agent/agentdevdl.asp*, provided that these engines are only downloaded and installed for use with Microsoft Agent.

- You can load Microsoft's designated characters or images from the Microsoft Web site in your script code using the Microsoft Agent **Load** and **Get** (**Prepare**) methods, as described on the character data page at *http://www.microsoft.com/sitebuilder/workshop/imedia/agent/characterdata.asp*.

However, to add or include Microsoft Agent and any of its components to or with an application, or post Microsoft Agent and any of its components on a server, or distribute Microsoft Agent and any of its components using other electronic media, you must first obtain a distribution license for Microsoft Agent. The license does not include the Microsoft Agent Character Editor or the Microsoft Linguistic Sound Editing Tool. The Microsoft Agent character files and their images and designated speech engines cannot be used or distributed without Microsoft Agent and only as part of a Microsoft Agent-enabled page or application.

Note to licensees of Microsoft Agent version 1.5: Your license does not apply to version 2.0.

To obtain a distribution license, please see the following:

- Microsoft Agent Distribution License (*http://www.microsoft.com/sitebuilder/ workshop/imedia/agent/agentlic.asp.*)

  Information on licensing and distributing Microsoft Agent and the files for Microsoft Agent characters.

Distributing licensing for the speech engines supplied by Microsoft that can be downloaded from the Microsoft Agent web site is covered in license agreement displayed when you install that engine. If you have a valid license agreement for Microsoft Agent, no additional license must be submitted for those speech engines. If you are using a speech engine supplied by a vendor other than Microsoft, check with your vendor for their distribution licensing requirements.

For further information, contact the Microsoft Agent Product Group at msagent@microsoft.com. Do not send technical support questions to this address.

APPENDIX F

Microsoft Speech Engines for Microsoft Agent

Microsoft provides a set of speech input (recognition) engines and speech output (text-to-speech or TTS) engines you can use with your Microsoft Agent-enabled applications or Web pages. Use of these engines is subject to the Microsoft Agent license agreement and the supplemental addendum displayed when you install the engines. This license entitles you to distribute the engines, but only when using them through Microsoft Agent API and using a visible character.

This document describes the procedure for installing and accessing the speech engines supplied by Microsoft for use with Microsoft Agent. For speech engines supplied by other vendors, check your vendor's information for this information.

Installing a Speech Engine

The Microsoft supplied speech engines can be installed by downloading the engines from the Downloads page at the Microsoft Agent Web site. When done using the Microsoft Internet Explorer you get the option to Run This Program From Its Current Location or Save This Program To Disk. If you choose Run This Program From Its Current Location, the engine will be installed directly. If, instead, you choose Save This Program To Disk, you can save the installation file to your disk. Opening this installation file will also install the engine.

For Web pages, you can author your page to automatically download install the engine by including an HTML Object tag on your page specifying the CLASSID and CODEBASE parameter.

```
<OBJECT width=0 height=0
CLASSID="CLSID:XXXXXXXX-XXXX-XXXX-XXXX-XXXXXXXXXXXX"
CODEBASE="#VERSION=X,X,X,X">
</OBJECT>
```

For the CLASSID parameter, specify the CLSID for the installation file. For the CODEBASE, specify the engine's version number. If you are not downloading the engine from the Microsoft site, you need to also include a URL.

The following are the installation file CLSIDs for the Microsoft supplied engines.

Engine	CLSID	Version #
L&H TruVoice Text-To-Speech	B8F2846E-CE36-11D0-AC83-00C04FD97575	6,0,0,0
Microsoft Speech Recognition	161FA781-A52C-11d0-8D7C-00A0C9034A7E	4,0,0,0

The descriptions of programming interfaces in this document follow the conventions for Microsoft VBScript. However, they should be generally applicable to other languages as well.

Accessing a Speech Engine in Your Code

To use a particular speech engine in your code, use the Agent API to set the engine. For speech input engines, use **SRModeID**, specifying the mode ID for the engine. However, note that the engine must be installed. To determine if the engine is present, you can query **SRModeID**. The engine must match the character's **LanguageID** setting. For example, you cannot set **SRModeID** to a German speech recognition engine mode ID for a character whose **LanguageID** is French.

Speech Input Engine Mode IDs

Voice	Mode IDs
Microsoft Speech Recognition Engine v4.0	{D8905400-B5C8-11D0-B968020AFDB1B9C}

Check and set the character's **LanguageID** and **SRModeID** in your code before you attempt to define grammar for the voice parameters of **Command** objects your application. Also consider checking the browser or system language so you can be certain to match your users' configuration. The engine may fail if you attempt to define a grammar for a language that the engine does not match.

A character set for text-to-speech (TTS) output can be compiled with a default speech output engine's mode ID preference. When the character is loaded, if the engine is installed and matches the character's **LanguageID**, Agent will attempt to load that mode ID for speech output. If the engine is not present or has a different **LanguageID**, Agent will attempt to load the first mode ID it finds that matches the character's **LanguageID**, but still sets the character's compiled speed and pitch setting.

To query for or set an engine's mode ID, use **TTSModeID**. With **TTSModeID** you can set a mode ID that is different from the character's **LanguageID**. For instance, you can set a German character to speak using a French mode ID. Speech output engine mode IDs not only define which engine you use, but also correspond to specific voices supported for an engine. You can also use the Microsoft Agent Character Editor or the tools included in the Microsoft Speech SDK to query for the mode IDs of TTS engines installed on your system.

Speech Output Mode IDs

Voice	Mode IDs
Adult Female #1, US English, L&H TruVoice	{CA141FD0-AC7F-11D1-97A3-006008273008}
Adult Female #2, US English, L&H TruVoice	{CA141FD0-AC7F-11D1-97A3-006008273009}
Adult Male #1, US English, L&H TruVoice	{CA141FD0-AC7F-11D1-97A3-006008273000}
Adult Male #2, US English, L&H TruVoice	{CA141FD0-AC7F-11D1-97A3-006008273001}
Adult Male #3, US English, L&H TruVoice	{CA141FD0-AC7F-11D1-97A3-006008273002}
Adult Male #4, US English, L&H TruVoice	{CA141FD0-AC7F-11D1-97A3-006008273003}
Adult Male #5, US English, L&H TruVoice	{CA141FD0-AC7F-11D1-97A3-006008273004}
Adult Male #6, US English, L&H TruVoice	{CA141FD0-AC7F-11D1-97A3-006008273005}
Adult Male #7, US English, L&H TruVoice	{CA141FD0-AC7F-11D1-97A3-006008273006}
Adult Male #8, US English, L&H TruVoice	{CA141FD0-AC7F-11D1-97A3-006008273007}

Note There is a difference between a speech engine's installation CLSID and its mode ID. Similarly, a speech engine also has an engine ID, but this ID is not applicable in the Agent API.

Bibliography

Axtell, R. *Gestures: The Do's and Taboos of Body Language around the World.* New York: John Wiley & Sons, 1998.

Ball, G. et al. "Life-Like Computer Characters: The Persona Project at Microsoft Research." *Software Agents.* Ed. Jeff Bradshaw. Cambridge, MA: MIT Press, 1996.

Bates, J. "The Nature of Character in Interactive Worlds and the Oz." *Technical Report CMU-CS-92-200.* School of Computer Science, Carnegie Mellon University. Pittsburgh, PA. October 1992.

Bates, J., Loyall, A., and Reilly, W. "An Architecture for Action, Emotion, and Social Behavior." In *Proceedings of the Fourth European Workshop on Modeling Autonomous Agents in a Multi-Agent World* (S. Martino al Cimino, Italy, 1992).

Bates, J., Loyall, A., and Reilly, W. "Integrating Reactivity, Goals and Emotions in a Broad Agent." In *Proceedings of the 14th Annual Conference of the Cognitive Science Society* (Indiana, July 1992).

Cialdini, R. *Influence: The Psychology of Persuasion.* New York: Quill, 1993.

Cassell, J. "Believable Communicating Agents: The Relationship Between Verbal and Nonverbal Behavior in Autonomous Communicating Agents." In *Siggraph '96 Course Notes.* Reading, MA: ACM Press, 1996.

Foner, L. "What's an Agent, Anyway? A Sociological Case Study." *Agents Memo 93-01.* Agents Group. Cambridge, MA: MIT Media Lab, 1993.

Grice, H. "Logic and Conversation." In *Syntax and Semantics 3: Speech Acts.* Ed. P. Cole and J. Morgan. New York: Academic Press, 1975.

Herman, J. *Newstalk: A Speech Interface to a Personalized Information Agent.* MIT Master's Thesis, Program in Media Arts and Sciences. Cambridge, MA. June 1995.

Koda, T. and Maes, P. "Agents with Faces: The Effects of Personification of Agents." In *Proceedings of HCI'96* (London, 1996).

Lassiter, J. "Principles of Traditional Animation Applied to 3-D Computer Animation." In *Proceedings of SIGGRAPH '87*. 35-44. Reading, MA: ACM Press, 1987.

Laurel, B. "Interface Agents: Metaphors with Character." *The Art of Human Computer Interface Design*. Reading, MA: Addison-Wesley, 1990.

Maes, P. "Agents that Reduce Work Overload and Information Overload." In *Communications of the ACM*. 31-40. July 1994.

Marx, M. *Toward Effective Conversational Messaging*. MIT Master's Thesis, Program in Media Arts and Sciences. Cambridge, MA.. June 1995.

Nass, C., Steuer, J., and Tauber, E. "Computers are Social Actors." In *Proceedings of the CHI '94 Conference* (Boston, MA, April 1994). 72-77. Reading, MA: ACM Press, 1994.

Nass, C. and Reeves, B. *The Media Equation: How People Treat Computers, Televisions, and New Media as Real People and Places*. Cambridge University Press, 1996.

Negroponte, N. "Hospital Corners." *The Art of Human-Computer Interface Design*. Ed. Brenda Laurel. Reading, MA: Addison Wesley, 1990.

Oren, T., et al. "Guides: Characterizing the Interface." *The Art of Human-Computer Interface Design*. Ed. Brenda Laurel. Reading, MA: Addison Wesley, 1990.

Parke, F. and Waters, K. *Computer Facial Animation*. Wellesley: AK Peters, 1996.

Perlin, K. and Goldberg, A. "Improv: A System for Scripting Interactive Actors in Virtual Worlds." In *Proceeding of SIGGRAPH 1995* (New Orleans, 1995).

Picard, R. *Affective Computing*. Cambridge: The MIT Press, 1997.

Schmandt, C. *Voice Communication with Computers: Conversational Systems*. New York: Van Nostrand Reinhold, 1994.

Syrdal, A., Bennett, R., and Greenspan, S. *Applied Speech Technology*. Boca Raton: CRC Press, 1995.

Thomas, F., and Johnson, O. *The Illusion of Life*. New York: Abbeville Press, 1981.

Thorisson, K. "Dialogue Control in Social Interface Agents." *InterCHI Adjunct Proceedings* (Amsterdam, Holland, 1993). Reading, MA: ACM Press, 1993.

Creating Personalities for Synthetic Actors: Toward Autonomous Personality Agents. Ed. R. Trappl and Paolo Petta. New York: Springer-Verlag, 1997.

Yankelovich, N., Levow, G., and Marx, M. "Designing Speech Acts: Issues in Speech User Interfaces." In *Proceedings of CHI '95* (Denver, CO, May 1995). 369-376. Reading, MA: ACM Press, 1995.

Yankelovich, N. "How Do Users Know What to Say?" *Interactions*, Vol. III.6. 32-43. November/December, 1996.

The Windows Interface Guidelines for Software Design. Redmond, WA: Microsoft Press, 1995.

Index

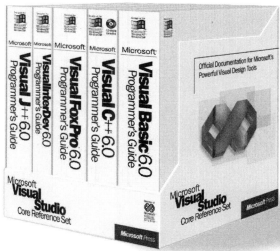